Doing Prison Work

The public and private lives of prison officers

Elaine Crawley

Routledge
Taylor & Francis Group

LONDON AND NEW YORK

First published by Willan Publishing 2004
This edition published by Routledge 2011
2 Park Square, Milton Park, Abingdon, Oxon OX14 4RN
270 Madison Avenue, New York, NY 10016

Routledge is an imprint of the Taylor & Francis Group

First published 2004

Hardback (published 2004)
ISBN-13 978-1-84392-035-9
ISBN-10 1-84392-035-2

Paperback (published 2006)
ISBN-13 978-1-84392-216-2
ISBN-10 1-84392-216-9

British Library Cataloguing-in-Publication Data

A catalogue record for this book is available from the British Library

Typeset by GCS, Leighton Buzzard, Bedfordshire
Project managed by Deer Park Productions, Tavistock, Devon

Doing Prison Work

Contents

In memory of my father, Captain Sidney Leonard 1919–2000

Acknowledgements

This book is based upon PhD research I carried out between 1997 and 2000. A large number of people helped me to produce my PhD thesis, and there is insufficient space here to name everyone who gave me their support as I tried to turn my tentative ideas about prison work into a thesis and now into this book. I hope that the people I do not specifically mention will take it as read that their kind assistance is very gratefully acknowledged.

I would like, first of all, to thank Richard Sparks for recognising the value of the project from the outset, and for supervising my PhD thesis with discernment and good humour. Thanks are also due to Alison Liebling and to Evi Girling who examined the thesis and provided me with invaluable comments and advice.

I also wish to express my deep gratitude to the prison governors who allowed me into their prisons. Without their kind co-operation and assistance the fieldwork on which this book is based (and hence this book) would not have been possible. Special thanks are, of course, due to all the prison officers who took the time to talk to me, put up with me hanging around their workplaces for almost two years, made me endless cups of coffee and trusted me with their stories. I am also very grateful to each of the kind and hospitable women who invited me into their homes to share with me some of the ups and downs of being a prison officer's wife, and who were generous enough to provide me with food, drink and, on occasion, a bed for the night.

My thanks are also due to the Economic and Social Research Council for their financial support for the project, and to Brian Willan for showing faith in the book and for his kind support and patience during its (rather lengthier than anticipated) production. For various forms of practical help during the preparation of the manuscript I would also like to thank Sue Humphries.

On a more personal note I want to thank my friends and colleagues in the Department of Criminology at Keele University. The twelve years I have spent there, first as a student and now as a research fellow, have been happy and productive ones thanks to their collegiality and support. Anne Worrall has been a particularly steadfast source of encouragement throughout those years. I want also to thank my friends and colleagues Susanne Karstedt and Ruth Jamieson, two very special women who have each, in their own ways, given me inspiration, fortitude and a sense of perspective. Thank you Susanne and Ruth, for providing friendship, affection and laughter when I needed it the most.

Finally, and especially, I want to thank my family. To my daughters Heaven and Fay, and my son Lol, thank you for your unstinting love, humour and support during the good times and the not so good. To my husband Peter, I hardly know what to say. To you I owe the greatest debt: without your love, wisdom and patience I would be in a very different place. Thank you, Pete, for igniting in me, so many years ago, an interest in sociology and a love of books, and for providing steadfast emotional and intellectual encouragement (and a million other things) ever since. I owe you everything.

Elaine Crawley
June 2004

Introduction

Prisons are at once extraordinary and ordinary institutions. They are extraordinary in that they are places in which large numbers of strangers are forced to live, in close proximity with each other, often for sustained periods. On entry to the prison, these strangers are stripped, searched and relieved of their personal possessions by other strangers – prison officers acting on behalf of the state. These officers are obliged to regulate prisoners' behaviour and ensure that they do not escape. Once inside, assigned to a cell and dressed in prison clothing, the strangers-now-prisoners are under almost constant surveillance, and instructed as to how they should conduct themselves, what is expected of them, and at what time, throughout the period of their sentences. In old prisons which stand in the centre of towns, all this may take place only yards from where people are freely going about their daily business – shopping, visiting the hairdressers or the pub, taking children to school, walking in the park. Whenever I step into the sunshine after spending the day in one prison or other, I rarely fail to be struck by this thought and by the apparent invisibility of this other world to passers-by.

Yet in many respects, prisons are also very ordinary. They are ordinary in that much of prison life, especially long-term prison life, revolves around those mundane matters which concern all of us in our non-prison lives – eating, sleeping, cleaning and tidying, doing the laundry, working (or looking for work), thinking about family and friends, attempting to alleviate boredom. All these concerns occupy prisoners because the prison is where prisoners must *live* and, as such, the prisoner is a member of what Clemmer (1940) terms the prison 'community'. As a result of the large body of work focusing on the lives of prisoners (notable examples include Serge 1977; Cohen and Taylor 1972; Boyle 1984; Carlen 1983; Liebling 1992; Toch 1977) we now know a good deal about the impact of prison on its prisoners, about the ways in which prisoners attempt to adjust to living in a prison and the ways in which they cope with (and sometimes are unable to cope with) the routines, demands and pressures of prison life. In contrast, very little is generally known about the impact of the prison on uniformed staff. What psychological and emotional adjustments must ordinary men and women make in order to become prison officers? How do *they* adjust to the prison environment? What aspects of the prison environment and the prison role do prison officers find most difficult to cope with? What conflicts and tensions do prison officers face when attempting to move between the prison world and home? In 1996, when I began the PhD thesis on which this book is based, these questions had already begun to interest me a great deal, and I was determined to find the answers.

This book, then, is a book about what it means to *do* prison work. It is not, however, simply a book describing the work that prison officers do, nor is it simply about the kinds of people who do it. Rather, it is a book that explores, using prison officers' own accounts, what officers *think* about their work and how they *feel* and *act* when they are doing it. In directing the research focus to these questions, it has been possible to make a number of interesting revelations. First, that prisons are extremely *domestic* spheres, and that, in consequence, much of the work that prison officers do is domestic in character. This aspect of the prison officer role rarely figures in new recruits' early imaginings of what the job is about. Secondly, that prisons are *emotional* arenas. In consequence, working in prisons demands a performative attitude on the part of staff, an (often significant) engagement in emotion work and the employment of a range of emotion work strategies.

The rationale for the book

The sociology of criminal justice occupations is an important subfield of criminological/socio-legal research. Yet by comparison with the large research literature on, for example, policing, the body of work on uniformed staff working in English prisons has remained small. Despite a great deal of academic interest in the prison *as an institution* (see, e.g., Sykes 1958; Mathieson 1965; Foucault 1979) and in the experiences of those sentenced to serve time behind its walls (see above), with the exception of the work of Thomas (1972), those whose job it is to keep prisoners captive were, until very recently, more or less ignored in British criminology, despite their pivotal role in prison life. On the rare occasion the spotlight *was* turned on uniformed staff, the prison officer was invariably a stereotype (see, e.g., Barnes and Teeter 1943; McCleery 1960) – an unintelligent, brutal and insensitive individual who, although urged to be 'professional' in his dealings with prisoners, was generally perceived as too under-educated, unsophisticated and biased to rise to the challenge (Toch cited in Lombardo 1981). Stereotypical accounts of the brutal and insensitive guard, media reports of prison officer abuses and officers' perceptions that 'nobody cares' about them have added to officers' wariness and mistrust of 'outsiders'. As a result, prison officers are generally unaccustomed to talking to researchers about themselves and their work. In the main, they have largely understood prison researchers as uninterested in *them* and *their* needs, perhaps largely because most prison researchers *have* tended to focus on the quality of prison regimes, the effectiveness of specialist programmes and on the needs and experiences of prisoners. Throughout my research, prison officers expressed surprise that I wanted to explore their role and the emotional and psychological challenges that it presents.

The paucity of scholarly work on this occupational group has represented a significant omission from the sociology of the prison, not least because it overlooked the contribution of uniformed staff to producing and reproducing the institution of the prison itself. Fortunately, following a lengthy period of neglect, the issue of the prison officer at work has once again begun to be acknowledged as an important one. There is now an important (albeit relatively small) corpus of research literature from the USA (see, for example, Crouch and Marquart 1980; Duffee 1980; Poole and Regoli 1980; Lombardo 1981; Kauffman 1988) and a less pronounced, but growing interest amongst British criminologists (see especially Hay and Sparks 1991; Liebling and Price 2001). This book aims to develop and extend this body of work by demonstrating – using prison officers' words – what prison work is *really* like for those who do it. It also allows the reader to follow prison officers home after work to see the extent to which the prison can 'spill over' into personal and family life. As Morgan (1997: 180) observes, on important questions such as the impact of prison work on health and home life, we know astonishingly little, despite the fact that prison officers typically spend a far higher proportion of their lives in prison than do many of their charges. This is, however, hardly surprising, given that few researchers (the American work of Kauffman (1988) is an important exception) have thought to ask prison officers such questions.

The broad and somewhat eclectic range of literature drawn upon in this book reflects both the paucity of scholarly work specifically on uniformed prison staff and my interest in theoretical concepts initially developed in other areas of study. In the absence of a developed literature on the prison officer I have explored a range of intriguing sources from other areas of sociology to develop my analysis. Consequently the reader will find that I have drawn upon literature in the sociology of emotions, the sociology of occupations and from dramaturgy to 'make sense of' what prison officers say, feel and do.

Organisation of the book

This book is organised in the following way. Chapter 1 'sets the scene' for the empirical chapters that follow. The chapter begins by examining the long-standing problem of staff discontent (and the central issues around which this discontent continues to revolve) and highlights those changes to prison policy, management and practice that have, over the last thirty years, affected the working conditions and role of the prison officer. Relatedly, this chapter explores the (relatively recent) desire on the part of prison managers to 'change culture' in the pursuit of better (and cheaper) prisons. The chapter then shifts its focus to the performance of power in the prison setting – or rather the 'myth' of total power as elaborated by Sykes (1958) – to argue that the ways in which power is *actually* performed has important implications for how prison officers carry out their mandated tasks and for their relationships with prisoners. The chapter then begins to sketch out the components and dynamics of occupational cultures more generally. Finally, the chapter introduces the key theoretical threads of the book. Readers will see that I employ Hochschild's (1983) concept of 'emotional labour' in my analysis of how prison officers 'manage' their emotions in the emotional arena of the prison. I suggest that as a *way of seeing* the social world of the English prison officer, the sociology of emotions is invaluable in that it permits insights into the complex intertwining of bureaucracy, rationality, dramaturgy and emotion in prisons. Similarly, I draw from Goffman's (1959) dramaturgical analysis of the structures of social encounters in order to explore how prison officers 'perform' their role in their interactions with prisoners and with other uniformed staff. Chapter 2 provides a summary of my research methods, and brief descriptions of the prisons in which my research took place. Using prison officers' own words and drawing upon my own fieldwork observations, the remaining chapters of this book demonstrate the complexities of prison work and the challenges that the work presents. Chapter 3, for example, focuses on the experiences of the new recruit to the Prison Service. Here we follow new recruits through the basic training process and then through their first days on the prison landings. The chapter demonstrates that the process of 'becoming' a prison officer is a slow, difficult and sometimes painful one, involving a significant degree of culture shock and a complex process of acculturation. The chapter demonstrates that through an internalisation, over time, of prison rules (formal, craft and feeling rules), social practices (which generally involves nick-names, various 'initiation rites', being given the worst jobs on the wing and just being 'left to get on with it'), formal and informal routines and occupational norms, ordinary men and women 'become' prison officers. During this 'process of becoming', new recruits learn the 'appropriate' ways of working with, and relating to, those who have become prisoners and with officers already accustomed to prison work. The chapter demonstrates how the process of becoming a prison officer is inextricably tied up with the management of certain emotions – particularly anxiety, sympathy and fear.

Chapter 4 explores prison officers' attitudes towards, and interactions with, prisoners, and their perceptions of the 'right' relationship between prisoners and themselves. As we shall see, the question of where power resides is of perennial concern to officers. The chapter also explores officers' perceptions of the 'good' officer and the 'culture shock' officers often re-experience when transferring to other prisons and other regimes. Chapter 5 presents a fuller exploration and analysis of the significance of emotion, emotional labour and performance in prisons, particularly the ways in which emotion and its management and display 'play out' in day-to-day interactions between prisoners and prison officers and between officers themselves. Drawing upon interviews with, and observations of, experienced and inexperienced officers, this chapter demonstrates that prison work generates a range of powerful emotions, all of which must be, in some way, managed. As this chapter demonstrates, however, officers do not always manage to manage their emotions. On the contrary, sometimes the performance fails and this can be a great shock, with implications for work identity and relationships with colleagues.

Chapter 6 discusses dissent and resistance in prisons, focusing on two types of incident that have the potential to impact significantly on staff emotions. First I explore prison officers' responses to prisoner suicide and, secondly, their (informal and formal) responses to prisoner dissent. Finally the chapter highlights the ways in which responses to collective dissent have the capacity to maintain the more 'traditional' occupational cultures of prison and raise staff morale. Chapter 7 elaborates my claim that prison officers are a diverse group who defend distinctly different visions and versions of the prison officer role, in terms of what that role should consist of, how the job should be done and who should be doing it. Perhaps unsurprisingly, this generates staff rivalries, resentments and conflicts. Drawing upon interview and observational data collected in three specialist regimes (a sex offender treatment wing, a therapeutic community for young offenders and a unit for elderly prisoners), the chapter examines these conflicts, exploring not only how officers see prisoners, but, more significantly, how officers see each other. Chapter 8 moves out of the prison setting to explore the impact of prison work on prison officers' families. Drawing upon interviews with officers' wives and children, this chapter demonstrates that the prison inevitably 'spills over' into the home, where it can 'contaminate' home life and spoil personal relationships with spouses, families and friends. Finally, I draw together the key threads of the book and consider what its findings can offer to the sociology of the prison.

Chapter 1

Setting the scene:
the research in context

This chapter 'sets the scene' for the empirical chapters that follow. My discussion is divided into five main parts. In the first part I consider the long-standing problem of prison officer discontent, and the central issues around which this discontent revolves. Staff resentments and frustrations about their working conditions, status and purpose are particularly pertinent here. The second part notes the substantial and far-reaching changes to prison management, organisation, practices and regimes that have taken place over the past two decades in a drive towards 'improving' the service. The nature of some of the changes that have taken place, and the pace at which they have been introduced, have impacted significantly on the day-to-day working lives of prison officers, on their perceptions of themselves and their work role and on the occupational cultures of prisons. With regard to the latter, managers of the Prison Service, like managers in other organisations in both the public and private sectors, are making efforts to change uniformed staff cultures in an effort to improve service delivery. This part of the chapter also notes certain *continuities* within the organisation, focusing on aspects of the prison officers' world that have remained constant for over a century, and which continue to shape action, emotion and culture at work. The third part discusses the performance of power in prisons. As I shall try to show throughout this book, the ways in which power is *actually* performed have important implications for how prison officers carry out mandated tasks, for officers' relationships with prisoners and ultimately for the 'legitimacy' of prison regimes. Staff–prisoner interactions are moderated by the fact that power in prisons is a *negotiated* affair, with prison officers having much less power than is often pretended, and prisoners rather more. The degree to which an officer accepts this (the notion of shared decision-making is anathema to many prison officers) determines his choice of working 'style' or 'credo'. In the fourth part of the chapter I explore cultures at work, drawing upon Skolnick's (1975) concept of the police 'working personality' in an attempt to identify similarities and contrasts between the occupational cultures of police beat officers and those of uniformed prison staff. Making such a comparison is helpful, because prison officers and police officers are the only blue-collar, predominantly working-class occupational groups in the criminal justice system. As such, one might expect there to be similarities in the ways that they think about their work. As I shall show, these similarities do exist, but there are also certain important differences, and these are largely determined by 1) the key function of each occupational group; and 2) the environments in which each occupational group works. In the final part I suggest that the prison should be read as an emotional arena. I apply Hochschild's (1983) concept of 'emotional labour' and Goffman's (1959) dramaturgical analysis of the structures of social encounters to explore the ways in which, in addition to being places for the confinement of law-breakers, prisons are highly domestic spaces in which prison officers must perform and manage emotion.

A century of staff discontent

For much of the past hundred years the Prison Service of England and Wales has simmered with staff discontent. In the late 1800s that discontent was focused around certain key issues; these issues, as well as more general questions about prison regimes, were addressed by a number of major committees during the period 1880–95. I do not intend to rehearse, here, the full remit or findings of these committees as this has been done adequately elsewhere (see, for example, May 1979). Rather I want to focus on the key concerns that emerged from two major inquiries of the time, namely the Rosebery Committee of 1883 and (more particularly) the Gladstone Committee of 1894. Both are of significant historical importance in tracing the development of the modern Prison Service. The Rosebery Committee was the first to report on staff problems seemingly common to prison systems, and which had (and continue to have) a significant impact on the morale of uniformed staff, namely: 1) the apparent inability of central administrators and staff 'in the field' to communicate with each other; and 2) prison officers' perceptions that the 'authorities' were more interested in the welfare of prisoners than in the welfare of staff. British prison officers are apparently not alone in these feelings: reports from America have also portrayed guards as feeling that 'administrative and operational changes are tending to favour prisoners over staff and that every political or administrative intervention weakens the prison guard's position' (Poole and Pogrebin 1987). The other committee of interest here, the Gladstone Committee, is perhaps the best known investigation into the history of the English prison system. The report of the Gladstone Committee had a significant and enduring impact in terms of both the purpose of the service and the uniformed officers' role within it. The central significance of the Gladstone Report was that it placed the reform or rehabilitation of prisoners as a primary objective of the penal system, *along with* retribution and deterrence. As the rehabilitative task increased in importance, so the uncertainty and confusion of discipline staff about their 'proper' role in the prison increased. They were given more discretion in their dealing with prisoners, but at the same time the move towards the increased association of prisoners, which the report had initiated, made the task of controlling prisoners more complex. For the first time, discipline staff found that they had to seek conformity through systems of remission and other 'privileges' instead (May 1979: 13; but see also Thomas 1972 for a fuller discussion of this process). This is a crucially important point for contemporary staff–prisoner relations, and one I shall return to below.

Prison officers' dissatisfaction with their role and with their managers has been expressed practically in a series of industrial actions over the years, some of them serious, in terms of their disruption to regimes (see, for example, Fitzgerald and Sim 1982) and all of them rearticulating the concerns outlined above (see, for example, Thomas 1972; May 1979; Home Office 1985; Hay and Sparks 1991; Woolf 1991; POA 1991, 1996; and virtually any copy of *Gatelodge*, the magazine of the Prison Officers' Association (POA)). By 1977, staff disputes had arisen over a number of local issues – in particular the increasing number of protests by prisoners. Of the various types of industrial action taken by the Prison Officers' Association from that period onwards, some interfered with the administration of justice (e.g. the refusal to escort prisoners to and from courts and to allow lawyers, probation officers or police to visit prisoners); some interfered with the administration of prisons (e.g. the refusal to co-operate with civilian and welfare staff); and some of it directly interfered with prison regimes (thus denying prisoners' statutory entitlements) such as late unlocking, bans on visits, education classes, bathing, laundry and association (Fitzgerald and Sim 1982: 122).

The concerns that led to these disputes seem remarkably persistent.

3

Indeed, as I shall demonstrate throughout this book, many prison officers feel unvalued, undirected and unsure of their role; not a single officer who took part in my research felt that his or her manager attached any real value to 'sharp end' knowledge of prisons and prisoners. Few had ever been asked by their prison managers to provide input into the regimes in which uniformed staff work; as a result, there is, amongst prison officers, significant dissatisfaction with, and to some extent, alienation from the work itself. Increasing numbers of prison officers are also reporting work-related stress. From a management point of view, many of the strains within the service can be laid at the door of uniformed staff themselves. From this perspective, the problem of inadequate service delivery is largely a cultural one.

Continuity and change

Managing the prison service: problems of culture

The desire to *change* the culture of the Prison Service, on the grounds that it is preventing the service from moving forward, is made explicit in the 1997 *Prison Service Review*. This internal review of the service was launched in March 1997 against a background of rapid expansion (a result of an unprecedented growth in the prison population) and increasing pressures to become more effective (in both custodial and rehabilitative terms) and efficient (in terms of controlling costs). The review focuses on proposals for improving the delivery of prison services in accordance with the Prison Service's *Statement of Purpose*[1] (Prison Service 1997). According to this document, prison services will not improve unless the Prisons Board embarks on a programme of 'cultural and behavioural change' (*ibid.*: para. 10.1). To this end, the review team recommended that the Prisons Board carry out a 'culture audit' to identity current staff behaviours and styles (the 'staff' in question appear to be discipline rather than managerial) in order 'to identify the distance to be travelled from where the Prison Service is now to where it needs to be' (*ibid.*: 134). It was proposed that this audit could easily run alongside the staff survey due to commence in the autumn of 1997.[2]

The review team's proposed *method* of identifying (with a view to changing) particular staff cultures and styles is a curious one. It is difficult to see how the richness, diversity and complexity of the social world of the prison officer can be captured through the audit process – a process normally associated with the official examination of accounts.

The *rationale* behind such a move however is common to many other large organisations wishing to improve their performance (I will return more specifically to the issue of culture in a moment). I do not intend here to provide yet another meditation on modern forms of management (cf. Pollitt 1993; Mclaughlin and Muncie 1994) nor an overview of penal policy and prison management and organisational change within the Prison Service itself. Rather my aim is to highlight those policy and organisational issues which are of most relevance to my own research interests and contribution, in order to explore the less discussed issue of what it means to undergo these changes from the point of view of uniformed staff. I turn first of all to the rise, and impact, of 'managerialism'.

Management, measurement and accountability

Briefly put, managerialism can be described as 'a set of beliefs and practices, at the core of which is the assumption that better management is an effective solvent for a wide range of economic and social ills' (Pollit 1993: 1). At the broadest level, there are a number of principles which underpin this ideology, and at the centre is the view that management is 'the fundamental co-ordinating force' and that managers must be 'free to manage' (Clarke *et al.* 1994: 1). Prescriptive formulae on 'how to be a good manager' are numerous and varied, but they commonly include 'the need to set clear objectives, allocate resources to ensure their achievement, control costs, motivate staff and improve efficiency' (*ibid.*: 5). In short, the successful organisation must be *efficient* and *effective*, and it should be run as *economically* as possible.

Driven by the philosophy of the 'three Es', Prison Service management has radically changed (see Evans 1990; Liebling and Price 2001 for useful elaborations of the service's recent management history). Oriented primarily to cutting expenditure, the Prison Department has allowed (via the Civil Service Bill 1992) the devolution of budgets to the governors of individual establishments, devised a strategy of objectives and targets for the service – measured annually by 'Key Performance Indicators'[3] (KPIs) – and quantified service delivery through a standardised process of 'regime monitoring' (Jones 1993). So how had all this come about?

The move towards modernisation and managerialism within the Prison Service has its roots in the early 1980s, the period following the May Inquiry which was intended as a major review of the entire prison system. It was clear from the subsequent *Report of the Inquiry* (Home Office 1979) that the service not only had practical problems of budget

5

management, but was also shot through with problems concerning the proper role of prisons (and by extension the proper role of prison officers). Within the Prison Department, concerns about poor management and escalating prison costs were already being expressed, not least because of the deteriorating industrial relations discussed above, increasing prisoner unrest and an ever-expanding staffing bill. In 1986, a report commissioned by the Home Office concluded – much to the chagrin of the POA – that officers were working excessive – and unnecessary amounts of overtime. According to this report, prisons could be run safely and efficiently if officers worked on average eight hours less but with revised shift systems and working practices. The government's response, in 1987, was a new scheme called 'Fresh Start'[4] under which prison officers were to work without overtime but with an improved basic salary. Fresh Start had a significant impact on the service. The impact of Fresh Start on pay and attendance alone was too great for many 'old hands', for whom, as one of my interviewees put it:

> Fresh Start was like the tide coming in. The first wave got all the old-style officers who used to virtually live in the prison. They just couldn't cope; not only did they miss the overtime money and the company, they had to spend a lot more time at home than they'd ever been used to. (Long-serving senior officer)

Before Fresh Start, many prison officers' wives brought up their children virtually single-handed. When overtime ceased, husbands and wives were thrown together and many found that they had grown apart:

> because they were at work all the time, they were suddenly finding more time to be with their family, and, it's, it's a similar thing happens in the army; people are away and they come back and they're suddenly livin' with their family all the time … It became a matter of getting to know somebody again. (Male officer, Lancaster Farms)

Some found that they barely knew their children:

> Working massive amounts of overtime brought in the money, but the downside was you never saw your kids. I still don't know my eldest – it's damaged my relationship with him, actually. (Senior officer, Garth)

Four years later, on 1 April 1993, the Prison Service became an executive agency in a move designed to give the service greater independence and a clearer sense of purpose (see POA 1991; King and McDermott 1995; Prison Service 1995; Lewis 1997 for competing views of agency status). The creation of the Prison Service Agency also brought with it an attempt to measure the performance of the service in a quantitative way. As I indicated above, each of the service's goals is now supported by one or more KPIs and each year the Secretary of State sets out the key targets[5] in respect of each KPI, measuring the achievements of the service against them.[6] While some have criticised the emphasis[7] of the KPIs, others claim that the system has really focused attention on improving performance (for a succinct and interesting discussion of this, see Bryans and Wilson 1998).

One of the more visible aspects of managerialism within the Prison Service has been the privatisation or 'contracting out' of prison management wherever service delivery was deemed to be poor. This 'market-testing'[8] of the prison estate has been an important strategy for exerting pressure on individual establishments to become more economical, effective and efficient, since those prisons that fail to do so can simply be contracted out. To put it simply, 'the explicit promise of market testing is that the public sector, goaded by the presence of the private sector, can and will improve its performance' (Harding 1997). Many of the prison officers who participated in my research were of the view that the threat of privatisation *has* improved the performance of public sector prisons, and that it represented the 'kick in the pants' the Prison Service deserved. Relatively high costs and inadequate facilities (the practice of 'slopping out' was still in place until the late 1990s) are of course the more *visible* indicators of inefficient and ineffective prisons. There are also many less visible factors to be addressed in the improvement of prison regimes, such as the attitudes and behaviours of prison staff. It was in this context of increasing pressures to improve service delivery that the Prison Service turned its attention to the impact of staff cultures.

Occupational cultures

It has become increasingly common to hear people talk about organisational and occupational 'cultures'. Indeed, over the past two decades an impressive array of management books and articles on the subject have been published (see, e.g., Smircich 1983; McLean and Marshall 1988; Williams *et al.* 1993; Fineman and Gabriel 1996), each noting the impact of occupational cultures on the performance of organisations and corporations. As a result, top levels of management in private corporations such as Abbey National and Rank Xerox attempted to identify (with a view to changing) the cultures of their own organisations, primarily to implement reform (i.e. improve performance and increase profit) but also to address issues such as staff retention and morale. The changing of informal work cultures has now become a priority in many types of organisation, with managers in both the private and public sector implementing new initiatives in recruitment, training and staff appraisal in an attempt to achieve this.

So what, precisely *is* 'culture' in this context? Culture is not easy to define. In anthropology, culture refers to the 'way of life' of a society or community, including codes of manners, dress, language, rituals, norms of behaviour, stock of myths and stories, customs, rituals and systems of belief. Generally speaking, definitions of culture tend to deal primarily either with the way we act or the way we think (Williams *et al.* 1993: 14). Writing from an organisational perspective, Williams *et al.* note that between these two extremes, culture has also been defined in terms of both thought and behaviour. A working definition of 'occupational culture' could thus be 'the commonly shared beliefs, values and characteristic patterns of behaviour that exist within an organisation' (*ibid.*: 12). Put more simply, occupational culture could be described as 'how things are done around here'. In his study of the British police, Holdaway (1983: 134) defines *occupational* culture as ' ... the officers' construction of what constitutes (and should constitute) police work i.e. what police officers think they *should* be doing and how they think this can best be achieved'. This pattern of meanings is historically transmitted; as people interact the norms and practices of the organisation are lived out, enforced and reinforced. The culture of an organisation has the capacity to be both a force for stability and an impediment to change. At its most fundamental, culture serves to reduce uncertainty; we draw on cultural knowledge to establish what kinds of behaviour are acceptable and how to present ourselves to different people. By the same token, cultures have the capacity to stifle difference and change, and to reinforce those ways of thinking and acting that are consistent with the historically shared and reinforced way of doing things. When managers try to achieve cultural change, this can often lead to the 'trenches response' 'whereby people keep their heads down until all the fuss has quietened down and then slowly re-emerge to carry on much as before' (McLean and Marshall 1988).

In the context of policing, the culture of the 'rank and file' was identified as a major obstacle to securing improved value for money, and concerted attempts were made to change it (Jones 1993). Delegated responsibility and individual initiative were to take the place of hierarchical decision-making, junior officers were to be involved in the formulation of higher-level aims and every officer was expected to know how he or she could contribute to the overall aims and objectives of the force. A range of training schemes were adopted by the Metropolitan Police in an attempt to 'modify' the attitudes of police officers (Bull and Horncastle 1986). A few years later, Sir Peter Imbert, having set himself the goal of changing police culture, abandoned the term police *force* and adopted the title of Metropolitan police *service*. The 'Plus Programme'[9] was set in train in an attempt to 'turn the inward-directed, self-interested focus of the lower ranks' occupational culture outwards to the public and their defined needs' (*ibid*). Similarly, for the first Director General of the Prison Service, the primary task was 'to jolt the service out of [its] complacency'. To do that he had to reinforce the concept of performance, and did so through the introduction of the performance targets described above.

Changing the culture of an organisation, however, is no easy task. It is clearly more difficult in organisations such as the Prison Service and the Police Service, where low-ranking members operate with a great deal of discretion. While organisational theorists had encouraged the view that cultures are a 'controllable variable' that managers can manipulate at will (see, for example, Peters and Waterman 1982) they neglected to highlight the fact that employees may not *like* to be manipulated. Although employees strive for meaning at work, that does not mean that they will embrace *any* meaning. Moreover, in most organisations there are usually some individuals who are too disillusioned, too cynical, too frustrated, too despondent or simply too old to 'buy into' the organisation's new ideal; these individuals fail to internalise it and make it their own (Gabriel 1993: 135). This is undoubtedly true in regard to the Prison Service, where it became clear during my own research that many long-serving officers have created an *alternative* ideal, one built not around galvanising utopias for the future but around re-constructions of the (cherished) past. As is clear from the growing literature on nostalgia (see, for example, Davis 1979; Lasch 1980; Sohn 1983; Daniels 1985; Kaplan 1987) memories and sentimental yearnings are important, even at work; in the context of increasing change they serve to soothe and console individuals who are feeling alienated, insecure and who no longer feel that they *belong*. As we shall see in subsequent chapters, lapses into reverie – about the 'characters' that once trod the landings, the days when the service was a *disciplined* service and when prisoners 'knew where they stood' – are commonplace amongst uniformed prison staff.

Tradition and the production of culture

The dominant occupational culture of uniformed staff in any one establishment (there are, as we shall see in subsequent chapters, a multiplicity of staff cultures in prisons) is dependent upon a variety of elements, including the history and function of the prison and its (formal and informal) identity within the service. The occupational cultures of each establishment have evolved over time and in different ways; moreover, different cultures can be identified amongst staff of the same grade and working in the same prison. Old, large, local prisons tend to have particularly durable traditions, customs and ideologies about the 'proper' role of the officer (and the status of the prisoner). In the 1970s, officers working in such prisons often 'thought along the lines of "if it's not broke, don't fix it"' (principal officer pers. comm.). Today, prison officers are increasingly being called upon to 'fix' their working practices whether they regard them as broken or not. Significant changes in staff attitudes and behaviours have occurred over the past two decades, not least because of serious prison disturbances and a significant increase in legal intervention in prison life. In addition, the introduction of policies such as cross-posting and what Martin and Jurik (1996: 172) call the 'reform-professionalization ethic' have to some degree undermined solidarity based on social similarity, and begun to fragment the 'old guard' or 'dinosaur' culture which associated competence with masculinity, physical strength and emotional toughness. None the less, as we shall see, there remain a significant number of male officers who fiercely resist change; these officers do not, for example, want women working in 'their' prisons and generally believe that prisons have become 'too soft'.

Until the late 1970s, and the landmark case of *St Germain* (see below) the treatment of prisoners reflected, to a large degree, the fact that prisoners were perceived (by prison staff and more significantly, by the courts) as having no recourse to any legal authority. As a result, when a prison officer told a prisoner seeking redress that *he* was 'the law here' (Livingstone and Owen 1995) the officer was more or less correct. Courts did not say that prisoners had no rights:

> only that the assurance of such rights as they had could safely be entrusted to their custodians. Behind this lay ... an assumption that in any contest the custodian would be stolidly in the right and the prisoner a mendacious troublemaker, so that nothing was to be gained by giving a prisoner a day in court. (*Ibid.*)

It was in this context that staff assaults on prisoners regularly took place. As one of my officer interviewees (a long-serving senior officer) put it, many prison officers of that era 'thought nothing of giving an obstreperous inmate a battering, or dragging him down several flights of stairs'.

Changing culture?

The ethos of a particular prison *can* be altered, although the *pace* of change may be slow. Policy changes and particular events – the removal of excessive overtime and the sale of staff 'quarters' (in the mid-1980s these policies dispersed staff and to some extent reduced solidarity as a result); the shift from national to local recruitment; the introduction of early retirement and severance packages such as VERSE[10]; the transferring out of large numbers of officers (and the subsequent transferring in of new ones) in the aftermath of serious disturbances; and the introduction of female officers into men's prisons – can have a significant 'diluting' effect on the more obdurate aspects of prison officer culture, for example the emphasis on seniority by 'time in' in addition to rank. As we shall see in subsequent chapters, when sufficient numbers of new staff are transferred en masse from the training college or from another establishment they are likely to have sufficient confidence (through the support of their peer group) to resist working practices and customs that they find disagreeable and to develop their own.

The need for image work

The review team also recognised the need to improve the public *image* of the Prison Service, noting that 'Prison Services across the world tend to have a negative public image and this plays back into the standing and self-image of the staff' (Prison Service 1997: para. 10.25). Since most of the work that prison staff do takes place behind the prison walls, the general public have little appreciation of what they actually do (*ibid.*). Moreover, media reporting of failure (of both security and control and the delivery of justice) has exacerbated the difficulty of conveying to the public the positive work that is done in prisons (*ibid.*: para.10.26). Arguably, efforts to change staff cultures and regimes have been prompted, at least in part, by the 'crisis of legitimacy' in prisons (see below). In recent years the Prison Service has made strenuous efforts to improve its public image (engaging in what Mawby 2002 terms, in the policing context, 'image work'). Much of this effort has been directed towards being 'more open and accessible to the media ... in order to convey a more balanced picture of the work that staff do' (Prison Service 1997: para.10.27).

The Prison Service now has its own website and has permitted numerous 'fly on the wall' prison documentaries. Arguably, both these would have been inconceivable thirty years ago (even if the technology had been available). Some prison officers are now working outside the prison setting and becoming involved in community crime prevention through the delivery of schemes such as 'Prison! Me! No Way![11] These officers go into schools with the primary aim of deterring children from crime. In the process, however, these officers manage to enrich their own working lives and give themselves an additional sense of purpose.

Improved working conditions

There have also been significant changes to staff working conditions over the past three decades. Notwithstanding the tendencies towards staff nostalgia that I have already noted, it is clear that working in prisons in the 1960s and 1970s was, for many officers, a depressing experience. In the 1960s, many prisons were 'still lit solely by gas lamps, technology was virtually non-existent, there were no two-way radios and no alarm bells, and staff who worked in them were often violent, depressed and demoralised' (principal officer pers. comm.). Officers who had worked at HMP Wandsworth (where a silent regime was imposed on prisoners until the mid-1970s) recalled that a restrictive regime was imposed on officers too. They, like prisoners, were not supposed to speak on the landings nor were they allowed to smoke or even bring cigarettes and matches into the prison. Those who wanted to smoke at work – which many did – hid their cigarettes and matches in their caps, hid round corners and kept an eye out for each other (senior officer pers. comm.) in case the chief officer[12] should appear. For the long-serving officers in this study, the chief officer, in his gold-braided cap, 'was God' (all ranks pers. comm.). Despite their veneration, however, officers *did* bend rules and develop informal strategies to cope with the long hours and the tedium of what was then a largely 'turnkey' role. The following extract, from an account published in the *Prison Service Journal* (Waplington 1996: 19) illustrates quite beautifully the ennui and disaffection of uniformed staff during that period. Describing his first days as a newly joined officer at Leicester in the 1970s, this former governor recalls:

> I resolved to fall in line with what I observed from the other officers to be the normal practices on the wing. The normal practices on the wing didn't take long to learn. They involved standing by an alarm bell and watching the prisoners in the wing. Standing by an alarm bell and watching prisoners in the workshop. Standing by an alarm bell and watching the prisoners on exercise. This

monotonous routine was only broken up by such tasks as the locking and unlocking of doors, collecting food or occasionally exchanging the alarm bell position for a radio position. We were not allowed to sit down, remove articles of uniform, smoke or stand and converse with other officers, and although one did all these things the numerous CCTV cameras made them risky practices ... Our only real compensation was money. A main shift of 8 hours 45 minutes was a short day and rest days almost non-existent ... a pleasant distraction for some officers, especially on Sundays, was to work out how much they had earned as each minute passed. Crosswords preserved the sanity of the rest of us, however, which were quite good in that you could extract them from the newspaper and conceal them in the palm of your hand. Periodically filling them in was made to look like a check on inmates and even made one appear conscientious ... Alienation par excellence!

Recruitment and investment

Management efforts to modernise and professionalise the Prison Service are evident from its involvement in a variety of initiatives taken from outside the prison environment, including the National Vocational Qualifications[13] framework (new officers are now expected to achieve NVQs in Custodial Care). The service has also introduced a policy of involving all establishments in the Investors in People[14] initiative, has encouraged establishments to enter staff in the Butler Trust Award Scheme (which aims to reward staff initiative and hard work) and made significant changes to recruitment criteria, in an effort to recruit staff with better observational, analytical and written communication skills than those possessed by some of the officers joining the service in previous years. New entrant officers are now required to have five GCSE passes (at grade A–C) or equivalent, including English and Mathematics (www.hmprisonservice.gov.uk). Arguably, the raising of educational standards *is* likely to ensure better-quality written reports (an increasingly important issue given the range of prisoner reports that officers are now expected to write). Improved educational standards, however, do not necessarily ensure a fair, just and tolerant staff approach towards prisoners[15] – or, as Jurik and Musheno (1986) put it, the recruitment of better educated officers does not guarantee better prisons. In the USA, changing patterns of guard recruitment, explicitly identified by managers as a key means for 'reforming' the prison, met with little success. On the contrary, more highly educated officers held no more positive attitudes towards inmates and inmate rehabilitation prospects than did many veteran staff with relatively little formal education (*ibid.*).

Moreover, more highly educated officers were found to be significantly less satisfied with the prison work environment than less educated, security-oriented officers, a finding that concurs with similar studies on the police (see for example, Stirling 1974; Swanson 1977; Talarico and Swanson 1982). Similarly, when ethnic minority prison guards were recruited on the assumption that they would treat minority prisoners more humanely, and relate to them more effectively, it was clear that staff attitudes towards prisoners and correctional goals bore no relation to whether guards were white or black (Jacobs 1983). One explanation for the latter may be that 'the status of prison guard is a "master status" that washes out extra-organisational allegiances' (*ibid.*: 176). Indeed, according to Jacobs, '[c]onflict between prisoners may be so structured into the organisational roles that only a certain kind of "working personality" enables the officer to survive' (*ibid.*) (I shall return to the concept of 'working personality' in a moment).

None the less, the new requirement for prison officers in England and Wales to possess GCSEs may have *some* impact on staff–prisoner relations, in that far fewer ex-services personnel will now be eligible for recruitment into the service (the lack of educational qualifications has never been a bar into the ranks of the armed forces). Although the exclusion of ex-services personnel is not an explicit aim of the new recruitment criteria, what is clear from my own conversations with both prison officers and prison managers is that such personnel (soldiers in particular have traditionally viewed the Prison Service as an obvious 'next step' after military life) are often too inflexible and discipline oriented to rise to the challenges of the 'modern' prison officer role (I return to this in a moment). Prior to the 1980s, however, the vast majority of prison officers were recruited from the armed forces. The Prison Service favoured ex-military recruits because they were perceived as sufficiently disciplined to turn up on time, obey and deliver instructions and be smartly turned-out and tidy. By the mid-1980s, however, the proportion of staff with a military background was already declining and a greater number of non-military staff recruited from outside industry. As I have already indicated, this had significant implications for the occupational cultures of individual prisons, and, ultimately, relationships, training and regimes.

Staff resistance

There is no doubt, however, that many prison officers resent many of the changes that have taken place within the service. In that so many officers perceive change as a threat to familiar and comfortable ways of working one could argue that they share police officers' tendency towards 'conservatism'. As in many other well established organisations, tradition and nostalgia have an extremely important place in the occupational cultures of prisons. Many of the older, long-serving officers who took part in this research lapsed into reverie, recalling a 'golden age' of heroic achievements and remarkable colleagues – 'characters' who had made the job special. In the Prison Service there is a distinct generational divide between experienced and new, between young and old. That divide is cognitive and normative, but it is also emotional – the past routinely described as fine and good, the present as disappointing. Prison officers who have experienced the change from the old practices to the new tend to see themselves as radically different from those who joined the Prison Service more recently; their past has become a shared heritage which binds them together and excludes those who never knew the 'old days'. Employing the past to comment on the here and now, these officers share a painfully felt sense of loss.

That change is *so* disliked is, in part, a consequence of the plethora of initiatives introduced by the Prison Service in recent years. Over and over again during my research, officers – even those with relatively liberal attitudes and with a relatively short time 'in service' – commented that too many initiatives have been set in train in too short a time. Virtually all complained that they had 'no stand-still time' – no time to 'take stock' of what they were supposed to be doing and why they were supposed to be doing it. As in other organisations, however, change has unfortunately been (and continues to be) implemented in a 'top-down' directive fashion – that is, fast but very prescriptive (Fisher 1998). As McLean and Marshall (1988: 16) note in their discussions of organisational change more generally, there is a tendency for senior managers, in their attempts to improve the performance of their organisations, to concentrate rather too much on shaping and presenting high-profile activities and rather too little on the (low-profile) working realities of those 'on the ground'. When this happens, 'the numerous exhortations, declarations of intent, charters or mission statements can sound like very hollow and meaningless rhetoric to their staff, and risk alienating them' (*ibid*.). As we shall see in subsequent chapters, such an approach leads to little 'ownership' of cultural change, particularly at the lower levels of the organisation (on this see especially Chapter 7). Instead it generates considerable cynicism, particularly towards those initiatives that profess to enhance officers' careers.

The benefits of change

This is not to say, however, that all prison officers resist change, nor that all changes are resisted. On the contrary, it is clear that many officers are embracing new working practices and opportunities, particularly the opportunity to do more rehabilitative work with prisoners, as this in turn makes their own job more interesting and fulfilling. Most officers acknowledge that certain changes have greatly improved the service and have made the job more enjoyable. The 'opening up' of the service to recruits from non-military occupations, for example, was regarded by many officers as a particularly important step because it improved the general *atmosphere* of prisons. Because recruits from civilian occupations have no military model to refer to, they have a non-military demeanour and as such tend not to expect blind obedience from prisoners. Moreover these officers are likely to be less concerned than their ex-military counterparts to present and maintain a 'macho' front. The traditional inclination of ex-military staff working in prisons in the 1970s to 'bull'[16] their boots, extend their key chains so that they clattered on the steel landings and 'slash'[17] the peaks of their caps so that their eyes were covered more fully were devices to intimidate and hence maintain the social distance between prisoners and staff. These are practices most officers working in prisons today are glad to be rid of. As this long-serving senior officer put it, 'The atmosphere [of prisons] has lightened up tremendously. The introduction of women, the loss of hats and slashed peaks ... its much better now. You were just uniforms before'.

The introduction of women into male prisons has had a considerable impact on the nature of prison regimes. Up until 1982, and the introduction of the Prison Service Cross-posting Policy, the prison was populated solely by men. In this environment, indifference and bellicosity were to the fore. As this senior officer reflected:

> ...You've got to bear in mind that there were no females in prisons when I joined [1967]. I don't mean female officers, there were no females, full stop. It was a very, very male orientated, dominated environment. So the only people inmates saw were male prison officers in uniform and other inmates. And its hard to get that message over ...to get people to understand what that was like. It was a harsh and often brutal environment.

Competition from the private sector and the loss of Crown Immunity have also been important elements in the 'humanising' of prisons and the development of accountable regimes. According to this principal officer, both have been particularly significant:

We needed a kick up the backside because we were not forward thinking. We were stuck in the past. [So what got in the way of forward thinking?] Secrecy. Now we're more transparent and accountable. [What kinds of secrets did you keep?] Well, about health and safety for example – don't forget we had Crown Immunity then – we didn't have health and safety audits. Also there was secrecy about regimes, about punishments, about what work was available, about the sort of training you could do. Nobody knew what we did. Private prisons have opened us up to public scrutiny. In the past, we had lots of ex-military staff [who were] all institutionalised already, and in secrecy mode already. They had blinkers on for what was expected, and what they would tolerate. It was bad really.

This officer, however, and indeed most of his colleagues, are well aware that 'outposts' with outmoded values and practices remain, and that officers working in such prisons tend to maintain 'an entrenched ideology which is very hard to break'. A newly built prison has, of course, no established 'culture' or identity to begin with; both emerge as regimes are developed, as staff 'find their feet' and as the ethos of the prison is established. In such circumstances, the senior management of a prison may well be able to persuade uniformed staff to engage in unfamiliar working practices. Moreover, they may be able to persuade them that change can actually benefit them, not just management and prisoners (new recruits, of course, are easier than experienced staff to 'mould' into desired ways of working).

And yet ...

Although most of my interviewees said that they felt overwhelmed by the pace of change within the service, they were also acutely aware that some things have not changed at all. Like their counterparts of the late 1800s, few of the prison officers who participated in this study felt valued, either by their managers or by the general public. Certainly they had rarely been consulted about the regimes in which they are expected to work. The belief that prison managers are more interested in prisoners than in them remains strong amongst officers working in English prisons. In my view this is an important issue, because positive staff–management relations are also surely an important element of getting prisons 'right'.

The second continuity I want to mention here is, unfortunately, outside the control of the Prison Service. I am referring to the increasing size of the prison population and the subsequent overcrowding of the prison estate.[18] As we know, the Prison Service has no say in who goes to prison; individual establishments must simply receive the prisoners sent to them by the courts. The key continuity, of course, lies in the prison's core function, the successful performance of custody. That this should remain its core function is largely undisputed. It is the question of the *purpose* of imprisonment that generates disagreement, and here we come to the second key continuity, the (ongoing and unresolved) tension between containment and reform/rehabilitation. Arguably, this ambiguity of purpose may never be resolved since the (modern democratic) state is itself ambiguous. Democracy implies the potential for competing perspectives; at varying times a particular perspective may be dominant and others not. The rehabilitation of prisoners is *in itself* problematic. When we expect that task to be achieved by uniformed prison officers (whose primary orientation is one of security) it is, as we shall see in subsequent chapters, even more so. None the less, despite the apparent demise of the 'rehabilitative ideal' in the 1970s, a plethora of treatment and assessment programmes have now been introduced into prisons, and these are as likely to be delivered by uniformed staff as by psychologists and staff from probation. This rehabilitative work – the delivery of which must meet annual targets – takes place in the context of rapidly expanding prisoner numbers. This ever-growing population includes larger numbers of mentally disordered prisoners, larger numbers of female prisoners,[19] larger numbers of elderly prisoners[20] and larger numbers of young people.[21]

Concluding comments

As we have seen, there have been many changes to prison policies and practices over the past three decades and, consequently, changing demands on prison officers. As I shall demonstrate throughout this book, prison officers are now expected to engage in what they (often disparagingly, it must be said) describe as 'social work', in addition to their basic custodial tasks. This is a far cry from the prisons of the 1970s when, as one principal officer (YOI) put it: 'Prison was *supposed* to be harsh; cons went into prison *for* punishment, not as punishment. Now, of course, its recognised that prisoners need help and support.' Today's prison regimes do reflect (albeit to widely differing degrees) a greater sensitivity towards the problems and needs of prisoners. As this senior officer notes:

The whole emphasis of how jailing is done has changed. When *I* joined, the emphasis was on keeping men banged up; on mass-bathing etcetera ... [With regard to bullying] At Lancaster Farms there are structured anti-bullying courses. When I worked at Strangeways, it was a case of 'Name names or forget it!'

Prison officers are increasingly aware that they are required to do more for their money. Most are trying hard to satisfy the new demands made upon them, in the hope that this will help them *survive* in the service (in a time of 'downsizing' they recognise that the acquiring of skills beyond basic jail-craft may give them an 'edge' over less adaptable officers). Many, on the other hand, find it difficult to cope – not simply with the changing nature of their role but with change more generally. For many officers it is the plethora of 'initiatives' from headquarters that makes prison work unnecessarily stressful; for others it is the bullying behaviours of some of their managers (and indeed some of their fellow officers), the presence of women officers in a traditionally male environment, inadequate staffing levels, overcrowding or the ethos of a particular wing. It is in this complex and changing environment that prison officers must do their work.

Power in prisons

Coercion, co-operation and compliance: control and inmate solidarity

As a reflection of the concern with prison disorder, a great deal has been written during the past three decades on the maintenance of control[22] in prisons. In 1990, reviewing the wealth of literature written on the subject was the remit of a Home Office research study (Ditchfield 1990). Ditchfield notes that one of the most common aphorisms of penology is that order[23] in prisons ultimately depends upon the co-operation or agreement of inmates (*ibid.*). This is, of course, something of a paradox, given that in modern society, prisons represent social systems which hold 'a grant of power which is without an equal', and that they attempt to create and maintain total or almost total social control over their inmate populations (Sykes 1958: 45). As Sykes notes, prison officials should not, on the face of it, experience great difficulty in converting their rules and regulations into reality, yet in practice the difficulties they face are many and varied and the struggle to maintain order is ceaseless. Moreover, it is a struggle in which the custodians frequently fail. The appearance of total control is thus, as Sykes observes, contrary to the reality of prison life, and for a number of important reasons. The first is that prison officers are greatly outnumbered by prisoners. In the second place, prison staff cannot rely upon prisoners' internalised obligations to obey. In examining the forces that undermine the power position of staff in an American prison, Sykes states that the most important fact to consider is that 'the power of the custodians is not based on authority' (*ibid.*: 46). Power based on authority is, to quote Sykes, 'a complex social relationship in which an individual or a group of individuals is recognised as possessing a right to issue commands or regulations, and those who receive those demands or regulations feel compelled to obey by a sense of duty'. It is this second element of authority – the sense of duty as a motive for compliance – that is lacking in the general inmate population (although see Lombardo 1981 who argues that this can be *earned* through the process of personal interaction with inmates). For Sykes, the prisoner's primary preoccupation is to compensate for/adapt to the various deprivations imposed by the fact of confinement – what he terms the 'pains of imprisonment' (on this, see also Clemmer 1940; Mathiesen 1965; Cohen and Taylor 1972; Toch 1977). Imprisonment is indeed painful for prisoners. The pains of imprisonment are not limited to the loss of physical liberty; they reside in the frustrations or deprivations which attend the withdrawal of freedom, such as the systematic deprivation of goods and services, heterosexual relations, personal security and autonomy (Sykes 1958). In relation to the latter, most prison regimes (there are exceptions as we shall see) deprive prisoners of any form of responsibility for themselves. Not only does this position the prisoner in a submissive or supplicant role that is in most other circumstances considered inappropriate for an adult, it also increases the potential for staff to increase the pains of imprisonment. As Goffman (1968) notes in his analysis of behaviour in another type of 'total institution' (a mental hospital), 'at almost every opportunity, the supplicant may be teased, denied, questioned at length, not noticed, kept waiting or merely put off'. For most prisoners (and perhaps especially for those serving long sentences) the pains of imprisonment are very difficult to bear. Loneliness, fear, sadness, frustration, regret, anger and depression are commonly felt emotions; joy, hope, satisfaction and happiness much less so. To survive psychologically, prisoners must find ways of coping with a wide variety of external and internal stress-producing conditions (Lombardo 1981: 111) (see also Clemmer 1940; Cohen and Taylor 1972; Fitzgerald 1977; Serge 1977; Toch 1977; Parisi 1982; Liebling 1992; Liebling and Krarup 1993; Bottoms 1999) and it is with the men, women and teenagers who suffer such pains that prison officers spend their working lives.

For Sykes, the inmate culture of code of norms and system of values arises as a direct consequence of the pains inflicted by imprisonment. On this view, the inmate norms position the solidarity of inmates against prison staff; in the process they function to make imprisonment less painful. Custodial power must, as a consequence of all this, be based on something other than internalised morality, and the custodians 'find themselves confronting men who must be forced, bribed, or cajoled into compliance' (1958: 47). One might ask why the administration does not ignore prisoners' lack of an inner compulsion to obey and simply force them into conformity. Addressing himself to this question, Sykes concludes that the use of physical force by the custodians has many limitations as a basis on which to found the routine operation of the prison. Not only is it an inefficient method of securing obedience, particularly when prisoners are expected to perform a task en masse, the use of force is diminished in effectiveness by the realities of the guard–inmate ratio (in most regimes, prisoners significantly outnumber staff). Moreover, the use of force has the potential to spark off further violence; indeed, numerous analyses of collective disturbances focus on the significance of illegitimate use of force (see, for example, Coyle 1989; Cooke 1991; Scraton *et al.* 1991). There is also much evidence to suggest that if prison management insists upon an overly rigid, inflexible and authoritarian style – that is, if it provides a target to be knocked down – prisoners may resort to violence as a means of saving face, to show that they can resist the regime (Cooke 1991: 105).

That is not to say, however, that prison staff never attempt to secure compliance through force or coercion; on the contrary there is a great deal of evidence to suggest that many prisoners have, over the years, been subjected to a range of abuses by prison staff, ranging from departures from procedural and natural justice to serious physical (and indeed psychological) assault (see, for example, Fitzgerald 1977; Boyle 1977, 1984; King and McDermott 1990; Scraton *et al.* 1991; Woolf 1991; Ross and Jakubczyk 1992; Jameson and Allison 1995). By 1979, however, the perception that the rights of prisoners could be safely left in the hands of their custodians was no longer valid; the Court of Appeal decision in the case of *R v. Board of Visitors Hull Prison ex parte St Germain* [1979] paved the way for increasing judicial intervention into all areas of prison life.[24]

Unfortunately, staff assaults on prisoners do still take place, especially in those prisons where a 'culture of staff violence' exists (in 2002 HMP Wormwood Scrubs was described in such terms). The combination of a (misplaced) sense of 'brotherhood' and peer pressure from dominant individuals can make abuses harder to uncover (on this see especially

Kauffman 1988); it seems that at Wormwood Scrubs, fellow officers were simply too afraid of their colleagues to report the abuse. Why is this? And why do some officers think it is appropriate to assault prisoners? According to my interviewees, notions about the appropriate treatment of prisoners vary from prison to prison and from officer to officer, and are rooted, at least in part, in past prison experiences, relationships and interactions. As such they are an important element in the occupational cultures of uniformed staff.

It is important to note that in most accounts of staff brutality towards prisoners, officers engaging in arbitrary and oppressive behaviour are held to be in the minority (see, for example, Walmsley et al 1991; Woolf 1991) and that their actions are seen (by prisoners and fellow officers alike) as creating a divide between staff and prisoners and spoiling the good work that the majority of uniformed staff do. As numerous prisoners made plain to the Woolf Inquiry, 'bad officers' get away with bullying and assaulting prisoners because 'quiet life' officers do not make waves to stop them. Failure to 'blow the whistle' on abusive colleagues may stem from a genuine fear of staff retaliation. 'Rotten apple' explanations, however, fail to capture the nuances of staff relations and perceptions, and the compromises that are made to ensure orderly regimes. This issue, and the question of *why* some prison officers engage in oppressive behaviour and others do not, are explored more fully in the empirical chapters of this book.

Since they are unable to count on a sense of duty to motivate their captives to obey, and unable to depend on the direct and immediate use of violence to ensure submission to the rules, prison officers are obliged 'to fall back on a system of rewards and punishments' (Sykes 1958: 50). Unfortunately, the system of rewards and punishments is also defective, for two reasons. First, the punishments that custodians can inflict 'do not represent a profound difference from the prisoners' usual status', particularly if the regime is so depriving that very little remains for staff to take away. Secondly, the reward side of the picture may be virtually non-existent, particularly if the prisoner is provided with all his rewards at the time of his arrival, including time off his sentence for good behaviour.

Systems of power may, of course, be defective for reasons other than the fact that those who are ruled do not feel the need to obey orders. They may also fail because those who are supposed to rule are unwilling to do so. Officers may, for example, 'turn a blind eye' to certain infractions of the prison rules, in the belief that such compromises help in the development of a better working relationship with prisoners. For Sykes, unissued orders, deliberately ignored disobediences and duties left unperformed are 'cracks in the monolith just as surely as are acts of defiance in the subject population' (*ibid.*: 53). Prison officers, then, are not in a particularly powerful position; on the contrary, they encounter a series of pressures towards compromise and accommodation. The need to get routine jobs done, their personal proximity with inmates, the 'claims of reciprocity' in human relationships – all these have their effects. Sykes calls these compromises 'corruptions', but it might be more useful to suggest that the officer is simply 'placed in the position of seeking some tolerable arrangement with prisoners while having limited resources at his/her disposal' (Sparks *et al.* 1996: 42). In sum, prison officers 'must strike the delicate balance between enforcing the rules just enough to maintain the fiction of staff supremacy, and at the same time not antagonise the prisoners to the extent that they refuse to co-operate in the charade' (Murton 1976: 66).

Although prison officers are required strictly to enforce the Prison Rules, the emotional and domestic setting in which they work makes it almost impossible for them to avoid the claims of reciprocity. Because they are in close and relatively intimate association with prisoners throughout the course of the working day, officers can, as Sykes notes, remain aloof only with great difficulty (1958: 54). While new recruits are warned against being too friendly with prisoners lest this undermine their capacity to control (Crouch and Marquart 1980; Kalinich and Pitcher 1984), as we shall see this is difficult to achieve not least because officers are, to quote Sykes, often 'caught in a conflict of loyalties'. First, as Sykes points out, prison officers may feel alienated from supervisory ranks. The reprimands, the lack of ready appreciation, the incomprehensible order – all push the uniformed officer closer to prisoners who, suffering similar irritants, act as willing sympathisers. Moreover, officers and prisoners commonly share similar working-class origins, education and local ties. It is certainly not uncommon for prisoner and prison officer to come from the same neighbourhood, have attended the same school and have acquaintances and experiences in common (Colvin 1977). There may also be a discrepancy between the judgements of society and the guard's own opinions as far as the 'criminality' of the prisoner is concerned, since in one sense, crimes of even the most serious offenders can lose their significance once the offender is in prison (as we shall see in subsequent chapters, however, sexual offences against children are often the exception). A man's behaviour in the community may thus have little bearing on his behaviour in prison; on the contrary, men who have committed the most violent and heinous crimes prove, for the most part, to be ideal prisoners (SHHD 1971: para. 57). From the perspective of many prison officers, the prisoner's behaviour in prison is much more important than his behaviour on the outside; as Lombardo (1981) puts it, 'when deviants exist in a population that is deviant by definition, deviance ceases to be important, and behaviour in the new environment comes to be the most important factor by which a man is judged'. Knowing a prisoner's offence is thus not necessarily a priority with prison staff – a state of affairs that was confirmed by many of my interviewees.

It is for all these reasons that Sykes argues that the apparent 'monolith' of total power in prisons is fundamentally 'cracked'. As I have already suggested, the organisation of prisons and prison regimes dictates that prison officers actually have much less power than is pretended, and prisoners somewhat more, and staff–prisoner interactions are, of course, moderated by this knowledge. As Sparks *et al.* (1996) note, the importance of Sykes's work, and its continuing relevance to prison studies, lies in his recognition that order in prisons is always negotiated, and that prisons in their 'normal' state are far more orderly and calm than the public generally imagines them to be.

The achievement of 'legitimacy'

Prison officers, then, may not necessarily feel that they 'have' authority simply because they wear a Prison Service uniform, or because they have rules to fall back on. Indeed, some officers differentiate sharply between power and authority, viewing authority specifically as something to be acquired though the process of interaction with prisoners. From this perspective, the legitimacy needed to exercise authority effectively must be developed and, in a very real sense, earned (Lombardo 1981). This process of acquiring 'personalised legitimacy' is generally seen by officers as a long and arduous undertaking, and only comes about when an officer learns what he can realistically expect of prisoners (and indeed of himself) and when he is able to communicate these expectations. When personalised legitimacy is achieved, reliance on rules becomes unnecessary; formal rules are used 'only in extreme cases or to set an example. They are no longer a major source of authority' (*ibid.*).

Similarly, *prisons* which manage to achieve order over long periods of time are likely to be those that have managed to achieve some minimum degree of legitimacy in the eyes of their prisoners (Sparks *et al.* 1996). The issue of 'appeasement' should perhaps be considered at this point, since prison staff (both uniformed grades and governors) often (mistakenly) conflate the two concepts. (This is unfortunate since, as we shall see in subsequent chapters, a perception that the prison is engaged in a policy of appeasement generates, amongst prison officers, intense feelings of

indignation and resentment.) The question is, how, and in what circumstances, do negotiation, tolerance and goodwill (central components in
the achievement of legitimacy in prisons) become 'appeasement'? As
Sparks *et al.* (*ibid* · 329) were themselves asked by a prison governor, 'is
legitimacy just about pleasing prisoners?' They found their answer in
Beetham's (1991) formulation of 'legitimacy', a formulation they thought
preferable to the Weberian version whereby legitimacy is simply
subjects' 'belief in legitimacy'. Importantly, Beetham's claim that power
relationships are legitimated only when they can be justified in terms of
subjects' beliefs – has implications for the 'dialectic of control'[25] that
(recursively) takes place in all social systems. By injecting a moral
judgement into the dialogue (and bearing in mind that moral
judgements are, as Sparks *et al.* note, inevitably grounded in the
prevailing moral beliefs of the society in question) outlandish demands
by prisoners that have no basis of moral support in that society can be
justifiably rejected, but demands for decent standards and fair
procedures cannot. *Legitimacy* of prison regimes, thus understood,
'demands reference to standards that can be defended externally in
moral and political argument'. An ethos of appeasement, on the other
hand, entails prison staff making concessions and compromises to
prisoners simply to avoid upsetting them.

Staff–prisoner relations

Although to 'outsiders' prison officers might appear to be a
homogeneous body with little individuality for occupational members,
as we shall see throughout this book, prison officers actually differ
greatly in terms of their working 'styles' and 'credos'. In other words, the
officers' 'grey homogeneity' (Hawkins 1976) is but a facade: 'beneath it
are attitudes and responses to the prison world as distinct among officers
as are differences that exist among inmates' (Kauffman 1988: 244). In his
discussions with a variety of criminal justice practitioners, Rutherford
(1993) identified three dominant working 'credos', namely, the
punishment credo, the humanity credo and the efficiency credo, each of
which were dependent not only on individual maturity and professional
experience, but also on the broader social and political context in which
practitioners operated. While the punishment credo is associated with a
powerful dislike and moral condemnation of offenders ('appropriate'
punishment should thus be Spartan and depriving), the humanity credo
has, at its core, an empathy with offenders (emphasis is placed upon
constructive work with prisoners, and upon openness, accountability
and the rule of law). The efficiency credo,[26] on the other hand, 'has its

base firmly in an expedient managerialist approach, which favours smooth management and avoids any claims to a moral mission. The orientation of followers of this credo is towards institutionally defined managerial goals' (Bryans and Wilson 1998: 48).

In some accounts of prison work, uniformed prison staff are perceived as fitting into two distinct groups, namely the 'people worker' and the 'bureaucrat' (Lombardo 1989). The 'people worker' (a term coined by Goffman 1968) develops, and indeed demonstrates, human feelings towards his charges; he has a flexible approach to prison work and adapts the formal rules to obtain a better working relationship and prisoner compliance. The 'bureaucrat' prefers to stick to the rules and is 'quick with the pen'; he operates in a routinised and mechanistic way and makes no compromises for individual prisoners and situations. Just as the prisoner must find his or her own way to 'do time', prison officers must find their own ways of adapting to the demands of prison work. Establishing their own strategies and 'styles' enables them to deal with the everyday realities of life on the landings. Like the prisoner entering prison for the first time, the new recruit must first cope with the *culture shock* presented by the new environment (Kalinich and Pitcher 1984). As we shall see, the basis of this shock resides *inter alia* in the high level of noise encountered in the prison, in the sudden sense of panic at being surrounded by what appears to be hundreds of 'dangerous' people, in the confusing (and contradictory) signals from veteran colleagues (some of the organisation's policies will be faithfully followed while others will be totally ignored) and in the myriad requests from prisoners (many of whom can recognise a novice all too well).

The quality of staff–prisoner relations is inextricably tied up with the nature of the prison regime. In some prisons, particular emphasis is placed on what Sparks *et al.* (1996) term – adapting the terminology current in the crime prevention field – 'situational' measures for maintaining order. Situational approaches are predicated on the belief that some people have a 'disposition' to offend (or in this context, create disorder) given the opportunity. Situational approaches do not try to alter such dispositions; instead they simply limit opportunities for, and increase the risks associated with, offending. In the prison context, minimising opportunities for disorder to develop has involved paying attention to the architectural design of prisons and maximising surveillance of activity within them. It should be noted that situational control strategies can also function to regulate staffs' behaviour; officers working on wings which utilise CCTV cameras are well aware that the cameras regulate *their* actions as well as those of prisoners.

Managers of other prisons, in contrast, may conclude that excessive use of situational controls frustrates other objectives (for example the rehabilitation of prisoners) preferring instead more 'social' means of control. Regimes which take a more social approach aim to secure a higher degree of co-operation from prisoners; in pursuance of this they allow a greater level of negotiation to take place between staff and prisoners. In therapeutic communities[27] in particular special emphasis is placed on social measures in an attempt to encourage inmate responsibility, co-operation and self-restraint (see Chapter 7). In such regimes, it is possible for prison officers to evolve and play roles that substantially transcend purely custodial ones (for example working running personal development courses for prisoners) to the benefit of both prisoners and themselves. In practice, however, most prisons tend to utilise a mixture of both situational and social measures.[28]

As I suggested above, not all uniformed staff may wish to transcend their basic custodial role; many officers have no desire to engage in non-custodial activities, preferring instead to keep their interactions with prisoners to a minimum. Others 'take an alienating role and shape it to meet their personal needs as well as the inmates under their control' (Johnson 1998: 119). This requires effort and commitment. Prison officers, as the gatekeepers to virtually every element of the prison regime, are, of course, in a position to either aggravate or alleviate the inherent pains of imprisonment. Consequently, it is they who, 'through a kind word, a flash of humour, and a little insight … can alleviate a prisoner's distress, defuse impending confrontations and forestall suicide and self-harm' (Hay and Sparks 1991: 7). Officers who do so 'provide human service rather than custodial repression' (ibid.: 137). Although some officers approach the human services aspect of their work grudgingly, calling themselves 'baby-sitters' and 'nursemaids', as we shall see there are others who approach the service aspect of their work with a positive attitude. As a 'human service' worker (the equivalent of Goffman's 'people worker') these officers become involved with inmate problems. In this role, many officers see themselves as being like psychiatrists, doctors, social workers or even father figures (Lombardo 1981). Such human services account for much of the 'real substance' of correction officer work in prison. Although the social distance[29] found between officers and prisoners varies significantly amongst officers, generally speaking, it is 'not as great as one might expect' (ibid.: 63). Similarly, many prisoners display a relatively low social distance from officers, as I shall try to demonstrate in the empirical chapters of this book.

There is a good deal of evidence that positive staff–prisoner interactions play a critical role in reducing violence and the management of dissent (see, for example, Boyle 1977; Zeeman *et al.* 1977; Gunn *et al.* 1978; Home Office 1984; Bottoms and Light 1987; Cooke 1991). Dunbar (1985) argued that 'dynamic security' is the starting point for maintaining secure and safe prisons. As Dunbar notes, improving regimes and relationships between staff and prisoners enhances security; prisoners will have less motivation to escape if they have trust and confidence in staff; moreover, intelligence about escape attempts will flow more readily where prisoners and staff have good, confident relationships. As the Control Review Committee (CRC) had concluded the previous year, 'relations between staff and prisoners are at the heart of the whole prison system and control and security flow from getting that relationship right' (Home Office 1984: para.16). Unfortunately, the committee did not elaborate how the 'general proposition' about 'getting that relationship right' was supposed to be translated by prison officers working on the landings. Nor is it even certain, as Hay and Sparks (1991) point out, that a consensus exists on what a 'right' relationship would be. What *is* clear is that until very recently, prison officers were rarely asked for their thoughts on the matter. Throughout this book I draw upon the CRC's primary observation to ask, *inter alia*, 'What is involved in establishing positive relationships in an institution as emotional and domestic as a prison?' 'What do prison officers consider the "right" staff–prisoner relationship to be?' 'Is the relationship that is "right" in adult prisons also "right" in young offender institutions?' 'How do prison officers work positively with prisoners such as sex offenders, whose crimes anger and disgust them?'

Cultures at work

Prison officers and the police

I want now to return to issues of culture. More specifically, I want to discuss the ways in which the occupational culture of prison officers compares (and contrasts) with the key characteristics of the occupational culture of rank-and-file police officers. Making such a comparison is helpful, because prison officers and police officers are the only blue-collar, predominantly working-class occupational groups in the criminal justice system. As such, it is perhaps unsurprising that there are certain similarities in the ways that police and prison officers think about their work. There are however certain important differences, which I shall outline below.

The working personality of the police officer

In contrast to the dearth of scholarly work on prison officers, there is an abundance of sociological literature on the work of the police (see, for example, Banton 1964; Bittner 1967, 1970; Cain 1973; Skolnick 1975; Manning 1977; Holdaway 1983; Punch 1985; Reiner 1985; Brogden *et al.* 1988; Heidensohn 1992; Mulcahy 1995; Chan 1996; Loader 1996; Mawby 2002). As an analysis of the occupational culture of rank-and-file police, the work of Jerome Skolnick (1975) stands unrivalled. It is the *locus classicus* of sociological police studies. Skolnick is primarily concerned with one of the central themes of the sociology of occupations, the effect of an employee's work on his or her outlook on the world. Earlier work in this vein includes Ely Chinoy's (1955) study of employees in the American car industry, Janowitiz's (1964) study of professional soldiers and Walker and Guest's (1952) study of assembly-line workers. Skolnick's focus of interest lies with the demands placed on the rank-and-file police officer. The core of his argument is that these demands 'result in tendencies general enough and similar enough to identify a distinctive "working personality"[30] among police' (Skolnick 1975: 71). That is, they generate distinctive cognitive and behavioural responses – distinctive ways of thinking about and doing police work – that amount to a distinctive occupational 'culture'.

Skolnick identifies the police officer's working personality as being generated in direct response to three important variables: 1) the (unpredictable) dangers of the job; 2) the authority invested in the office of constable; and 3) the constant pressure to be 'productive' and 'efficient'. Although Skolnick does not suggest that all police are alike in working personality, he does argue that there are 'distinctive cognitive tendencies in police as an occupational grouping', including a tendency towards cynicism, suspicion (the need to be preoccupied with potential violence encourages the police officer to develop a perpetual shorthand to identify symbolic assailants), a strong sense of group solidarity and 'clannishness' (professions which are continually preoccupied with the threat of danger require a strong sense of solidarity to operate effectively), conservatism (police officers have a strong need for order, routine and predictability) and a liking for potential danger (particularly its associated excitement). Interestingly, Skolnick places rather less emphasis on machismo than does Reiner (1985) a decade later.

As Skolnick notes, some of these tendencies may of course be found in other occupations sharing similar problems; so far as exposure to danger is concerned, the police officer may be likened to the soldier. The police officer's problems as an authority, on the other hand, bear a certain similarity to those of schoolteachers, and the pressures they feel to prove

29

themselves efficient are not unlike those felt by the industrial worker. It is the combination of these elements, however, which Skolnick argues is unique to rank-and-file police. As a result of combined features of their social situation, police officers 'tend to develop ways of looking at the world distinctive to themselves; cognitive lenses through which to see situations and events. The strength of these lenses may be weaker or stronger depending on certain conditions, but they are ground on a similar axis' (Skolnick 1975: 42).

It is important to note that the characteristics which make up the police officer's working personality are not, from this perspective, psychologically pre-dispositional, as Skolnick's use of the term 'personality' appears to imply. As Brogden *et al.* (1988: 29 emphasis added) note, it is more meaningful 'to talk of *performance* rather than personality traits, and of the social construction of attitudes rather than natural pre-dispositions'. The working personality of police officers is perhaps best described as a result of a 'process of acculturation'; '... the outcome of situationally specific interactions [and values] which get picked up informally by watching older more experienced hands at work' (*ibid.*: 6). Although police officers initially go through a period of formal training, it is *after* basic training – through the absorption of the 'commonsense', 'recipe' or 'craft' rules of the police subculture – that new recruits are transformed into 'practical coppers'. In the eyes of his colleagues, the competent officer is one who can give the *impression* of competence in a way that is acceptable to the occupational group, the wider community and the courts; in short, policing is a 'performance' constructed with particular audiences in mind (*ibid.*: 42 but see Manning 1997). In sum, the old hand explains to the new recruit how it is not always possible to work to the book (Chatterton 1979). Through the use of stories and through early experiences shared with more experienced colleagues – what Brogden *et al.* (1988) term 'situationally located learning' – the new recruit learns how to get the job done in ways that are acceptable to his colleagues. When newcomers are 'learning the ropes' – which consists largely of learning the shortcuts around, and resistance to, organisational controls (Thompson and McHugh 1995: 337 but see also, for example, Punch 1985) – they are, in part, learning the (sub)culture of the organisation. Microsociology (which encompasses theoretical frameworks such as symbolic interactionism and phenomenology) has been invaluable in drawing attention to these processes. Microsociology, in short, led to the 'discovery' of informal police cultures; that is, to an uncovering of the rules, norms and values which construct and guide the attitudes and behaviours of police officers (Brogden *et al.* 1988: 31). These informal police cultures are often portrayed as a pervasive, malign and potent influence on the behaviour of officers and which mobilise the lower ranks to resist enlightened change (Waddington 1999: 287).

The occupational culture of the police is by no means universal or static. On the contrary, researchers of the police have pointed out that there are multiple cultures within police work in the sense of distinct differences of outlook between and even within police forces, according to variables such as personality, age, rank, past experience, specialisation and so on (Skolnick 1975 but on this see also, for example, Reuss-Ianni 1983). Indeed, given the variety of cultures identified by researchers of the police – Websdale and Johnson (1997), for example, draw distinctions between rural and urban police, while Reuss-Ianni (1983) note the hierarchical divisions between 'management cops' and 'street cops' and Fielding (1995) the division between beat officers and 'community constables' – Waddington's (1999: 290) claim that the occupational culture of policing, as a set of shared artefacts, has almost disappeared completely may not be far from the truth. It therefore makes more sense to speak of police cultures. Similarly, as I shall go on to argue, it is probably more useful to speak in the plural when discussing the culture of prison officers, given that here too researchers have thrown doubt on whether a single prison officer culture exists or indeed *ever* existed (see, for example, Lombardo 1981; Poole and Regoli 1981).

None the less, those working in the Police Service and the Prison Service are often described in terms of particular occupational 'types'. In the police world we find, for example, the 'enforcer' (who emphasises law enforcement at all costs, even if rules must be bent in the process); the 'professional' (who is ambitious and career conscious); the 'uniform carrier' (the cynical and disillusioned time-server who avoids work); and so on. Similarly, prison staff refer to the 'black-and-whiter' (who sticks to the rules), the 'give-and-taker' (who *might* allow something, depending on the individual inmate and his circumstances) and the 'care-bear' (who enjoy interacting with and helping prisoners). Yet for Skolnick and Reiner the 'craft' of police work does incorporate distinctive and core features that seem to remain intact both over time and whichever force is studied. Building on Skolnick's work, Reiner maintains that the core characteristics of what he terms 'cop culture' are 'mission–action–cynicism–pessimism'. When combined with 'suspicion', 'isolation/solidarity', 'conservatism', 'machismo', 'racial prejudice' and 'pragmatism' 'the result is a recalcitrant occupational culture that enables and justifies police (mis)behaviour' (Ellison 1997: 64). Police misbehaviour includes the bending of formal rules. In his study of police culture, Holdaway (1983: 134) found that the various legal and policy instruments available to police personnel staff are modified as the rules in the book are translated into rules on the ground. Rules thus become merely guidelines for action. In the prison setting, rules include not just the formal Prison Rules but also the informal rules borne of local culture and tradition. These constitute the 'ethos' or 'way' of individual establishments (Sparks *et al*. 1996: 80). I will return to this in subsequent chapters.

The biased character of policing along class, race and gender lines (stories of police oppression and brutality have tended to centre on particular social groups), the 'bending' of formal policing rules to 'get the job done', the sexist treatment of female officers by some male officers (ranging from verbal hectoring and sexual propositioning to over-protectiveness) and the prejudice directed at gay officers are rooted in the informal, traditionally macho 'canteen' cultures of policing (see, for example, Holdaway 1983; Punch 1985; Reiner 1985; Brogden *et al*. 1988; Heidensohn 1992; Burke 1993; Chan 1996, 1997). The norms of this informal police culture can have a significantly negative impact on the organisation and upon the individuals working within it; they encourage cynicism and a lack of commitment to organisational goals. In addition, they often condone physical violence and encourage the protection of individual aggressors (Van Maanen 1975; Toch 1977a). On the other hand, they may also benefit the work group in that they generate solidarity, provide enjoyable interactions on the job and thus improve morale. As Waddington (1999: 295) astutely observes, 'the canteen is the "repair shop" of policing, and jokes, banter and anecdotes the tools'. Although I am not persuaded by certain other aspects of Waddington's argument, I share his interest in the potentially positive impacts of informal work cultures and this is a point I shall return to later.

Foremost among the values, attitudes and practices of both the informal cultures of police officers and prison officers is the bond of solidarity between officers (for discussions of the former see, for example, Skolnick 1975; Punch 1979; Bittner 1980; Reiner 1985; Young 1991 and for the latter, see Lombardo 1981; Johnson 1988; Kauffman 1988). According to Bittner (1980), loyalty to one's colleagues is *the* defining feature of police culture. It is perhaps unsurprising that prison officers, who also work in environments they perceive as (always) unpredictable and (often) violent, also attach a high value to solidarity. The bond of solidarity performs three central functions for both occupational groups; first it ensures that they can rely on colleagues in a 'tight spot' (i.e. when they are at risk of harm from assailants). The obligation to go to the aid of a colleague is the most important positive responsibility of any uniformed officer; in the prison as on the beat, it is 'the norm on which officer solidarity is based, the foundation of their sense of brotherhood' (Kauffman 1988 but see also Lombardo 1981). Secondly, solidarity sustains against criticism by groups who do not understand the pressures of the job (namely, the general public, 'do-gooders', the media, prisoners' legal advisers and prison officers' own managers). Thirdly, staff solidarity ensures that colleagues will maintain secrecy in the face of both internal and external investigations against them, either as individuals or as a group (see, for example, Holdaway 1983; Kauffman 1988). In relation to the second of these, Skolnick (1975) rightly notes that staff solidarity 'is very closely related to lack of public support and public apathy'. All occupational groups do of course share some degree of inclusiveness and identification; people are brought together simply by doing the same work and having similar career and salary problems. What is clear, however, is that the police show an unusually high degree of occupational solidarity (Westley 1953; Banton 1964). The dangers inherent in the work not only draw police officers together as a group but separate them from the rest of the population (Skolnick 1975: 54 but see also Bittner 1970; Manning 1977 and, in relation to prison officers, see, for example, Webb and Morris 1980). It is important, however, in any discussion of staff solidarity, not to neglect the importance of staff *conflicts* within the organisation; in my view, Skolnick's failure to do so is one of the few flaws in his analysis. Staff conflict is an important component in the day-to-day lives of prison officers, and as such it is an issue that I return to throughout this book.

Because of the nature of the work, the police officer also tends to be a suspicious person (Skolnick 1975). Indeed, the police officer is specifically trained to be suspicious. The police officer (and his prison counterpart) is also a cynical individual; he has developed 'a hard skin of bitterness, seeing all social trends in apocalyptic terms' (Reiner 1985: 113). In the prison setting, officers' shared perception of limited support from the general public (and from their own superiors), combined with the difficulty of maintaining control over increasing numbers of (often recidivist) prisoners can foster cynicism towards correctional work, an attitude that grows with time in the job (Regoli *et al.* 1979; Crouch and Marquart 1980; Poole and Regoli 1980). Police officers are also socially isolated; they become 'tainted' by the character of the work they perform (Skolnick 1975 but see also Bittner 1970) and thus less desirable as a friend to those in the wider community. This rubs off on their wives who 'experience a kind of vicarious contamination' (Finch 1983: 37). As a result, police officers and their partners tend, in the main, to socialise with 'their own kind' (on this see, for example, Banton 1964; Finch 1983). To overcome their feelings of social isolation, and to retain normal relationships with 'ordinary' people, it is not uncommon for officers to conceal their police identity. In their efforts not to become 'a police family', attempts are made to try to put police work into the background; to 'try not to let people know I'm a policeman' (Skolnick 1975). Similarly, Banton (1964: 198) found Scottish police officers attempting to conceal their identity when on holiday, because they recognised – as did their wives – that 'a sort of invisible wall was up for conversation purposes when a policeman was there'. Prison officers and their families experience strikingly similar feelings of contamination, and this is one element in the 'spillage' of prison work that I address in Chapter 8.

Although the element of danger, like the element of authority, contributes to the solidarity of rank-and-file police, police officers themselves do not necessarily emphasise the dangers associated with their work when questioned directly, and may even have well developed strategies of denial. This is because the element of danger 'is so integral to the policeman's work that explicit recognition might reduce emotional barriers to work performance' (Skolnick 19: 47). Thus, while police officers may talk a great deal about danger, they tend not to talk about being afraid. Fear must be suppressed at all costs. Because overt displays of fear by occupational members can be detrimental to the entire work group, occupational norms and values stress the overcoming of fear through displays of masculinity and machismo (see, for example, Haas 1977). A type of stoical attitude develops. I shall argue that just as high-steel construction workers must continually demonstrate their fearless-ness by flaunting danger as they 'walk the irons' hundreds of feet in the air (to express fear is to raise doubts, among their co-workers, about their trustworthiness) prison officers *perform* fearlessness at work. Just as 'running the iron' is a managed performance, apparently confident and blasé interactions between officer and prisoner are often performances intended to disguise real feelings, particularly fear (see especially Chapters 3 and 5). Fear, in short, must never be expressed; it can be felt, and *is* felt, but it is 'hidden, controlled and privately lived' (*ibid.*: 156). As we shall see, to respect a potentially dangerous situation is also an occupational norm of great importance. The prison officer who never *feels* fearful is regarded as a liability by his colleagues – as someone who may put *them* in danger.

It is partly because police*men* have traditionally enjoyed an enhanced solidarity created by external dangers that women officers were (and often still are) perceived as a threat by many of their male colleagues. As Martin (1989) observes, the entry of women officers into the police threatens to disrupt prevalent norms, dismantle group solidarity and challenge occupational identities based around 'manliness' and physical strength. Likewise, Martin and Jurik (1996: 175) argue that women threaten the close association between the prison officer's job and the production of masculinity. Clearly, if women can do the job as well as men, the job is no longer a viable resource for constructing masculinity. In a more general sense, it can be argued that the social order of the institution itself is sustained and reproduced through deeply embedded discourses around masculinity and femininity; that is, the daily experience of prisoners can be seen to be consistently and continuously mediated by their relationship with, and expectations of, the other prisoners and their guards as men (Sim 1994: 102).

The working personality of the prison officer

As I shall try to demonstrate throughout this book, prison officers possess distinct cultures within individual prisons and these can have significant impacts on the 'climates' or 'atmospheres' of those prisons. That is, the values, beliefs, attitudes, customs and working practices that influence the quality of the regime, the 'tone' of the prison and the consequent relationships between prison officers and prisoners and between officers themselves.

As an occupational group, the prison officers who participated in the fieldwork for this book claimed certain group norms and assumptions – about what should and should not be done by group members in specific circumstances – as central. Like the American prison guards studied by Kauffman (1988), they believed that an officer should adhere to a number of specific norms, i.e. 1) always go to the aid of a fellow officer in distress; 2) never 'rat' on a colleague (i.e. testify against another officer); 3) never criticise a colleague in front of a prisoner; 4) always support an officer in dispute with a prisoner; 5) always support officer sanctions against a prisoner; 6) maintain solidarity against all outside groups; 7) never demonstrate sympathy for prisoners; and 8) show positive concern for fellow officers (i.e. don't leave problems for officers on the next shift to deal with). These norms are not, however, adhered to to the same degree and by all officers. For example, norm 1 (always go to the aid of a fellow officer in distress) is generally described as inviolable; as the norm upon which solidarity is based, new recruits are judged by their willingness to uphold it. However, prison officers told me that in practice – i.e. whenever an officer calls for assistance – there are invariably some officers who 'hang back', e.g. by stopping to fasten a shoe lace that has suddenly come undone or responding so slowly to the officer's call for help that he is sure to be overtaken. If these officers are in their later years, their reluctance is likely to be tolerated by colleagues as long as they do not breach the remaining norms. Similarly, a breach of norm 7 by an officer (never demonstrate sympathy for a prisoner) may be overlooked if the officer has demonstrated that he can be relied upon to adhere to norm 1.

Prison officers work in an occupation that is highly sex-typed male and which has long been thought to require the traditional male qualities of dominance, authoritativeness and aggressiveness. It is a job in which, for many male officers, the traditional female qualities of nurturance, sensitivity, and understanding 'are thought to be not merely unnecessary but actually detrimental' (Zimmer 1986: 3 but see also Martin and Jurik 1996; Pogrebin and Poole 1997). Likewise, Crouch (1980: 217) notes that the occupational culture of the prison officer stresses the importance of 'machismo' for successful job performance, to the extent that 'the prison guard who cannot muster some version of this masculine image before both inmates and peer is in for trouble'. This 'cult of machismo' (Ryder 1994: 86), however, does have a tendency to steam-roller the sensitive, compassionate and caring side of individuals; as we shall see in subsequent chapters of this book, not only do prison officers learn not to show compassion towards prisoners (except in specific circumstances), many also learn not to feel it.

The psychological and emotional impact of prison work was noted, albeit very briefly, in a Prison Service staff attitude survey carried out in the mid-1980s (Home Office 1985). Commenting on the social costs of prison work, the survey reported that many officers felt that the job had changed their attitudes; that they had become 'more cynical and suspicious of others' and 'somehow harder and more retributive' (*ibid.*: 100 but see also Colvin 1977; Poole and Regoli 1980; Kauffman 1988 on this). Kauffman has noted, in rather more depth, the capacity of prison work to disrupt family life. This is an important issue that I return to in Chapter 8. Meanwhile, I want to make a brief detour towards an issue that is of increasing concern to both prison officers and their managers – the apparently increasing incidence of occupational stress.

Occupational stress

Occupational stress has been studied scientifically for nearly half a century. Research investigations into the effects of occupational stress[31] began in the 1950s (cf. Beehr and O'Hara 1987). Initial studies were spurred by a concern in the private sector that uncontrolled employee stress affected morale, efficiency, productivity and job turnover; one result was the development of the concept called burnout (Kalinich and Pitcher 1984). Today, it is generally accepted that a wide range of occupations expose workers to stress. Stress (including dramaturgical stress) has been demonstrated to impair the social, psychological and physical functioning of the individual; stressed individuals are more likely to experience job dissatisfaction, decreased productivity, increased rates of error and accidents, poor judgement and delayed reaction times. Psychological changes such as increased irritability, anxiety, feeling 'uptight' or 'flying off the handle' can seriously affect working relationships with colleagues and personal relationships outside work. Continued stress may result in drug dependency and substance abuse (usually alcoholism), and it may also increase the likelihood of marital breakdown and suicide. The long-term effects of stress include chronic disease such as high blood pressure, heart disease, diabetes and asthma attacks (see especially Cheek and Miller 1983; Kauffman 1988) which can result in early retirement on health grounds and, in extreme cases, in premature mortality. In addition to the physical and emotional costs of stress on employees, the costs of stress-related illness to employers – high absenteeism, high employee turnover – are considerable and increasing (Brown and Campbell 1990).

Employees in certain occupations suffer from stress at a greater rate than other occupational groups. Research by Territo and Vetter (1981) and Cooper *et al.* (1982), for example, suggests that in terms of both routine stressors and traumatic incident stress, police officers suffer disproportionately. There has been a considerable growth of interest in the causes and effects of stress amongst police officers (see, for example, Kroes *et al.* 1974; Kirmeyer and Diamond 1985; Loo 1986; Martin *et al.* 1986; Brown and Campbell 1994; Lowenstein 1999); perhaps the most significant factor contributing to this interest is the increasing pressure on public services in general to be economically rational (Brown and Campbell 1990). High levels of sick leave are, of course, inconsistent with managers' desire to be efficient, effective and economic, i.e. provide value for money. Whilst the incidence of stress amongst prison officers has provoked much less academic and in-house research than the police, what research there has been has suggested that working with prisoners can also give rise to considerable stress-related problems which are exacerbated by shift systems (and, up until 1987, high levels of overtime within the service). The Home Office survey into the attitudes of prison staff towards their work found that a significant proportion of prison officers experience high levels of stress and anxiety – as well as feelings of isolation, alienation and anomie – in their place of work. These findings have been confirmed and reiterated by others since; from within the Prison Service itself (see, for example, Norman 1986) and in the field of criminological research (see, for example, Hay and Sparks 1991).

Neither is exposure to traumatic incidents unique to police officers; prison officers also have to deal with violence, suicides, serious injuries and situations of collective disorder, all of which engage the prison officer in emotion work. In recent years the Prison Service, like the Police Service, has formally acknowledged that prison work can be extremely stressful (HM Prison Service 1996; *Prison Service News* 15 (154) 1997). UK and European employment legislation now requires organisations to assess all risks to employees' health and take steps to reduce them if necessary. As well as physical factors, this can include 'psychosocial' hazards – harmful aspects of the design, organisation and management of work. The prison disturbances of 1990 were a severe blow to the morale and the image of the Prison Service, yet officers working in the service today have benefited from that period of upheaval (Thomas 2000: 14). As Thomas notes, the physical and psychological problems suffered by uniformed staff as a direct result of these riots acted as the catalyst for the facilities that exist today. Every prison in England and Wales now has a Post Incident Care Team[32] – described by most officers as the 'Care Bear' team – which takes care of staff following traumatic experiences in addition to offering more general support and advice. Some members of these teams are trained to Diploma level in post-traumatic stress counselling and others are qualified in critical incident debriefing. The Prison Service Staff Care and Welfare Service (PSSCWS) will also engage private sector counsellors whenever an element of workplace stress is present and it is inappropriate to use in-service counsellors.

As we shall see, however, prison officers do not find it easy to admit to feeling 'stressed'. The (long-standing) cultural expectation that prison officers will be courageous, resilient, authoritative and fearless in all situations and that they will suppress those emotions thought to be 'non-masculine' (for example, anxiety, fear and depression) prevents officers who are experiencing such emotions from seeking help. It has been interesting to note, moreover, that some of the stress felt by prison officers is generated through interactions with colleagues and managers and not through interactions with prisoners. New recruits to the service are particularly vulnerable in this regard. Not only must they learn to deal with the day-to-day problems of prisoners, and to conform to the values of the occupational cultures operating in the prison in which they work, they will also have to cope with the (often disagreeable) attitudes and behaviours of their colleagues. Staff hostility, when it arises, is not only directed towards prisoners. On the contrary, officers often allege intimidation of staff by staff, directed at keeping in line those, for example, who would provide human services to prisoners and inform on the misdeeds of their fellows (on this see also Canada 1977 cited in Wright 1982: 64).

Many prison staff *do* manage to resist the more negative values, beliefs and attitudes of the 'guard subculture', particularly the emphasis on masculinity and the notion that prisoners cannot be trusted (Zimmer 1986). They may also prefer not to socialise with co-workers after work hours. As Zimmer observes, these individuals, many of whom desire to move up through the ranks, are usually more committed to organisational goals than to fellow officers. While the dominant occupational culture may fail to enmesh all prison guards (see various chapters of this book) that is not to deny its significance. On the contrary, as Zimmer notes, 'its definitions and values remain powerful because they provide the only clear, consistent philosophy for guards'. There is substantial pressure on new recruits to adopt 'subcultural' values, beliefs and moral outlook, and if they do so they are rewarded with the collective support of many of their peers.

As I have already suggested, the occupational cultures of specific establishments evolve over time. Their precise character is dependent on such things as the type and function of the prison; the prison's history (for example, the number of disturbances and the quality of industrial relations); the ratio of young to old and experienced to new staff; the nature of the regime; the ratio of staff to prisoners; the rate of staff turnover; and the architecture of the prison itself (see, for example, Home Office 1984; Bottoms and Light 1987; Woolf 1991; Fairweather 1995: 19). Arguably, external factors such as the political and economic climate are also important. Indeed, the present level of consciousness in any prison (and indeed that of any other institution) can only be understood by reference to the series of historical situations in which it has developed (Cohen and Taylor 1972: 122–3). For these reasons, the occupational culture of prison officers is not a reified *thing*: from an actor-network theory[33] perspective (see Law 1994) it could be described as an 'achievement', a 'process', a 'consequence', a 'precarious *effect*' produced by a network of heterogeneous materials – including texts, materials, architecture, paperwork, uniforms, rules, jargon, customs, ideologies, technologies and human beings. In consequence, the degree of solidarity, the value placed upon machismo, the nature of the staff–prisoner relationship and so forth vary significantly from prison to prison. As I shall go on to show, policies and practices designed to 'reconstruct' prisoners also reconstruct prison staff. In that they impose new demands as to what officers should accomplish, they impose, by extension, new demands on how officers are supposed to conduct themselves.

Some of the core characteristics of the occupational culture of prison officers are strikingly similar to those that comprise the occupational culture of rank-and-file police. As we shall see, cynicism and suspicion are commonly felt and practised at every rank and in every prison. This is perhaps unsurprising since both police and prison officers work in environments that pose similar problems and make similar demands, and that both groups are under constant criticism from the public (and, to some extent, from their managers). This has significant consequences. In particular, when an in-group perceives that it is constantly under attack from an out-group, the morale and solidarity within the in-group may, ironically, be increased. Criticism is considered a prerogative of group members; criticism from outsiders, except in special instances, is fiercely resisted (Goldstein and McGhee 1972: 120). An important effect of criticism from groups as varied as the media, the general public, politicians and prison reform groups has been the development of a laager mindset – a tendency, on the part of uniformed staff to 'circle the wagons' against unsympathetic outsiders. Sensing hostility from all sides, prison officers *as a group* have, over the years, taken an aggressive and confrontational stance. Feeling besieged from all sides they turned in amongst themselves (see Chapter 7).

In addition to the similarities, there are some significant differences between the organisational priorities of the police and those of prison officers, and significant differences between the environments in which each work. First, the pressure upon individual prison officers to 'produce results' – especially during times of moral panics around specific types of crime – does not impact on prison officers in the same way that it does upon the police (as I indicated above, however, prison officers are now also expected to achieve certain targets in terms of efficient and effective performance). Within police work, this pressure to 'get results' has implications for miscarriages of justice; in relation to prison work it does not. Pressures exerted by the occupation culture, however – peer pressure – may lead to departures from natural and procedural justice and to the de-legitimation of prison regimes. As we shall see in Chapter 4, however, making the decision to challenge such pressures, particularly when this entails reporting a colleague, is a complex issue, involving feelings of loyalty and empathy and (prisoner) desert.

Secondly, the police and prison officers also have very different roles. A medical analogy might be useful here: police officers deal with the *acute* illnesses of the body politic. When their services are called upon, emergency treatment is required, namely, the removal of the offender (the illness) from the streets (the social body). Prison officers, on the other hand, deal with more *chronic* problems – particularly problems of recidivism – involving long-standing and ongoing problems of containment and rehabilitation. The contrast, then, is one of surgery versus long-term care and convalescence. Whether prison officers have a sense of 'mission' is less clear. Whilst police officers' perception of themselves as 'the thin blue line against anarchy' is quite pronounced, the 'mission' of prison officers is blurred, as we shall see, by competing opinions about what a prison officer is supposed to do or be. Whatever their opinion, however, all prison officers agree that *numbers* – in the sense of preventing escape – is the primary task of the prison, with 'the objective of maintaining internal order ... a close second' (Sykes 1971: 22).

The chief pressure on prison officers, then, is to prevent escape. This is their primary task and the most important of the key performance indicators introduced to measure performance. In addition to this primary task, however, prison officers are expected to maintain order within the prison and to provide prisoners with a proper degree of care. While many officers may, particularly in high-security prisons, feel 'at risk' on a day-to-day basis (those of my interviewees who had worked in dispersal prisons recalled being constantly 'on guard' against assault) in general, prison life 'is not continuously suffused with imminent violence' (Toch 1994: 94). Rather, staff and inmates, perhaps particularly those in long-term prisons '... evolve an uneasy tolerance' of each other (Cohen and Taylor 1972: 130). In young offender institutions, the biggest problem for many officers is coping with the domestic tedium, and with the childish demands of young inmates, some of whom, by legal standards, *are* children. It is perhaps for this reason that stories of heroes and villains, and reminiscences about past dangers and risks, are often told when officers get together; they inject excitement into a job which is often as interesting as 'watching paint dry' (numerous officers pers. comm. but see also King and McDermott 1990 on this).

Significantly, the social world of the prison officer is smaller, more intimate, more *domestic* in character than the world in which the police officer moves. The prison is still a relatively secret world whose workings are generally hidden from view. In the past, the Prison Service has made sure that things stayed that way; when researchers have asked for access, it has often been refused them (see, for example, Cohen and Taylor 1972). Police officers, in contrast, have greater visibility and a much wider network of contacts; their social world is relatively large. They deal with law-abiding members of the general public (people who have lost their children, pets or property, relatives of those injured or killed in road traffic accidents and victims of a variety of crimes) as well as with offenders. In their working lives, prison officers deal, in the main, with people convicted of, or awaiting trial for, a criminal offence (although they do of course deal with prisoners' visitors). Moreover, as I shall demonstrate in subsequent chapters of this book, the degree of *intimacy* involved in working with prisoners is great in comparison; a prison officer may have close contact with a specific prisoner for a significant proportion of that prisoner's sentence (particularly if he is that prisoner's personal officer), unlike police officers, most of whose relationships with suspects are relatively fleeting. A police officer may not have to spend time with an individual he has treated roughly or unfairly; a prison officer does. For these reasons, prison officers are likely to be much more aware of the value of building positive relationships with those in their charge.

In all prisons (except perhaps local prisons in which there is a rapid turnover of inmates) uniformed staff are likely to spend substantial periods of time – sometimes several years – in close proximity with the same prisoners. In dispersal and Category B training prisons, the turnover of the prison population is relatively slow. Whilst it might be relatively 'safe' for an officer working in a busy local prison to be dismissive or cavalier with a prisoner since the latter is unlikely to be spending long in the prison, officers working with long-term prisoners can ill-afford to establish relationships in which conflict and resentment are to the fore. That prisoners are able to influence the actions of their keepers is made much more explicit in the more 'laid back' regime of the training or (more particularly) the dispersal prison, not least because staff here know that 'a refusal often offends' (King and McDermott 1990: 65).

It is now widely recognised that su.pervisory techniques and styles and positive staff–prisoner relationships are major factors in establishing the climate of any correctional institution (Kalinich and Pitcher 1984: 34 but see also Hawkins 1976; Henning 1976; Shover 1979; Duffee 1980). As the Control Review Committee (Home Office 1984) rightly concluded two decades ago, 'relations between staff and prisoners are at the heart of the whole prison system and control and security flow from getting that relationship right' (see also, for example, Bottoms and Light 1987). Certain consequences flow from all this. For example, prison officers working with long-term prisoners have to do things much more 'by the book' in some respects and yet be more flexible in others. Doing things 'by the book' includes providing prisoners with their full entitlements, not least because long-term prisoners (whose periods of confinement may exceed the working experience of staff) often know the rules and their own rights and entitlements better than the officers in charge of them do. On the other hand, because of the need to 'get along' on a long-term basis, officers working with long-termers have to be much more reflexive in their interactions with prisoners than they do in busy local prisons where 'the staff have got it so screwed down that they make *me* jump!' (male officer, Garth pers. comm.). In short, prison officers working with long-termers have consciously to monitor and modify those working practices and attitudes that tend, in more traditional settings (and indeed in the wider society), to exacerbate resistance and confrontation, namely, unfairness, bullying, intolerance, inflexibility and the tendency 'to treat grown men as if they were little boys' (on the latter, see Woolf 1991: 475). It could be said that these officers are consciously engaged in what King and McDermott (1990: 65) term 'a game of diplomacy' (or as many officers would say, they are 'more laid back'). The further up the security scale ones goes, the more laid back staffs' interactions with prisoners tend to become (*ibid.*), a situation which, as we shall see, many officers are uncomfortable with (see Chapter 4). Getting the staff–prisoner relationship 'right' is even more pressing (and perhaps rather more difficult) in this prison context than in any other, since it is here that concerns about security, appeasement and 'conditioning'[34] are particularly pronounced.

Emotion and performance

Organisations as emotional arenas

There is much more going on in organisations – including heavily bureaucratised organisations such as the Prison Service – than getting the job done. Organisations are also emotional places. Although the role of emotion[35] and its management are aspects of organisational life that are conspicuously absent from more traditional texts on organising and organisational behaviour, more recent work in the sociology of organisations has foregrounded emotion, arguing that 'the workplace represents an important part of social existence, and encapsulates the range of human feelings – the loves, hatreds, fears, compassions, frustrations, joys, guilt and envies – that develop over time wherever any social group interacts' (Noon and Blyton 1997: 124). In the prison as elsewhere, workers also make friendships, fall out, get disappointed, have arguments, gossip and so on. The longer I spent with prison officers, the more interested I became in the emotional and performative character of prison work. It became clear to me that emotions are right at the heart of prison life. It also became clear that prison officers' emotions must be managed, and that they must develop strategies for doing so. As a strategy for conveying, disguising and managing emotion, humour plays a significant (if somewhat unexpected) role in prisons. I was struck by the nature and volume of humorous exchanges between prison officers (and indeed between officers and prisoners). I was also struck by prison officers' penchant for practical jokes, their willingness to gossip about fellow officers and their proclivity to tell and retell (often highly embroidered or fictitious) organisational stories and myths – what Goffman (1959: 25) calls 'anecdotes from the past'. These reveries and cautionary tales do, as Goffman observes, serve a variety of purposes; they are a source of humour, a catharsis for anxieties and a sanction for inducing individuals to be modest in their claims and reasonable in their projected expectations. As in the policing context (see Waddington 1999) prison officer humour is *palliative*. This is an important point, and it is one that I return to throughout this book.

In a similar vein, Schwartzman (1993) notes that occupational stories are an important form for 1) communicating experiences; 2) socialising new members; 3) documenting success and failure and indirectly communicating information about issues too sensitive to be discussed directly; and 4) shaping and sustaining individuals' images of the organisation in which they work. In short, individuals tell stories to make sense of their world and their life at work. In the policing context, the police folk narrative exposes the reality of policing – the adaptations to the formal structure made by the lower ranks – and affirms its supremacy. Although some might think of police stories as 'just talk' between police officers, in reality, 'such talk is essential if their world is to retain any semblance of order' (Holdaway 1983). Story-telling is particularly important in the socialisation of new recruits (see Shearing and Ericson 1991). As we shall see, in the prison setting, stories – about failures to cope, about 'convict-shy' staff, about the blunder made by so-and-so and about who did and said what and to whom – abound: they constitute the folklore of individual establishments and are passed down from one generation to the next. As such they help to constitute a prison's (informal) identity within the service.

Social life as 'theatre'

The metaphor of social life as 'theatre' is extremely useful for making sense of how people operate in organisations. It is, essentially, 'a device for uncovering and de-mystifying the constructed nature of action' (Mangham and Overington 1987). As Goffman observes in his classic analyses of the theatrical character of everyday life, in constructing ourselves we perform a variety of roles, as actors do in theatrical performances. But exactly what roles we are to play, and how, in various organisational encounters is not always clear. As a result, we may 'get it wrong'. We must therefore attend to how we *present* ourselves; we must learn how to foster impressions that others will see as normal or acceptable (Fineman 1993). When an individual appears before others, he will have many motives for trying to control the impression they receive of the situation (Goffman 1959). He may, for example, wish to foster sympathy, disguise fear or inspire confidence. In everyday life there is a clear understanding that 'first impressions' are particularly important, for it is on the basis of this initial information that the individual starts to define the situation and starts to build up lines of responsive action (*ibid.*: 22). As Goffman notes, when the interaction that is initiated by first impressions is itself merely the initial interaction in an extended series of interactions involving the same participants, we speak of 'getting off on the right foot'. Individuals in positions of authority over others often feel that in 'starting out tough' and letting others 'know who is boss' much future difficulty will be prevented.

Playing a part and creating the right impression is thus not something confined to the theatre. In our everyday work lives we take up roles on the organisational 'stage' and there are 'scripts' for different people in different circumstances – between bosses and subordinates, in job interviews and personnel appraisals, in committees and in corridors (Fineman and Gabriel 1996). It follows that 'performances' are not just of the grand sort, such as when standing in front of an audience delivering a talk or lecture. Rather they are part and parcel of all face-to-face encounters as we strive to present ourselves in ways that create certain impressions in the eyes of others; as authoritative or knowledgeable, caring and concerned, or in control of events. Importantly, these impressions may or may not be how we feel or normally are, but they reflect what seems right for the situation. The new member of an organisation, for example, must quickly learn the correct mannerisms, dress and mode of speaking that are associated with his or her position. Impression management[36] is not a *false* process, however; rather it is a process that makes all social interaction possible. As such it is necessary for all organisations to operate smoothly. Crouch and Marquart (1980) note that in the prison context, impression management is functional for a prison officer's career in two fundamental respects: 1) when a prison officer learns to present himself in the 'approved' manner he is better able to control prisoners; and 2) reflecting appropriate behaviour to fellow officers indicates that the recruit is, or can become, an officer that can be trusted. As this book attempts to show, on a day-to-day basis every prison officer is always 'on stage'; each and every one is concerned to define himself as someone who can 'do the business', and careful not to be defined as the weak deviant in the group.

Performance, impression management and emotion work

Goffman's dramaturgical approach to social inquiry has been taken into specific organisational settings by organisational culture researchers such as Mangham and Overington (1987) and Giacalone and Rosenfeld (1991). Their work focuses attention on how the performing actor performs on the organisational stage. Of particular interest here with regard to prison officers' work is research such as that conducted by Fineman (1993) who discusses the 'social defence system' created by nurses – a strategy of keeping a check on their emotions in order to practise relatively protected from the emotional anxieties which threaten to overwhelm them in their everyday work. To be effective, emergency room workers must be cool and clinical when faced each day with an overflow of sick or bleeding bodies. Clearly, hospital workers who are overly distracted by cries of pain, or who panic at the sight of blood, will be of little value in this occupation. By the same token, if prison officers became upset or angry every time they passed by a convicted murderer or rapist, they would be unable to perform their duties properly (Dilulio 1987: 169). 'Professionalism' means doing the job in a fair, legal, confident and neutral manner. For the prison officer, this is not always easy, not least because, as Dilulio points out, prison officers are obliged to deal on a daily basis 'with people whom most of us would be both frightened and disgusted to be near'. But prison officers cannot afford such feelings; their job is to forget the crime and work with the prisoner. As Dilulio goes on to observe, 'this might be a lousy sort of professionalism, but being a professional in corrections means being able to work with these sorts of people'. This, I want to argue, is where emotion management comes in.

Whilst it has become commonplace to distinguish between jobs involving mainly physical tasks, and ones that primarily call for mental performance, a growing proportion of the workforce (including rescue workers, nursing staff, debt collectors, bank staff, police, undertakers and fire-fighters) are engaged in occupations that involve the performance of particular emotions. For these employees the management of their own – and other people's – emotions represents a key aspect of their job. As social actors, we all learn, through processes of socialisation in families, schools and elsewhere to manage our emotions in a range of contexts. For example, as children we are often taught not to be overwhelmed by adversity, but instead to persevere by 'putting on a brave face' or 'grinning and bearing it': that is to say, by creating an emotional 'mask' behind which real feelings can be hidden. In most work situations, individuals are required to suppress some emotions and to display others. Emotional expression is constrained by the 'feeling rules' [37] of the organisation – implicit rules about the kinds of emotions it is appropriate to express and indeed, to feel at work. Feeling rules are the subtle product of working arrangements and the social history of each workplace; unspoken and largely invisible, they regulate a myriad impression management behaviours, as well as the open expression of feelings. Thus, medical staff must learn to control their emotions towards pain and death – to remain neutral and detached. Similarly, people in authority often regard it as prudent to maintain an emotional distance between themselves and their subordinates, so as to avoid any compromising of their ability to exercise discipline over those under them (Noon and Blyton 1997).

Although much of the theatre is about *feeling*, surprisingly little attention has been given to that issue by dramaturgical sociology (Mangham and Overington 1987). Hochschild (1983) addresses this omission, dealing with emotions and emotion work through a dramaturgical understanding that is partly derived from Goffman (1959) and partly from Stanislavski (1961). In her book *The Managed Heart*, Hochschild discusses the ways in which people manage their emotions while at work. She terms this process 'emotional labour', and by this she means 'the management of feeling to create a publicly observable facial and bodily display' (1983.: 7). Originally identifying emotional labour in occupations where individuals have to manage their emotions in order to serve the commercial purposes of the enterprise (flight-attendants are seen as having to smile and maintain an air of friendliness and calmness for the benefit of passengers), Hochschild explores the ways that individuals suppress or re-present their own private emotions to make them appropriate or consistent with a situation, a role or an expected job function, and with socially accepted norms. An essential feature of the job is to maintain the organisationally prescribed demeanour or mask (see also Hochschild 1998). Taking the lead from Hochschild, Putnam and Mumby (1993) explore how the job of debt-collecting demands a suspension of sympathy and trust. Training is an important factor in all this; through the use of scenarios and role-playing sessions, debt-collectors learn how to deal with angry and anxious people. In this way an organisation develops – through recruitment, selection, socialisation and per-formance evaluations – a social reality in which *feelings become a commodity* for achieving instrumental goals.

Most organisations contain 'emotional zones' – places or settings which become understood, by those who work in them, in terms of different emotions. The funeral parlour, pit-head bath, factory canteen – each space is socially constructed for particular forms of social display, whether it be tears, solemnity or laughter. Different zones offer different degrees of emotional freedom (Hearn 1993). As we shall see in Chapter 5, emotional zones in which it is possible to let off steam are of vital importance to prison officers who work in regimes where emotion management is particularly intensive. It is important to note that those who engage in a high degree of emotional labour often find that, in the process of managing their emotions, they have become estranged from their own feelings (Thompson and McHugh 1995), and that identification with the job itself has incurred considerable socio-emotional costs, including stress, anxiety and depression (I return to this in subsequent chapters of this book). What is often ignored by managers is the role of the organisation in all this. Thus we find systems of stress management reinforcing the notion of stress and anxiety 'as *personal* problems to be coped with rather than *structural* issues to be contested' (*ibid.*: 340 emphasis added but see also Parkin 1993). The recent growth of counselling services inside the workplace is a way in which emotions are dealt with, controlled and confined. However, employees are often wary of such services because they may symbolise a service for those 'not being up to the job'. Moreover, employees may fear that when they make use of these services, their 'problems' may be divulged to those who can give or withhold promotion (Parkin 1993: 184). This consigning of emotions, and their expressions, to the counselling arena is often a further way in which the expression of certain emotions is stigmatised and pathologised. In this way emotions are controlled by those in power defining what is meant by emotionality, and then imposing a pathology on expression of emotions which does not fit the criteria of organisational strength (Parkin 1993).

There are certain significant similarities between the emotion work of medical staff and that of prison officers. That medical staff and prison officers share the same type of humour, and that they use it in similar contexts is particularly interesting. I indicated earlier that I was struck by the extent and type of humour in prisons. As we shall see, the type of humour prison officers appreciate is what they themselves call 'sick', 'black', 'toilet' or 'gallows' humour (various officers pers. comm.) and it finds its expression in day-to-day banter and joshing, pranks and practical jokes. Such humour may also be employed in tragic and shocking situations, such as when a prisoner has committed suicide or 'cut up'. It is here that its form and function most resembles the humour employed by those in the medical profession. Like the nurses interviewed by Lawler (1994) and the medical students interviewed by Lella and Pawluch (1988) prison officers use humour during certain hands-on, dirty, messy tasks, particularly where there is blood, excreta or vomit to be cleared away. Just as many nurses tell 'dead body stories' (Lawler 1994: 190) and make 'dead body jokes' when confronted by dead patients, many prison officers joke during, and after, dealing with dead or seriously injured prisoners. In the nursing literature we find that nurses often use humour as they lay out bodies after death. Although they are aware of the expectation that the corpse should be handled with respect, their composure often deserts them, especially when unexpected things happen, for example if the body groans as it is turned. This often gives rise to uncontrollable laughter which stems from uncertainty and, sometimes, from fear (Meerabeau and Page 1998: 298). Similarly, Lella and Pawluch (1988) refer to the ways in which medical students use humour as a coping strategy when dissecting cadavers; in the apparent calm of the dissecting room, medical students are often disturbed by their work; the sight of the lab and the cadavers produces a myriad of emotional or 'gut level' responses. Individuals develop 'coping' strategies in distressful situations, particularly in those situations of heightened dramaturgical stress in which a 'sincere' or authentic performance that belies distress is demanded. In the dissecting room, one such strategy is to joke about and nick-name the cadaver; such behaviour is often used 'to lighten what may be a tense and anxiety-laden situation' (Lella and Pawluch *ibid.*: 135). Resorting to humour in such circumstances may strike one as unprofessional and callous; when prison officers do so, 'outsiders' may assume that they are simply performing true to the stereotype of the callous, insensitive guard. It is not so easy to rely on stereotypes when nurses joke about death and dying, since nurses are generally thought of as compassionate and caring individuals.

Humour as communication

Humour neutralises, and thus makes bearable, the fear of death (Mercier 1926). Through laughter and joking, 'emotional experiences which are hard to express verbally are made *collective*, and *communicative*; cognitive and emotional dissonances are lifted, and reality is restored' (Zijderveld 1983 emphasis added). Joking and humour can thus *unite* the members of an occupational group. The integrating and communicative function of humour is, of course, of special importance when the group is somehow endangered or threatened. Under threat or in danger, an occupational group might easily disintegrate in panic, but humour and laughter usually manage to keep its members together: they talk, as it were, some common sense into each other, providing energy and even hope, and thereby strengthen their morale (*ibid.*: 47). Humour puts things into perspective and restores social reality.

Humour also establishes and maintains informal work hierarchies; for example it provides a vehicle for identifying the workplace 'butt' (as we shall see, in the prison setting the butt of jokes is usually the new recruit). Humour, often in the form of teasing, is an informal initiation device employed by a team to train and test the capacity of its new members to 'take a joke' – that is, to sustain a friendly manner whilst perhaps not feeling it. When an individual passes such a test of expression control he can thereafter venture forth as a player who can trust himself and be trusted by others (Goffman 1959: 211). In the prison setting, experienced officers claim the new recruit's capacity to 'take it' (the style is deliberately earthy and the jibes are deliberately provocative) reassures them that the new recruit will be able to exercise emotion management with prisoners (see Chapter 3). If the new recruit retains his composure he will be regarded as 'okay'.

It should be noted that humour has two modes; pure humour which is produced for its own sake and applied humour which is produced for a hidden or veiled purpose, such as a put-down, sarcasm, reprimand or compliment (Zijderveld 1983). Applied humour, therefore, usually has a serious point to it (Fox 1990: 431). As we shall see, much of the humour employed by prison officers is applied humour, focused around stories of misdemeanour, faux pas, deception and blunder. Interestingly, but perhaps unsurprisingly, there are similarities between prison humour and the humour used in other work where there is a preponderance of males (I have already mentioned policing and fire-fighting but this also applies to, for example, coal-mining, construction work and the military). In all these occupations there is what Fox (*ibid.*) terms a 'constant football locker room style of combative, competitive banter and repartee'.

A more general defence mechanism for coping with the demands of emotion work and emotional labour is simply to 'switch off' or 'go robot'. Traditionally, an occupational characteristic of a 'good' nurse was the ability to hide emotional reactions and to cultivate an air of detachment – to develop a professional distance from the work. Formal nursing training dictates that staff displays of emotion are inappropriate to the hospital setting; they demonstrate that the nurse is 'not made of the right stuff' to be a competent nurse. Nurses are confronted by suffering in the way that most of us are not. Their work involves carrying out tasks which, by ordinary standards, are distasteful, disgusting and frightening and the work situation arouses very strong and mixed feelings in the nurse – pity, compassion and love, guilt and anxiety, and even hatred and resentment of patients who arouse these strong feelings (Menzies-Lythe 1988). Nurses create a social defence system in which they can practise, relatively protected from the anxieties threatening to overwhelm them; an important element of this is the reduction of familiarity. Depersonalisation – patients are often known by their bed number or disease type ('the pneumonia in bed 15') – and a rhetoric of coping and detachment ('a good nurse doesn't get too involved') help to reduce these anxieties (for rather different reasons doctors wear the mask of 'relaxed brilliance' which enables patients to feel that they are 'in good hands'). The problem is that lack of affect can become *the* standardised and expected emotional response, in which case it excludes the possibility of sharing difficult moments in a way which allows the nurse to 'make contact' with the patient 'existentially' (Lawler 1994: 130). Although there is now a recognition that the expression of some emotions in hospitals is therefore desirable, historically, the occupational ethos of emotional control remains relatively pervasive (*ibid.*: 126). As we shall see throughout this book, an occupational ethos in which emotion management is a distinctive, central feature is also to be found in prisons.

Notes

1 According to the Prison Service's *Statement of Purpose*, 'Her Majesty's Prison Service serves the public by keeping in custody those committed by the courts. Our duty is to look after them with humanity and to help them to lead law-abiding and useful lives in custody and after release.' While the review team concluded that, in terms of service delivery, the first half of the statement is valid, the second half is not. Rather, the team believed that 'the time is ripe for a reassertion of the equal importance of care and rehabilitation, without diminishing the importance of security, safety and order' (para. 6.47). The team concluded that 'as presently organised and managed [the Prison Service] lacks the capacity to deliver effective regimes and to work with the Probation Service, other statutory agencies, and the private and voluntary sector on sentence management and through-care and that this is where the thrust of managerial effort now needs to be directed' (para. 6.48).

2 This survey was not actually carried out until May 2000, when uniformed staff from a selection of prisons were invited to take part (the prisons selected were the same prisons that were surveyed in 1994). The findings of the survey were never published.

3   By 2000 the number of Key Performance Indicators (there were intially six, relating to escapes, assaults, purposeful activity, visits, cost per place and prison conditions) had risen to fifteen.

4   Fresh Start was a package of measures concerned with issues of pay and attendance, the rationalisation of 'line management', the division of personnel management and the co-ordination of uniformed prison staff into 'groups'. The concept of 'group' working was that instead of being centrally deployed, effectively by the chief officer (the chief officer rank was abolished with Fresh Start), officers were to work as teams within certain functions (residential, visits, security and operations) and were to be deployed and managed by the principal and senior officers in charge of their group who, in turn, reported to their line managers in the governor grades. The increased emphasis on accountability subsequently resulted in the loss of Crown Immunity.

5   These targets are contained in the annual *Prison Service Business Plan*.

6   These achievements are published in the *Annual Prison Service Report and Accounts*.

7   Sir John Learmont, for example, took the view that the KPIs showed a strong bias towards care issues (five KPIs) to the potential detriment of custody and control (two KPIs).

8   Broadly speaking, 'market testing' describes 'the process by which the public authority seeks to ascertain the true price at which its own agents can deliver given services, so that this may be compared with the price offered by the private sector' (Harding 1997: 144).

9   The 'Plus Programme' included the development of the *Statement of Common Purpose and Values* and attempted to win the hearts and minds of the workforce through a series of seminars to all 44,000 staff members at a cost of £5.5 million (Fleming 1994 but see also, e.g., Chan 1996).

10   During the period 1996–7 the Prison Service introduced VERSE (Voluntary Early Retirement and Severance) in order to reduce the number of posts in the service. The scheme was part of an overall cost-reduction strategy but prison officers and their managers also recognised it as an attempt to get rid of the 'dead wood' in the service.

11   The 'Prison! Me! No Way!' initiative was intended to encourage youngsters away from criminal pursuits. While this is a relatively new initiative in English prisons, American prisons have been running such programmes for some time. In the 1980s, New Jersey State started a programme called 'Scared Straight' which involved taking groups of young people on a tour of a maximum security prison, where they were lectured by inmates 'about the horrors of life behind bars' (Dilulio 1987: 262). Launched nationally in England and Wales in November 1996, this project was developed by a group of prison officers concerned at the growing number of juveniles received into prison. Officers involved in the project visit schools to talk to children about prison life. The aim is to steer children away from crime and hence from prison; team presentations, usually held in the school hall,

involve the use of props such as prison clothing, weapons and even a mock cell.

12 Since Fresh Start, this rank no longer exists.

13 As part of the Investors in People initiative (see Endnote 14) new officers who join as from September 1997 have to achieve a National Vocational Qualification (NVQ) in Custodial Care to the standard of Level 2. This takes between 12 and 18 months to complete. It is a basic custody course; although officers would have learnt most of these skills at the training college, they are not assessed on them there. Under the NVQ system, they will be assessed on their standards within the prison in which they work.

14 Investors in People is a national strategy, recently taken up by the Prison Service, 'for organisations committed to improving business performance through their people'. Organisations that take part in this initiative have to provide evidence that they meet the national standard which consists of four principles: 1) a commitment to develop all employees to achieve its business objectives; 2) regular reviews of the training needs and development of all employees; 3) a commitment to the development of individuals throughout their employment; and 4) a commitment to evaluate the investment in training and development to assess achievement and improve future effectiveness.

15 Interestingly, the May Committee (1979: para. 7.28) considered whether there would be an advantage in increasing the required educational standard for entrants into the service, but came to the conclusion that there was 'no reason to suppose that higher academic standards are necessarily a good indication of a person's potential as a prison officer'.

16 This is an Army term. To 'bull' one's boots is to engage in excessive cleaning and shining.

17 Many ex-military officers slashed or cut the peaks of their caps to give it a more downward tilt and thus obscure the eyes. As we know, lack of eye-to-eye contact impedes social interaction. It does not, however, impede the communication of an order or instruction.

18 The total prison population on 5th March 2004 was 74,960 (there were just over 66,000 people in prison in 2000).

19 The rise in average female prison population between 1987 and 1997 was substantially higher (51%) than the rise in the male population (24%). Female prisoners only accounted for 4.4% of the prison population in 1997 (3.6% in 1987). The average female population rose by 18% (males by 10%) from 1996 to 1997 (*Source: Digest* 4 Home office 1999).

20 On 30 November 2001 there were 1,379 prisoners aged 60+ in the prisons of England and Wales (Prison Reform Trust 2003).

21 On 5 March 2004 there were 10,515 young people between the ages of 15 and 21 years in prison. Of these, 504 were female.

22 Following Sparks *et al.* (1996) I use the term 'control' to mean 'the use of routines and a variety of formal and informal practices, particularly sanctions, which assist in the maintenance of order'.

23 Following Sparks *et al.* (1996) I refer to 'order' as 'the absence of violence, overt conflict and the reproduction of social routines'.

24 The decision of the Court of Appeal in *St Germain* (that the adjudications of boards of visitors are susceptible to judicial review) following on from cases such as *Golder* v. *United Kingdom* [1975] in the European Court of Human Rights proved pivotal in the courts' gradual acknowledgement that prisoners *do* have rights; rights that are not taken away by the fact of their imprisonment. Judicial intervention into prison life has not been uniform however; to date the judiciary have proved much less willing to intervene in issues of prison management (e.g. tackling unsatisfactory prison conditions) than they have in issues of sentencing (for example, the procedural rights and entitlements of discretionary lifers).

25 The exercise of power in prisons (as elsewhere) is extremely complex. Giddens (1984) uses the term the 'dialectic of control' to describe its two-way character. Simply put, the dialectic of control refers to the means or resources whereby subordinate players in a power relation may influence those in more powerful positions. From this perspective, the less powerful members of an organisation – and that includes prisoners – can always 'manage resources in such a way as to exert control over the more powerful in established power relationships'. In carceral organisations the significance of the 'dialectic of control' is considerable since, as I have already noted, the prison officer's close proximity with inmates and the 'claims of reciprocity' that arise in everyday interactions encourage compromise and accommodation. This two-way flow of power is particularly evident in therapeutic communities within prisons, where decision-making is *formally* shared between prisoners and staff.

26 In 'The prison governor: theory and practice' (1998), Bryans and Wilson discuss in detail how the efficiency credo that now pervades prisons (through the new sets of key managerial ideas, beliefs and behaviours outlined above) sometimes conflicts with the humanitarian credo of many practitioners.

27 The (now defunct) Barlinnie Special Unit (BSU) is the most well-known therapeutic community for prisoners. For fascinating discussions on both the setting up of the unit and its impacts on prisoners see, respectively, Scottish Home and Health Department (1971) and Sparks (1993).

28 See Bottoms *et al.* (1990) for a comprehensive discussion of these contrasting approaches.

29 Bogardus (1933) defines social distance as 'the degree of sympathetic understanding that exists between two persons and a person and a group'.

30 In many respects, the concept of 'working personality' corresponds to Pierre Bourdieu's (1990) notion of *habitus*. Both concepts are concerned with the acquisition of particular patterns of thought, behaviour and values and both suggest an *embodiment* of those values and ideas. Both concepts allow us to rethink the ways in which subjective psychological and bodily relations are shaped – through inscription, repetition and practice – by interaction with

the social world. When Bourdieu used the concept he was, of course, using it to illustrate *class* distinctions.

31 There is no single definition of stress; in the literature, the term carries a variety of different meanings according to the purposes of various writers. For the purposes of this chapter, I shall use the Prison Service Staff Care and Welfare Service's definition. The PSSCWS define stress as 'a response to experiencing demands which are out of balance with capacities and resources'.

32 The PSSCWS have a considerable workload dealing with a wide range of problems experienced by prison staff. A recent report stated that the service sees between 800 and 1,100 staff each month, and carries a constant 'live' caseload of 500, 60% of them uniformed grades. The most common presenting problems are physical illness, stress-related absences, medical retirement, discipline and debt.

33 The metaphor of *heterogeneous network* lies at the heart of actor-network theory (ANT). ANT provides a way of suggesting that society, organisations, agents and machines are all *effects* generated in patterned networks of diverse (not simply human) materials. Some of these materials are more 'durable' than others and so maintain their relational effect(s) for longer. Imagine a continuum – thoughts are cheap but they do not last for long, and speech lasts very little longer. When we start to *perform* relations, however, and *embody* them in inanimate texts and materials (such as texts and buildings) then they may last much longer. Like symbolic interactionism, ANT acknowledges that props are important. However, it argues that social agents are not located in human bodies alone. Rather, an actor is a *network* of heterogeneous relations, or an *effect* produced by such a network. For a fuller exposition of this theoretical approach see Law (1994).

34 In the Prison Service generally, 'conditioning' – the manipulation of staff behaviour by prisoners which results in loss of vigilance on security matters – is a widely acknowledged threat to staff and security. The potential for staff conditioning is regarded as particularly great in the relaxed atmosphere of dispersal regimes, and was cited as one of the most significant factors in the escape from Whitemoor Prison on 9 September 1994 (see Home Office 1994).

35 What *is* emotion? Puzzling over what constitutes an emotion has a long pedigree (Noon and Blyton 1997: 123). As these authors note, the subject of human emotion is a very wide one, just like the range of emotions a person can express. For the present discussion it is sufficient to note the widespread agreement amongst those writing on emotions in the workplace (see, for example, Hochschild 1983; James 1989; Van Maanen and Kunda 1989; Fineman 1993) that emotions centrally concern an individual's *feelings*.

36 Via 'impression management' (Goffman 1959, 1967) social actors aim to present themselves in a generally favourable light and in ways appropriate to particular roles and social settings.

37 All organisations have their own 'feeling rules' which set out those emotions deemed 'appropriate' to the occupational culture and setting; they

are rooted in the organisation's function, history, customs, values and traditions (see Hochschild 1983). Those who transgress the feeling rules of an organisation risk presenting themselves as unreliable, untrustworthy or simply unsuitable employees (on this topic see also Turner 1982; Mangham and Overington 1987; Fineman 1993; Bendelow and Williams 1998).

Chapter 2

Research methods

I could not have written this book if I had not been willing to spend time – a lot of time – with prison officers. From the outset, I felt sure that prison officers' 'ways of life' – their norms of behaviour, language, customs and traditions, values, rituals, stories and relationships – could only be uncovered by observing officers as they went about their work. By the end of my fieldwork, I sensed that my participation in the daily work lives of these officers – observing what happened (and where and when), listening to what was said (and by whom and in what manner) and by asking innumerable questions – had allowed me to uncover at least some of the subtleties and complexities of prison work.

For those who are interested in the 'inner life' of organisations, the key attraction of ethnographic[1] work is its ability to contrast the *formal* organisation with its *informal* counterpart. All organisations (schools, prisons, hospitals, biscuit factories, computer companies, etc.) are 'formal' in the sense of having specific tasks to accomplish and 'informal' in the sense that members of those organisations continually negotiate with one another in the interpretation and carrying out of such tasks (Schwartzman 1993). The promise of ethnography for a study such as this is the presentation of the work cultures that emerge from the *interplay* between the formal and informal aspects of organisational life. As I will try to show throughout this book, while control and security are dominant themes in the prison setting, domesticity, emotion and emotion management are also central features of the prison environment.

It was only through a dogged determination to 'hang around' in each of my selected prisons for extended periods, and on a regular basis, that

I began to understand the environments in which prison officers work and was able to observe specific events as they unfolded. I hope that I will not sound naïve if I claim that simply 'being with' groups of prison officers on a regular and sustained basis enabled me to overcome (at least to some degree) officers' wariness and mistrust of an 'outsider' coming in to 'do research'. I also hope that my interpretations of what I observed, and what I heard, 'make sense' to those who have participated in this study. The names of all those who participated have, of course, been omitted or changed to ensure anonymity. Although the rank of each participant is generally included after each quotation presented in this book, where anonymity could be compromised by this process (i.e. where only a few individuals in an establishment hold a certain rank), I have noted the rank of the officer but not the name of the prison in which the officer was working.

The prisons

This book is based on two years of intensive fieldwork in six public sector male prisons. I had originally intended to restrict my fieldwork to three prisons in the North West region, i.e. HMYOI Lancaster Farms (a young offender institution and remand centre), HMP Wymott (a Category C prison) and HMP Garth (a Category B training prison): taken together, these establishments provided a good working cross-section in terms of function, size of establishment and security category. They were also all geographically convenient to my research base (Keele University). However, at a later point I also gained access (via a local representative of the POA) into HMYOI Portland, a young offender institution in Dorset. For two reasons I also decided to carry out a limited amount of fieldwork in two other prisons, namely HMYOI Stoke Heath and HMPYOI Moorlands. First, it seemed foolish not to exploit the excellent working relationship I had already forged (during earlier research) with a number of senior uniformed staff at Stoke Heath, particularly as this establishment was only a few miles from my research base. Secondly, during my fieldwork at Lancaster Farms the then governor transferred to Moorlands and invited me into his new establishment to talk to uniformed staff there. The amount of fieldwork time spent at each establishment varied considerably; for example while I made dozens of extended visits to Lancaster Farms I visited Moorlands only twice.

Lancaster Farms is a young offender institution and remand centre located on the outskirts of Lancaster. It was opened in 1992. Designed along 'new-generation' architectural lines (which permits a high level of surveillance and supervision) it is a medium-security prison with a Certified National Accommodation (CNA) of 504. On opening, the goal of Lancaster Farms was 'to develop a model Establishment for Young Offenders and young people on remand'. In 1995 Judge Stephen Tumim, the then Chief Inspector of Prisons, described Lancaster Farms as 'well on the way to achieving its model establishment aim' (HMCIP 1995). As an example of best practice in relation to the treatment of young offenders, HMYOI Lancaster Farms was soon included in the Prison Reform Trust's list of 'Achieving Prisons'.

The ethos of Lancaster Farms was expressed in its mission statement to 'Prevent the Next Victim' through a regime prioritising (in addition to good security and a safe environment for both staff and prisoners) the addressing of offending behaviour. At the outset, the senior management team understood that to manage and control prisoners effectively, it is important to understand the behaviour and problems of those prisoners, and with this in mind the team developed, in partnership with the Trust for the Study of Adolescence and drawing upon uniformed staffs' own experiences, a training course for prison staff entitled 'Understanding and handling adolescents in custody'. This in-house training package was subsequently adopted by the Prison Service College and is now a national training package available to all Prison Service staff working with young offenders. It was interesting to note that before the establishment opened, the senior management team at Lancaster Farms also explored better ways of managing staff. NISSAN (GB) were approached by the then governor because the organisation was seen as having excellent shopfloor relations, and a rare ability to motivate and inspire staff. With this in mind, three principal officers visited NISSAN to see whether the ethos and management principles of the organisation could be adopted in the running of Lancaster Farms. Some aspects of the 'NISSAN way' *were* adopted, in particular the belief that 'people are an organisation's biggest asset'. For various reasons, however, little of this 'way' remains, except, notably, in terms of the continuing emphasis on 'teamwork' and on good communications between all grades.

At the outset, Lancaster Farms claimed a largely 'social' (as opposed to 'situational') approach to prisoner management. In developing the regime the then governor deliberately chose more social than physical measures for control purposes, considering that in a reforming regime, the co-operation of prisoners was a worthy goal as it allowed them to develop. It was interesting to note that, in keeping with the ethos of care, the wing of the prison allocated for the segregation of disruptive or vulnerable prisoners (variously known in most other prisons as the 'block', 'chokey' 'seg' and so on) was termed the 'Separation and Care' unit. It was also interesting to note that Lancaster Farms was the only prison where the governor-in-charge made a point of walking on to the wings every day and talking to staff and prisoners 'off the cuff'.

HMP Wymott is a Category C establishment located in Leyland, Lancashire. During its history (the prison opened in 1979), Wymott has suffered three riots, the last of which, in September 1993, virtually destroyed the prison. The damage to the fabric of the prison was so great that it was necessary to send 35 control and restraint (C&R) units (I will describe these units later) to the scene and evacuate the majority (707) of the prisoners to other establishments. Since then, Wymott has been rebuilt and its physical structure and regime radically altered to ensure more effective control. It is now effectively two prisons on one site. A and B Houses comprise the Vulnerable Prisoners Unit (VPU) while blocks C–F accommodate Category C prisoners on normal location. Wymott can hold up to 360 ordinary Category C prisoners and 460 vulnerable prisoners. Sentences range from six months to life. From a research perspective, HMP Wymott was an interesting establishment because it has such a large VP unit in which an intensive Sex Offender Treatment Programme (SOTP) was (and indeed still is) in operation. At the time of my visit, the prison also held a number of elderly prisoners; today many of those prisoners are cared for in the prison's newly developed Elderly and Disabled Unit.

HMP Garth is a Category B training prison, located on the same estate as Wymott. The prison opened in 1988, and a new residential wing opened in 1997. At the time of my visits the prison held an average of 560 prisoners, approximately of 100 of whom were lifers. Sentences ranged from four years to life (Garth did not normally receive prisoners serving less than four years). Amongst officers working in other prisons, Garth had a reputation for being an unsafe prison to work in, partly because of the physical design of the prison and partly because of Garth's relatively relaxed regime.

HMYOI Portland, which stands high on the cliffs of Portland, Dorset, was originally built as a convict prison in 1849, and later became a borstal. At the time of my fieldwork it operated solely as a closed young offender establishment for prisoners aged from 15 to 21. HMYOI Portland has a tradition of taking disciplinary transfers from other prisons, and its ethos is one of 'discipline'. Despite this ethos, Portland became home, in 1996, to a 'therapeutic community' (TC) for young offenders, which aimed to decrease drug use and drug-related crime. In 2002, however, the prison was described by the then Chief Inspector of Prisons as 'in a time warp as far as change and appropriate treatment of young prisoners are concerned', not least because its culture (known as the 'Portland Way') involved disciplining prisoners by fear and shouting. In 2004 seven young offenders received a total out-of-court settlement of £120,000 from the Prison Service over allegations that at Portland they had been assaulted by prison staff.

HMYOI Stoke Heath is a closed young offender institution located in a rural setting in Shropshire. The prison, which was built in 1964 on the site of a former RAF station, was originally a Category C adult prison. It was converted to a borstal two years later, and has been used to hold young offenders ever since. At the time of my fieldwork, Stoke Heath held both young offenders (17–21 years) and juveniles (15–17 years).

HMPYOI Moorland opened in 1991, built on land adjacent to the buildings of a former RAF station, now HMP Lindholme. The prison (which was designed for adult males but became a remand prison and YOI before it came on stream) opened in 1991. Within months of opening, the establishment experienced two serious disturbances.

It became strikingly clear, as officers in each of these prisons reflected on their work experiences, that the histories, functions, working practices and cultures of individual establishments have a significant bearing on both the nature and quality of regimes and indeed on staff–prisoner, staff–staff interactions.

The fieldwork

I spent two years 'soaking and poking' as Dilulio (1987) so aptly puts it, beginning, in the autumn of 1996, with an 'induction' week at both HMYOI Lancaster Farms and HMP Wymott. When I arrived at these prisons I found that the training officers had sent a memo round to all staff, informing them of my impending visit, the nature of my research and asking if any staff would be willing to participate. I was flattered that they had gone to so much trouble, and pleased to find that so many officers had given their co-operation. A schedule had been drawn up for the week and various members of uniformed staff (all grades) had been assigned to meet me on the different wings, introduce me to other staff and, after talking to me and giving me some idea of the routine, pass me on to another member of staff. I was, however, unaware that each officer on the list assumed that he would be interviewed there and then, and so when they each presented themselves as 'mine for about an hour', I had to (very hastily) decide what sort of questions I wanted to ask. I decided that the best strategy would be to ask the officers some very general questions about themselves (for example length of time in the service, which establishments they had worked in, etc.) so that I could then frame one or two questions around what they had already said. Although I was unsure how this would work out, fortunately the information they offered was abundant and extremely interesting, and this sustained me until the end of the week. By then I had carried out long, unstructured interviews with over a dozen officers, and had chatted informally to many more.

As the fieldwork progressed I shadowed officers on the day shift as they unlocked prisoners, supervised at the servery, inspected cells, received new prisoners, removed prisoners to the segregation wing, completed paperwork and delivered a variety of courses to prisoners. In addition I observed governors' adjudications, a staff promotion board (at the invitation of the candidate) and attended a variety of meetings (ranging from daily staff briefings to 'thrash out' sessions between senior management and the POA). I ate my sandwiches on the wings as officers played pool (I am a hopeless pool player so I was unable to join in), observed riot training at one of the Prison Service colleges, attended training sessions (such as anti-bullying and suicide awareness), went to a pantomime which officers performed for family, friends and the local community, accompanied a group of officers to a school to help with their 'Prison? Me? No Way!' presentation and socialised out of work hours with a small number of officers and their wives.

On four occasions I stayed on in the prison for the night shift, accompanying officers as they patrolled the landings and grounds and listening to officers' stories as others watched TV, read the newspapers, did their knitting (one evening, a female officer, surrounded by pink wool and knitting patterns, put the finishing touches to a baby's matinee jacket) or briefly dozed off, their coats thrown over them, across two easy chairs pulled together as a makeshift 'bed'. I went home when it was getting light and the day-shift staff began to arrive. I had been rather apprehensive about turning up at the prison on my first night, despite my invitation to do so by one of the senior officers who would be on duty. I hoped that the other night staff would not mind my being there; I had been told on an earlier occasion that some night staff 'liked to have a kip' at some point during the night, and so I wondered if they might resent the presence of a researcher. I also hoped that I could keep awake myself (I thought that falling asleep and snoring might undermine my credibility somewhat). Although I was offered the use of an easy chair in the rest room for a nap if I wanted it, I was determined to keep alert the whole night – not least because I was frightened of missing something. I heard a few days later from another senior officer that, far from being irritated by having me hanging about, staff on the night shift were impressed that someone had taken so much interest in their work that she was prepared to stay up all night to ask them about it.

Although my research proposal to the Economic and Social Research Council (ESRC) stated my intention to carry out interviews with a 10% sample of uniformed staff (stratified on the basis of age, length of service, grade and gender), I soon realised that this was unrealistic. In practice, interviews with officers were often difficult to arrange (and sometimes had to be rearranged) because of shift patterns, sickness and the general demands of the regime (on a number of occasions interviews had to be rescheduled because officers had been required to extend their shifts or because they had been asked to work on another wing). Instead, I had to seize any interview opportunity that presented itself. As Johnson (1990) remarks, ethnographers end up interviewing 'whoever they are able to convince to cooperate'. In terms of locating informants, my fieldwork proceeded, in the main, along the lines of 'seize anyone and everyone that offers help'. For example, when I was having a brief conversation with a principal officer, he suddenly volunteered an hour of his time to talk about his experiences working in a dispersal prison. Although I had intended to visit another part of the prison that afternoon, I jumped at the chance, not wanting to turn him down in case he did not offer again. Several other officers subsequently offered themselves for interview. Similarly, if I met anybody who said that they knew someone who might be willing to talk, I immediately followed the contact up. Several very interesting interviews were arranged through this informal 'snow-balling' process. At the end of two years of fieldwork I had observed and interviewed scores of prison officers (male and female, all grades) in a variety of settings.

Interviews ranged from spontaneous, informal conversations in places being used for other purposes (for example the wing office) to formally arranged meetings in rooms out of earshot of other people. Many informal interviews (conversations really) were punctuated by ringing telephones and the need for staff to answer inmate inquiries. As I said above, preliminary interviews were deliberately not recorded, in order to give officers the opportunity to find out more about the study and about me, in a relaxed atmosphere. I did not want them to feel they were simply being 'pumped' for information and then abandoned; anyway I was unsure at that stage about what I actually wanted to find out. At other times, when officers either offered or agreed to talk in more depth, they themselves sought out an empty room somewhere on the wing (on one occasion we ended up in the wing laundry surrounded by dirty washing) and we talked there.

Being with prison officers for sustained periods of time was a fascinating and illuminating experience. It was also, at varying times and to varying degrees, poignant, amusing, bewildering and disquieting. I found that the majority of officers I approached were extremely keen to talk about their work. Indeed all my interviewees claimed that our discussions represented their first real opportunity to speak at length about their working lives to someone who seemed genuinely interested in understanding prison life from *their* point of view. Most of my conversations with the officers who participated in this study took place in the prison setting, but I was also able to talk with some officers in their own homes and with their wives and children (see Chapter 8). Their stories, anecdotes and reflective accounts, along with my own observations of the officers at work, are the bedrock of this book. They bring into sharp relief the challenges, emotions, tensions and conflicts involved in doing prison work.

Note

1   The term 'ethnography' refers to a particular set of research methods. Ethnography has been variously described in terms of 'thick description' (Geertz 1973), as 'an interpretive act' (Van Maanen 1988) and as a method for grasping 'the native's point of view' (Malinowski 1922). For examples of classic ethnographic work see, e.g., Geerz (1973), Spradley (1979), Van Maanen (1988).

Chapter 3

Learning the rules, managing feelings: becoming a prison officer

The process of *becoming* a prison officer is a slow, difficult and sometimes painful one, involving a complex process of acculturation. In this chapter we follow new recruits through both the formal and informal training processes and into their first, anxious days on the prison landings. While the formal training programme sensitises new recruits to the need for vigilance in security matters, it is interesting to note how unprepared most new recruits were for the emotional and domestic demands of prison work. In other words, they found that working with prisoners (and indeed with other uniformed staff) was a rather more complex affair than they had anticipated. The complexity of prison work, and the emotional responses it can produce in new recruits, are graphically illustrated in the comments of these officers themselves, which I include below.

The first part of this chapter considers why people apply to be prison officers and the second part discusses officers' experiences of basic training. The third part explores the work realities of inexperienced prison officers and the ways in which they survive the culture shock of their new role.

Joining the prison service

People apply to become prison officers for a number of (related) reasons. For most of the prison officers in this study, 'the pay' and 'job security' were the primary motivating factors for both joining and remaining in the service. Many had been attracted to prison work simply because they needed a job and because 'the pay was relatively good'. Ex-services personnel had joined because they were accustomed to working in uniform and presumed that the Prison Service would offer similar benefits (and make similar discipline-oriented demands) to those of the Army and Navy. Some officers had joined because the job was second best to police work (they had applied to the police and had been rejected). A few of the officers I interviewed had joined because they 'wanted to make a difference' while others (an even smaller minority) said that they had joined out of a long-standing fascination with 'the criminal', or indeed the 'criminal mind'.

The vast majority of the prison officers who took part in the research had not planned a career in the Prison Service; rather they had simply 'fallen into' the job. As one male officer put it:

> This job is not one you plan to do when you're a kid, like kids say they want to be a train driver or a policeman. This job's usually something you do when something goes wrong – like if you're made redundant ... I was made redundant from British Leyland.

In short, prison work is the kind of work that many people simply drift into. Most of the officers who took part in this study came from blue-collar occupations. Male officers had previously been employed as factory workers, coal miners, engineers, car mechanics, long-distance lorry drivers, market traders, pig butchers, foundry workers and swimming instructors. A large proportion had been in the armed forces, and one or two had university degrees. Female officers had previously worked as shop assistants, care assistants, bank clerks, typists, sales-women, postal workers and telephonists. Large numbers of ex-services personnel continue to work in the Prison Service, but as I indicated in Chapter 1, decreasing numbers are now being recruited. Of those officers I interviewed who did enter the service from the Army or Navy, all said they joined because they wished to continue working in uniform and enjoyed the 'protection' of working in the services. Since these officers joined the service, however, one of the greatest 'protections' – rent-free staff housing – has been removed.

The recruitment process

In the 1970s, the common requirement for recruitment into the Prison Service was that the applicant should be over 21[1] years of age, of average, or above average height, and in good physical health. No formal educational qualifications were required[2] but candidates were required to pass simple tests in English, arithmetic and general knowledge. Advertising for recruits was mainly carried out through newspaper advertisements. Recruitment is now carried out locally, rather than nationally. Since devolution of the recruitment process, each prison is responsible for recruiting the officers they require. Jobs are advertised in local job centres, and those wishing to apply must contact the prisons directly. There are minimum eligibility requirements. In addition to the educational requirements already mentioned, candidates must be aged between 18½ years and 57 years at the time of appointment. Candidates must also be fully physically fit (the recruitment process involves a medical and fitness test); however the Prison Service operates a guaranteed interview scheme for disabled people (as defined in the Disability Discrimination Act 1995) who meet the minimum published criteria for appointment.

All applicants for the post of prison officer are required to complete an application form. A competence-based assessment follows; this is a structured sifting method where trained assessors, using a standard rating procedure, rate the candidates' accounts of their achievements in specific areas of experience. These areas of activity form part of the key competences required for the job of prison officer. The highest-ranking applicants are invited to an assessment centre where they undertake a series of work-related exercises which do not require experience of prisons.

The development of the prison officer role in recent years has heightened the need for conceptual and analytical skills and the ability to take a theoretical perspective. According to current recruitment literature, applicants are also required to possess a range of interpersonal skills; in particular they require assertiveness, good listening, influencing, negotiating and verbal communication skills. Contrast this to the following account by an officer who attended a recruitment interview 'at a big house somewhere in the country' in 1991:

> I remember at my interview, they asked me if I watched 'Porridge', and if I was a Mr McKay or a Mr Barraclough. I said I was some-where in-between. [That was a funny question to ask wasn't it?] Well it was, but I felt at ease then ... 'Porridge' is the most realistic programme on prison life – you *do* get your Ronnie Barkers who try to get one over on you. (Male officer, Garth)

The traditional interview was replaced on 31 March 1998 by exercises at a JSAC (Job Simulation Assessment Centre). JSACs require applicants to show a range of reasoning and interpersonal competences across standardised role-playing situations and to compete a report-writing task. Assessments are aided by video recording and made by trained assessors using consistent and detailed criteria (Prison Service Instruction 72/1997). The exercises assess skills such as calming, making a complaint, taking criticism, giving constructive criticism, dealing with requests for help, listening with a purpose and written/analytical skills. The following quotation from a young female officer illustrates the typical content of such assessments:

> We had to go into a room – and there was a psychologist there – and you had to go in the room with a television camera, and they give you some scenarios before you went in the room, but I think there were like, eight scenarios, with like eight situations and you had to just, you know, be yourself ... In one of the scenarios we were supposed to have been looking after a friend's plants but we were supposed to have forgotten to water them and they had all died. And he must have been six foot odd this bloke, and I walked into the room, and there was all dead plants on the floor ... and he was shouting and bawling and carrying on! I thought, oh no, what have I left myself in for?! But, in the past, what they used to do, they used to have a Board, and you used to go in there, and they used to say to you 'Right, what would you do if somebody ran out of a cell at you with a knife?' And that's what they used to do in the past. And what they're trying to do [now] is to try and bring it into everyday situations. Cos half of the people would just turn round and say I don't know! Cos you *don't* know ... So they've stopped using that method now.

Ten weeks at college: officers' experiences of basic training

Basic training takes place over a ten-week period. The first week of training consists of an observation week at the recruit's own establishment. During this period, the prison officer in training (known as a POINT) must be able to, *inter alia*, recite the requirements of the Official Secrets Act, be able to describe the purpose of the Statutory Rules and be familiar with the correct procedure for the use of radios. The next four weeks are spent at the training college (POINTS are allowed home at weekends); the officer then returns to his or her own establishment for one week. The remaining four weeks are spent back at the training college (again coming home at weekends). POINTS must sit and pass exams in weeks five and nine; they must also perform adequately in PE assessments and in control and restraint (C&R) training (I return to the latter in Chapter 6).

Although several recruits reported that tutors had emphasised the 'caring' aspect of the job, there was general agreement that security was emphasised above all else. Like police officers, prison officers are specifically trained to be suspicious; to be constantly on the look-out for potential, as well as actual, 'trouble'. For the prison officer, the ability to 'read' people and situations is crucial for the maintenance of order and indeed for his or her own safety, and the new recruit is taught during basic training not to trust any prisoner. New recruits are instructed to observe inmates carefully and constantly; to get into the habit of asking themselves, when supervising inmates: 'What is he doing?' 'Why is he doing it?' Summing up the advice of the trainers, a female officer commented that 'at training college, you're taught never to trust the bastards!' As we shall see in later sections of this book, the development of a suspicious 'mindset' has certain knock-on effects for officers' relationships *outside* as well as inside the prison. Within the prison setting itself: 'You get to think that everybody is out to do you harm if they get the chance … you lose your objectivity a lot. You get to think, well, they're all scroats. That's it. End of story' (senior officer, Lancaster Farms). Most of the new recruits I interviewed had generally enjoyed the classroom activities they had taken part in during basic training. In contrast, perceptions of the mandatory fitness training differed significantly. Much seemed to depend on the age and gender of the recruit, and the recruit's basic level of fitness at the outset. Descriptions of fitness training ranged from, at one extreme 'the best nine weeks of my life' (young male recruit), to 'an exercise in humiliation' (young female recruit).

Numerous new officers told me that when this part of the training programme began, they were shocked at the degree of verbal and psychological abuse meted out by their trainers (see below). They claimed that corporate promotions of 'excellence', 'caring', 'quality' and 'respect' – terms that they had heard a great deal during their initial interviews – were barely evident in the organisational realities that they had experienced during this element of their basic training. From my conversations with a number of new recruits, females appeared to fare the worst; for them, the 'punishment' for entering a male-dominated occupation entailed verbal abuse, ridicule and ritualised humiliation. Both female and male officers who had recently completed training told me that the PE element was geared heavily towards the physical capabilities of men. There is evidence that men enter basic training of this nature with a physical advantage: as Martin and Jurik (1996: 77) note in their discussion of women correctional officers in the USA, male recruits are 'usually larger and stronger than women and are more likely to have had previous athletic and bodybuilding experiences [and to have] played in contact sports'. From my interviews with new recruits, it appeared that at the Prison Service training colleges (as in American training academies) the content of physical training exemplifies the gendered nature of the organisation into which the new recruits are supposed to fit. As one female POINT put it: 'It was an eye-opener ... the PE seemed to be geared to ex-marines, and we were just piddly poddly housewives!'

Some – the ex-forces officers and those who were particularly fond of sport – claimed to have really enjoyed basic training, but others felt abused and hated it:

> I thought it was great! Mind you I used to be in the TA, and I thought it would be like that. But they do try to frighten you when you first get there – 'If you do so-and-so you're out' sort of thing. And I think two people left as soon as the introduction was finished. They just packed their bags and left. They must have thought 'I'm a grown man, I don't need this'. (Male officer, Garth)

Many of my interviewees, male and female, remarked upon the militaristic, paternal and abusive nature of their basic training:

> In the first week, we were dressed down in the lecture theatre [It was] You will *not* do this, you will *not* do the other ... I suppose they were setting the tone for the gravity of the job ... accountability and that. But it was a bit OTT. (Male probationer, Garth)

For these officers, the positive aspects of basic training – the growing sense of camaraderie, the sense that one was embarking on a pro-fessional career path and so on – were eclipsed by the common practice of being 'beasted'. Recalling his training experiences in the Army and now the Prison Service, this young male officer remarked:

> In the Army, to get beasted was to be given a lot of psychological pressure ... they absolutely reduce you to protozoic slime! The first six weeks is absolute pure beasting ... sleep deprivation, running for miles – if you can't run fast enough, you've got to go again – you get to such a stage that you do it [obey orders] without thinking. This is what the Army wants and needs ... You support each other *but* if some won't get it right – if they just give up – they get a good

kicking [from other recruits in the platoon]. [What do they do then?] Then they either buck up or they get out. It wasn't quite as bad as that at the training college but it was pretty hard. (Officer, Lancaster Farms)

Whilst not as extreme as military beasting, the 'beasting' that many officers said they had encountered during basic training with the Prison Service was none the less difficult to deal with:

They go 'Come on, you're fucking crap!' – to break you. They're in your face all the time. They try to get you to quit – to say 'Fuck you!' But you keep going 'cos you don't want to look stupid. (Male probationer, Garth)

Those who claimed to have enjoyed the physical aspect of training, for example this young female officer, did none the less realise that many of their counterparts – male and female – found it difficult to cope:

It was very strict at first, but they chilled out after the first couple of months … It was the best part of my life [but] they really beasted you … and I mean I'm fit 'cos I do kick boxing and that. But the instructors, they think they're God. Eighty percent of the recruits hated it, 'cos they'd really push you beyond your limit. One guy from here said 'They're gonna kill me in that gym' … he collapsed in the gym [afterwards]. I felt sorry for the unfit people I did. I trained for 12 months before it and *I* struggled. (Female officer, Garth)

Some reported feeling sorry for colleagues, particularly female POINTS who had arrived unfit:

We tried to slow things down so that they'd lay off them. For them it was straight from the kitchen sink to five miles then circuit training. Mind you, they did recommend you to get fit first 'cos it would be hard work. (Male officer, Garth)

A slightly built female officer in her early twenties put her feelings about the PE in the following way:

It was bloody awful. [In what way?] They treated you like the men. If you can't do it, you get humiliated. A woman in her mid-30s was really ridiculed; she was tearful a lot of the time. She nearly packed it in.

As in the soldiering context (on this see Hockey 1986) training officers became 'significant others' for new recruits. Fear of failure, of being discharged for incompetence (especially lack of physical fitness) was prevalent during the training period of my interviewees, as was the fear of being 'back-squadded' (in the Prison Service the preponderance of military terminology is quite striking) and having to repeat parts of the training programme. Being back-squadded involves, *inter alia*, the officer's removal from his or her immediate peer group and, as a consequence, having to make friends in a new one. These fears drive new recruits to put a great deal of effort into training, particularly the PE component. Several of the officers I interviewed admitted that this dimension of basic training had been a rather traumatic experience, not least because tutors had 'tried to impose competitiveness amongst the sections'. Because of this competitiveness, both tutors and recruits were sometimes unwilling to acknowledge injuries. Officers receiving an injury were apparently told by tutors 'If you've got to go to the doctors, for God's sake play it down, otherwise you'll be back-squadded'. Disturbingly, a few officers had stories to tell about POINTS who said that they had been pushed so far beyond their physical limits that they felt in danger of dying. One of these officers recounted how one young woman had collapsed and died during the first few weeks of the training period. Although it transpired that the officer had had a congenital medical condition, this officer attributed her colleague's death to the instructor's lack of sympathy when the woman had become distressed during previous training sessions. While this was clearly a rare event, various non-serious injuries are commonplace; during every programme of basic training, new recruits may incur broken fingers and a variety of sprains.

The sexualised training environment

Basic training for female POINTS can also be problematic in other respects. Disturbingly, it was alleged by a female officer who has since left the service that during her initial training, some of the PE instructors and senior officers actively encouraged, and indeed instigated, sexist behaviour towards female recruits (most male *recruits*, on the other hand, had been supportive to their female colleagues). Moreover, she alleged that some of the activities in which male and female recruits were expected to engage were degrading. For several of the female officers interviewed during the course of my research, the physical training aspects of the course had little to do with the visions, values or goals that had been drilled into them in the classroom. One officer described, for example, a game of 'shag-tag' that recruits were required to play in the gym in the guise of PE. A variation on the children's game of 'tag', in which one child chases the rest until he or she touches another, who then becomes the pursuer, 'shag-tag' requires each officer (male or female) who is 'tagged' to bend over and touch his or her knees. The officer can only be 'released' by three thrusts (indicating sexual intercourse from the rear) from another officer (again, male or female). Summing up this aspect of basic training, this female officer remarked:

> I expected it [basic training] to be vaguely militaristic and male-oriented, but it's how close to the wind they play ... [that shocked me]. They didn't realise that somebody might blow the gaff on them [So how would you sum it up?] It was an exercise in humiliation.

The same officer also recounted a scenario where, during a 'leap-frog' session:

> an eighteen-stone bloke jumped on the back of a nine-stone woman. Meanwhile, the instructions were deliberately being delivered very slowly, and the poor girl was trembling with the strain of holding up this eighteen-stone bloke.

Having been told upon arrival at the college that the first value of the Prison Service's 'Vision, Values and Goals' was 'integrity', she was ashamed that she had not had the integrity to report such behaviour. As she put it: 'Where's my integrity when I didn't have the courage to blow the gaff on my fellow colleagues being degraded? [As a result] Your self-esteem falls.'

Similarly, from a female officer who subsequently went to work at Lancaster Farms:

> The gym side was quite tough. I think they [the PE instructors] pick on women a bit. [Can you talk to me a bit about that?] They were trying to see how far they could push you really ... They insisted you had to wear shorts ... I felt they were leering at you. And one [instructor] asked me if I was getting shagged by anybody, and I felt I couldn't say anything. *Now* I wouldn't stand for it ... And I was told I should put weight on. One woman was told she was too old at forty-eight; they kept going on and on about it. They made her feel worthless really.

As far as this officer was concerned, some of the instructors responsible for PE at the time of her basic training abused their power. She argued that these men relied on the knowledge that new recruits would be bewildered and vulnerable, and that they would be unwilling to 'rock the boat' for fear of failing the course and hence losing their jobs. That female officers undergoing training had received abuse from male staff was borne out by the comments of a number of (male and female) officers I interviewed at a later point in my research. For example, a male officer with two years in the service said that he had been similarly un-impressed by the attitudes of some of the trainers. He commented simply that 'It was so unprofessional it was untrue. They were pig ignorant, arrogant bastards'.

Female officers with some years in the service may also suffer hostility when taking part in certain types of additional training. A male officer, reflecting on a riot-training course he had recently attended, commented on the hostile and abusive behaviour of some of his colleagues towards the women officers taking part:

> As soon as they knew there was women on the course some of the blokes said 'Oh no, fucking splits! I hope I haven't got one on my team'. They were looking for mistakes all the time. If the women fell over running up the stairs with their shields, they'd get called a stupid bitch, but if a bloke fell over they just laughed.

It is interesting to note that during basic training, it was the *trainers* who had given new recruits a hard time. On the riot-training course, in contrast – a course for more experienced officers (see Chapter 6) – 'it was their *colleagues* that gave them stick. The trainers were great' (male officer, Lancaster Farms pers. comm.). When I asked why he thought this might be, he reflected that during basic during, every officer is on the same level; none of them know what to expect or what is expected of them. Male officers undergoing basic training have not yet 'found their feet' or slipped into the macho culture that is prevalent in prisons. By the time they go on to do further training, they have often done both.

The confidence of female officers may be sapped by the bullying and derisory comments made by some of their male colleagues; as a result they may make more mistakes and their ineptitude then seems confirmed. Older male officers may also feel disadvantaged during the more physically demanding elements of basic training, and may recognise that in an environment where male strength is so highly valued, being older or being female carry similar stigmas. As an officer in his late fifties remarked: 'For the older officer, its a bit like a female in the job. She's got her own sexist pressures and we've got being old.'

Many officers were of the view that regular and ongoing fitness training should be compulsory for the uniformed grades. Although they had themselves become physically fitter during basic training, their eagerness to 'fit in' with their occupational group had led to them going to the staff club, where they drank a lot and, in consequence, had started putting on weight. Becoming unfit again, however, was seen as a fair price to pay for acceptance and camaraderie.

Culture shock

Generally speaking, new recruits' preconceptions of prison life are similar to those of the general public; they anticipate that violence will be an everyday occurrence, and that prisoners (most of whom are presumed to be violent and dangerous) will spend most of their time locked up. Moreover, they expect to find that prisoners are 'different' from them. The vast majority of officers who took part in this study had expected to be confronted daily by prisoners, and they had been given this impression of prisons by the media, especially films, newspapers and television 'soaps' such as *The Governor*. Asked whether he had any preconceptions about the job before he started, one officer remarked:

> Yeah, and it wasn't like *this*! I thought we'd be like guards, up on a tower, spying on 'em.' [So the reality was a surprise?] Yeah, but it was still daunting.

Indeed, without exception, every officer who participated in this study recalled that their first days as a prison officer were difficult and frightening ones. Their accounts of their first days on the landings speak for themselves. Here is a selection:

> It was very daunting at first. It was a big step coming to work in a prison ... A very big step. I remember the first morning here ... I was that nervous I couldn't stop shaking. Obviously I was scared stiff, like. [What were you scared of?] I don't know, it was a massive challenge, and I didn't know if I was up to it, to tell you the truth. When I was on the induction, we went round the workshops, and it suddenly hit me how outnumbered we were, and they [the prisoners] were shouting 'Rookies! Rookies!' I was *terrified* then. You had to keep your hands in your pockets so that they couldn't see your hands shaking. I was that frightened! [So how *did* you cope?] I was told by a colleague it would be about eighteen months

before I got confident – this is confidential isn't it? [Yes, of course.] I had dreams for about eighteen months. Not nightmares, and not very often now, but I have a re-occurring dream – I get it three or four times a year. [What's it about?] I'm locking the inmates in their cells, and the more inmates I lock up, the more appear ... But don't get me wrong, I wouldn't swap this job for anything now. (Male officer, Garth)

There was me and another officer in the dining room, and in walked about a hundred and odd inmates. I thought *fifty* officers are needed here! It was frightening. A lot of prison officers wouldn't tell you that, but I think deep down, everyone is terrified at first, until they get to know a few staff, and a few of the inmates. *I* can see it in new staffs' faces. (Male senior officer, Garth)

I was terrified 'cos I didn't know what to expect. I spent most of the previous day on the toilet. (Male officer, Wymott)

The first time you walk in that dining room and you see a hundred-odd inmates, it's a knee-shaker. You think 'What have I let myself in for?' And your first confrontation ... How you react is very important, 'cos things can escalate in seconds. The last thing you want is a slanging match, 'cos then the other inmates hear it, and the con then wants to – or feels he has to – put a show on. [So] When you first start in the job, you've got very mixed feelings. (Male senior officer, Garth)

Before going to the training college, new recruits spend an 'observation week' at the establishment in which they are going to work (before local recruitment, new recruits had no idea to which establishments they would be sent after completing their basic training). During this week, new recruits will be shown the layout of the prison and instructed in the kinds of tasks they will be expected to perform (such as cell searching and (what is commonly termed) 'feeding'[3]) and the routines they must follow. In the course of this they will also be introduced to the staff they will be working with, as well as staff working in other parts of the prison. New recruits also, of course, meet prisoners (often for the first time) and observe how more experienced staff interact with them. At the end of this first week, new recruits will usually know whether or not the job is for them. I asked all my interviewees what their first impressions of, and feelings about this first week had been. Without exception, they confessed that they had been 'daunted' 'bewildered', 'scared' or 'frightened'; the first week had been, in short, a culture shock. The degree of culture shock new recruits experience is to some extent dependent on the type of prison and regime they initially encounter: many who had started out in large, busy local prisons (which can hold well in excess of a thousand prisoners) had found the noise level itself overwhelming and had stared, disbelievingly, at the number of prisoners that uniformed staff were expected to deal with. None the less, these new recruits did go on to complete their basic training and returned to their establishment ten weeks later.

All the officers in this study reported that the need for impression management was intense from the start. They were keen to give senior officers the impression that they were coping, while at the same time recognised the dangers of keeping their fears too much to themselves. Some spoke of being 'flung in the deep end'; they felt that had received insufficient support from experienced officers and had anxieties about falling flat on their faces when dealing with prisoners. One officer recalled the experiences of other probationers who, in their attempts to feign competency with their colleagues and reporting officers, had kept quiet about threats of violence from certain prisoners. The result was that each of these officers had been 'panic-struck – a bag of nerves' (male officer, Garth pers. comm.). Unsurprisingly, the greatest anxiety about starting work with prisoners was: 'What the cons will be like with you [and] how you'll deal with the cons.'

Some new recruits felt fearful because of the type of prisoner they were required to work with. One such officer, whose first post was at Long Lartin, said that he had been perturbed to find that an inmate who was serving a life sentence for a murder involving a knife was allowed to use a knife whilst preparing his own food in the kitchen. It took this officer 'months to get used to that ... to stop looking over my shoulder'. The physical layout of a prison also has implications for officers' perceptions of their own safety. At HMP Garth, for example, which has a number of 'blind' spurs rather than open landings and where, in consequence, sight-lines are relatively poor (I return to this issue later), several officers confided that they had felt unsafe. As one put it: 'I was bewildered when I got here. It took me ages to work out where I was walking. The prison was designed wrong, and you can't see what's round the next corner.'

In the first few days and weeks of being employed as a prison officer (the 'culture shock' period) the new recruit is likely to experience a range of emotions, including surprise, panic, confusion, anxiety and fear. While surprise, panic and confusion usually disappear entirely as recruits become more familiar with their surroundings and with the routines of the prison (events initially experienced as bizarre and frightening eventually become accepted as normal and routine – as just part of the job) feelings of anxiety and even fear may well remain, although they usually diminish in intensity. Some officers, however, learn to enjoy confrontations with prisoners. While for most officers, confrontation is to be avoided at all costs, for some the threat of physical violence adds excitement to an otherwise humdrum and routinised day:

> Confrontations with inmates bother some [officers] … but it's no good worrying about them. And to be honest, staff get a buzz out of them. [Do they?] Sometimes. (Male officer, Lancaster Farms)

Reality shock

'Embryonic images' (Brogden *et al.* 1988) of what being a prison officer is about, then, take shape during basic training. These embryonic images are made more 'real' when the officer starts work in the prison itself; it is at this point that the officer begins to gain an understanding of the *informal* norms and values of the occupational culture. We fast-forward now to when basic training and induction are over, and the new officer takes his or her place on the landings.

Several long-serving officers reflected upon their feelings of disappointment when they realised that working in the Prison Service was not quite as it had been painted at the interview and in the recruitment literature.[4] They had, none the less, remained in the job, some for almost thirty years. Recalling his first experiences of HMP Strangeways, this senior officer reflected on the disparity between the formal and informal realities of his new post:

> The recruitment literature had lied. I thought it was a professional organisation, in which I would be able to make a difference to the people we locked up. *Wrong!* A fortnight at Manchester cured that. I couldn't imagine what I'd done. They'd had me over. They professed to being a professional service, and we had Strangeways, with strange ways. The smell, the noise, the attitude problems of some of the staff we had to work with – they were very macho-orientated. Sensitivity wasn't looked on with much favour I can tell you and they'd take the piss out of baby jailers. But some of them would help you. It was a culture shock. Staff were blasé with large numbers of prisoners – about 1,800 of them we had at one point. In the boys' prison, they were three'd up. There was about 700 of them, and it got so bad the smell used to knock you over. They

actually called the boys' prison the Animal House ... Within a fortnight I realised that it was a numbers game, and the object of the prison was to push in as many prisoners as possible. And when they went to work we'd sit in the weaving shed going quietly bonkers. There were 50 looms and ear-defenders were bits of cotton wool stuffed in your ears. That was the Modern Prison Service! The reality was nothing like the promotion; it was a different world to what they'd told us at the training college. [The slopping out must have been pretty horrendous?] Pardon my language but it was fucking awful. I did seriously wonder what the hell I was doing. I'd still got what was in the brochure in my mind – rehabilitation – and the reality was seeing the lads paddling about with buckets of crap. It was simply a matter of opening the doors and putting stuff in that end [points to his mouth] and waiting for it to come out the other.

The life of a sprog

Joining an organisation can either be a gentle, carefully orchestrated process or a sudden immersion in deep water. While some organisations have induction programmes to hold the recruits' hand and a mentor to guide them, more common is an entry with minimal assistance (Fineman and Gabriel 1996: 137). According to the long-serving officers who participated in this study, it was a matter of chance which experience a new recruit into the Prison Service got. Experienced officers still differ greatly in terms of the amount of support and guidance they are prepared to offer new recruits. To a greater or lesser extent (the inclination to help new recruits differs temporally and geographically) those joining the service in the 1970s tended to find that the learning process was one based almost entirely on observation. There was no alternative given; it was common practice for more senior officers to refuse even to *speak* to 'sprogs' (new recruits are traditionally called 'sprogs' by longer-serving colleagues, even if they are middle-aged and have children of their own). In the 1970s the occupational hierarchy was steep and unyielding; a new recruit asking for help from an experienced officer was likely to be told to 'Fuck off and find out for yourself, like I had to!' (numerous officers, all ranks pers. comm.). Unsurprisingly, this served only to exacerbate inexperienced officers' feelings of isolation: 'My first posting was Manchester [where] staff had no time for rookie staff like me. I don't know who was more frightening, the prisoners or the staff!' (male officer, Lancaster Farms).

Similarly, a principal officer (currently working in a young offender institution but previously an officer at Strangeways) commented that in the past, experienced officers:

used to treat probationers like shit. Even officers who only had a few more weeks in would tell new staff to piss off if they asked for help or wanted information. In fact, [because they wouldn't help you] they'd push you nearer to the prisoners! [Really?] Yes. It was them that'd warn you if they saw the Chief coming or anything.

And again, this time from a senior officer working at Garth:

It was a case of 'Stand in that corner … keep them open and that shut'. New staff were not expected to question the logic of anything that longer-serving staff did; it was their job just to keep in place the routine that had been in place for years and honed to perfection.

In some prisons, officers were not even trusted to be able to use their keys without help for the first few weeks:

For the first week, you'd just be told to stand in a corner. Perhaps by the second week you'd be told 'When I nod, you unlock that door'. By the third week, they'd say 'When I nod, you unlock that door and lock it again afterwards.' You knew you'd really arrived when they let you get your cell key out and open up a con. That night, you'd go home really chuffed! (Senior officer, Wymott)

Even officers who joined the service within the last few years had experienced being, as they put it, 'blanked' by longer-serving staff – a state of affairs arising out of the importance placed upon seniority, particularly in large, old locals such as Liverpool and Wandsworth.

Thank God for the old lags

New officers were thus exposed to a practice of learning as they went along. If they were lucky, and another officer had started on the same day, they might be able to reassure and help each other; otherwise, they relied on good fortune and the eyes and ears of 'old lags'. That prisoners played a large part in orienting the new recruit to his job is clear; even today, in prisons where new recruits are left either to sink or swim, learning to swim involves accepting help from prisoners. Describing his first experiences at Garth, this officer commented:

To be honest, when I first got here, I hated it for the first couple of months … There was what I thought to be the typical prison officer on there. Even the PO blanked me! And when you went in the staff room, they'd all stop talking … It was like being in a John Wayne film – the piano would stop playing! To be honest, I found the cons more helpful. The cons would say 'You wanna lock that door' or 'You don't wanna unlock *him*, he'll get a cob on … you'll get into trouble'. Thank God for the old lags that's all I can say. [Did it strike you as odd that the inmates helped you more than the staff?] Yes, it did actually.

Perhaps unsurprisingly, relying on prisoners could sometimes get prison officers into trouble:

We don't have so many work parties now, but there are work parties, and a new officer will often have to, er, say to the inmates 'What do we do now?' And I think I told you, here, not too long ago, a number of years ago, erm, there was an inmate on report for stealing bread from the kitchen. And the governor said to him 'Did you take the bread out of the kitchen?' And he says 'yeah.' The Governor says to him 'Why?' He says 'Well for the toast!' He says 'What do you mean, toast?' He says 'Well we make toast every morning.' And er, it turned out that what used to happen was that the lads used to bring bread, and they managed to get some margarine from somewhere, and when they got a new officer on the coal party, they'd say to him halfway through the morning 'We have our smoke break now, and we make a bit of toast.' It turned out they were making toast on the incinerator where all these shit parcels were being thrown on to and then sitting round having a fag and a bite to eat. And there was rubber, and, you know, all sorts of horrible stuff being burned. So then the officer got told off as well. (Principal officer, YOI)

Contamination avoidance: the mentor scheme

Generally speaking, today's new entrant officers are likely to be helped through the early days by their colleagues, at some prisons by a 'mentor'. HMP Wymott, for example, has a mentoring policy in operation which is described, in the *Notice of Guidance for Line Managers* (1996), as 'a means of providing support and guidance to individuals as they adapt to the new environment of their workplace'. As this document goes on to say, mentoring has been adopted through the industrial world 'as a successful means of furthering personal development, competencies and relationships between colleagues within an organisation'. In the prison setting, a 'mentor' is an experienced officer who is 'willing to share his/her knowledge with someone else in a relationship of mutual trust. [The mentor is, in short] a mixture of parent and peer' (*ibid.*). In practice, new recruits usually 'shadow' their mentors and the mentors point out their mistakes:

> Basic training does not fully equip people for working with prisoners. So many prisons have a 'buddy' scheme whereby the new officer can see how others interact with prisoners. They can see if he is confrontational, assertive or submissive. Clearly, he must be assertive only. (Principal officer, Portland)

On some wings, senior-ranking officers try hard to keep sprogs away from 'old guard' staff lest they 'contaminate' them with outmoded values and working styles. In a sense, this has parallels with the way that eighteenthth-century prison administrators separated young and old prisoners, in order to prevent the contagion of crime spreading from the experienced to the initiate (see, for example, Ignatieff 1978). Mentoring schemes could be described as a strategy for 'contamination avoidance'; those managers who want to keep new recruits from cynical dinosaurs – old hands who are likely to teach them undesirable working practices – are likely to have a mentoring scheme in place.

In practice, new officers also look for their own role models. In their attempts to 'learn the ropes' they emulate the actions, attitudes and behaviours of officers whose style of working they admire and whose values and beliefs they roughly share: 'I modelled myself at someone at Styal. I thought "God, she's good". She made it okay to talk to the inmates' (female officer, Garth). None the less, learning the ropes is still a fairly slow, hit-and-miss process. As this principal officer (Lancaster Farms) put it: 'Man-management skills are learnt "on the hoof". It takes two to three years to be proficient at it, 'cos no two days are alike.'

Similarly, this time from a male officer working at Wymott: 'It's like walking through a forest and picking up sticky-buds. I'd say it's at least a couple of years before you're actually confident.'

Getting used to the rules, routines and technology employed in the prison can be a stressful business, as this officer pointed out when describing her anxieties about learning the radio system:

> I heard a bleep alert and I didn't even know what a bleep alert was! I thought if I ignored it it would go away! I used to have to go to the toilet to join the NET, I did, I was that nervous! (Female officer, Garth)

The first few months in the job, then, tend to be anxious ones for all new officers. The same female officer recalled how much she relied upon her counterparts for support: 'When I started the job I hated it. I cried for six months. If it hadn't been for the other three lads that joined the same day, I'd have left.' Much of this officer's anxiety stemmed from there being so much to learn in an environment where one's mistakes are easily seen by both prisoners and staff. New recruits may also find the closed environment of the prison difficult to cope with: 'I worked on a submarine, closed in with twenty other men, but it wasn't half as claustrophobic as my first days on a landing. It was really oppressive.' (male officer, Lancaster Farms).

For many recruits, prisoners' apparent capacity for bare-faced lying comes as one of the biggest shocks of all:

> To me, it was a bit of a shock really – all these sob stories all the time and having to say no. 'Cos in your own community, you expect people to behave with good morals; here they tell you their mother's dying of cancer so they can get a phone call when they just want to phone their girlfriend! So you've got to be suspicious all the time ... It's in the back of your mind all the time. (Male officer, Garth)

To these officers this was evidence that prisoners were indeed 'different sorts of people' from them. They, and other officers like them, quickly learnt to acquire a hard shell to protect them from exploitation; they knew the consequences for those perceived by prisoners as 'soft': 'If you're a sucker for a sob story they would walk all over you' (male officer, Moorland).

Learning to survive: impression management

Although new recruits recognise that first impressions are important, they invariably find it difficult even to *look* confident at first. As this senior officer (Garth) put it: 'with his extra-shiny shoes and brand new uniform, the new recruit *looks* brand new out of the box.' More experienced staff often tell new recruits to pretend to prisoners that they have worked in a prison before (it is important to choose somewhere at the other end of the country where the inmate is unlikely to have been) so that they will be less likely to be taken advantage of. Prisoners, however, are not so easily fooled. They are usually able to spot a new recruit immediately because the body language of new officers gives them away. Newly recruited prison officers, like new recruits in any organisation, are unfamiliar with the routines, with other officers, with the layout of the prison and with prisoners. They tend to stand about, unsure of what to look for and where to look, yet trying to look nonchalant, just as I did when I started my fieldwork on the wings. One officer put his own recollections across quite beautifully:

> You turn up like a bloody new pin, and you haven't even got creases in your shoes, and you stand out like a sore thumb. It's flipping obvious you haven't done it before. Inmates aren't stupid, they can tell because new officers tend to hover. (Male officer, Garth)

The 'working personality' of the prison officer – the walk, the talk, the posture, jargon, mindset, values and beliefs – takes time to acquire. The social relations of, and informal hierarchies between, prison officers may serve to extend the learning process. As in most organisations, experienced officers tend to pass the most disliked jobs on to new recruits. For example at Garth, officers consistently sent new recruits up to the 'top landing' – an unpopular place to work because there were no other officers there (this was less likely to happen to new female recruits because they were seen as more vulnerable).

While the formal rules of each establishment (the Prison Rules and Standing Orders) are laid down for each officer to follow, the informal rules of the job are neither clear-cut nor articulated. Rather, they are 'embedded in specific practices and nuances according to particular concrete situations and the interactional processes of each encounter' (Kalinich and Pitcher 1984). New recruits are thus likely to find that when they start work in their establishment, they are told to 'forget what you learnt at college' and expected to fit into a particular working culture. In short, they are expected to understand 'the way we do things around here'. As Kalinich and Pitcher note, new recruits are likely to receive confusing signals from other uniformed staff. In brief, they:

> will find that some of the organisation's written policies and procedures will be followed faithfully, while particular policies and procedures will be totally ignored by veteran employees. Some experienced personnel will attempt to undermine formal training, leaving trainees in doubt as to how to conduct themselves in the performance of their personal interactions with more experienced colleagues. (*Ibid.*: xii–xiii)

Invariably, one of the first instructions received by the new recruit is to 'go in hard and soften up later on' on the grounds that it is better to appear hard than appear a fool. A new recruit's ability to say 'No' to a prisoner, and appear to mean it, is, for many officers, a signal that the recruit can be trusted. To be really trusted, however:

> You've got to be seen to perform – to respond to an alarm bell. In this job there's doers, followers and lazy bastards and new staff are quickly sussed out according to these criteria. And the label you get is hard to lose. (Principal officer, Portland)

New members of any organisation must quickly learn the correct mannerisms, dress and mode of speaking that are associated with their position. As I suggested above, this 'impression management' is a process that is required for all organisations to operate smoothly. Impression management (particularly the management of the *first* impression) is particularly important in occupations such as police work and prison work, where *presence* is often more necessary than action. Unlike in police work, looking and sounding in control must be *sustained* since the prison officer (unlike the police) has to negotiate and maintain 'appropriate' social relations with prisoners *over time*.

One of the fundamental aspects of prisoner supervision is that officers keep their personal lives to themselves. New recruits are instructed not to lose their perspective of their role as prison officers and become personally involved with prisoners. Divulging of personal information can occur suddenly and without the officer being aware that this rule has been violated. New recruits are, in short, socialised to be discreet.

Learning to banter: humour as survival strategy

New recruits also have to survive certain informal socialisation 'rites' before they are accepted by more experienced colleagues. This is part of what one long-serving officer described as 'a sprog's upbringing in the service – to make him into an officer'. This terminology suggests that the new recruit is perceived, by more experienced officers, as having a somewhat childlike status. The making of a sprog into a competent, trustworthy colleague involves, *inter alia*, the use of humour. Experienced officers argue that 'taking the mickey' out of new recruits is an essential part of the socialisation process; that learning to banter – 'to be able to take it and give it back ' – is crucial to *becoming* an effective prison officer: 'Your banter between the lads is a protective thing … we rib each other ... If you can take it from colleagues, you can take it from cons.' (male officer, Garth). In short officers 'practise' on each other in preparedness for the 'real thing', i.e. confrontations with prisoners:

> [The] Banter makes you think quicker; it makes you think on your feet. You've got to be ready for it ... your mind's always got to be active. But you've got to be careful not to take things too far. You get to know who'll take things the wrong way. And that's just basic jail-craft. (Male officer, Garth)

Learning to banter can be tough on new recruits; they may be teased unmercifully (particularly if they make a silly mistake) and become the butt of practical jokes. Much of what prison officers call 'banter' could be described, in anthropological terms, as 'ritual insult exchange' (Zijderveld 1983). Anthropology has provided important insights into this social phenomenon of self-consciously staged verbal contests. The kind of humour contained in these exchanges is often at least partly prepared (standard off-the-shelf material) and entirely 'hard' – that is, a humour of sarcasm and ridicule rather than clowning or whimsy (Goodrich *et al.* 1954 but see also Goldstein and McGhee 1972). Observational data gathered by Goodrich *et al.* on the staff of a psychiatric hospital demonstrate that 'bluntly derogatory remarks about colleagues accounted for 35% of all laughs'. Ritualised insult exchange must not, of course, be taken too far; in the prison setting officers have to be extremely careful in their verbal joustings with prisoners. As the above quotation makes clear, officers claim to be able to gauge which prisoners can appreciate this sort of banter and which cannot; as another of my interviewees went on to observe, this is the kind of knowledge that officers are alluding to when they talk about the 'common sense' nature of prison work.

Officers may also take affront at the jibes made by colleagues; on a number of occasions during my fieldwork, officers walked off in a huff following an insulting joke or remark made by another officer at their expense. New recruits spoke of experienced officers trying to find their 'soft spots', and then picking at them until they got them to 'bite' – a process described by one perpetrator as 'like picking at a scab'. Perhaps unsurprisingly, continued bombardment of abrasive humour can have a destructive effect upon the recipient (Goldstein and McGhee 1972: 12) while bolstering the morale of those who initiate it. Most of the time, however, the banter between prison officers is good-hearted, and insults and jibes are taken in good part. Importantly, banter generally lightens the atmosphere of a wing, and on numerous occasions I too dissolved into fits of laughter, and I found myself trying to think up funny and witty repartee.

As I indicated earlier, humour has a number of functions. Humour functions as a defence mechanism (to protect against the emotional distress of specific situations), a wit sharpener ('the banter makes you think quicker; it makes you think on your feet'), a morale raiser (the pre-shift 'gee up' or the release of tension as staff leave the gate for the day), an 'incorporator' (the mickey-taking of a new recruit to make him or her 'one of us') and a strategy of exclusion (for example, to reinforce the belief that 'deviant' officers are *not* 'one of us'). Humour is also therefore a monitor of staff performance on the terms established within the local staff culture: if officers perceive, for example, that a colleague is not pulling his or her weight they will attempt to say so via humorous jibes and digs. So while humour can be healing (promoting group solidarity and relieving tension) it can also be destructive and divisive.

Prison officers love to play pranks. Pranks are an important part of the life-world of uniformed staff and an important element in the ritualised induction of new recruits. They perform two functions on the prison wings: first and most obviously they provide amusement for the perpetrators of the prank and for onlookers; secondly they establish and maintain the informal hierarchy of the group and give the recruits 'clues' as to how they should perform. The following extract from my field-notes provides a typical example of the use of humour in the prison setting, and it illustrates the ways in which practical jokes or pranks are employed to socialise the new recruit:

One morning in the senior officer's office, I was privy to the mickey-taking of Martin, a young probationer [mid-20s] by longer-serving male officers. There are two desks in the SO's office; when the phone rang on one of them, Martin picked it up and asked who was speaking; there was a roar of laughter as he realised that an officer sitting at the other desk was on the line! Determined not to get caught out again, Martin kept his eye on the officers sitting at the other desk; when the phone rang again [internal telephones seem to ring constantly in all prisons] Martin presumed the call was 'kosher'; however he had not noticed that an officer had gone to the office next door and dialled from there; another roar of laughter – including from myself! Female officers also engage in mickey-taking; a little later in the day, following an intensive search throughout the prison for a pair of scissors that had gone astray from the Education Department, an experienced female officer told Martin [when he asked her what would happen if the scissors weren't found] that they would all be issued with flack jackets [rather than having a lock-down]. She told Martin that because he was new, he could expect to get a phone call asking him to go for a fitting for a jacket. He waited anxiously for a phone call; when I left the wing he was still waiting and his colleagues were stifling their giggles and contemplating how to proceed.

In the working lives of prison officers, humour is as important as it is ubiquitous. As the following comment demonstrates, humour is central to prison life: 'At Walton, I was told that the job runs on cups of tea and a sense of humour. And I'd say that was about right.' (male officer, Garth).

Virtually every officer I spoke to cited camaraderie (mutual trust and sociability) and what they called 'the crack' as the best aspects of the job. The 'crack' – those convivial and intimate moments of banter, joking, story-telling and high spirits that are borne out of shared experience and like-mindedness (and the reassurance that comes with it) – is highly valued, as is the ability to *tell* a joke, and the willingness to *take* one. Indeed, the 'crack' is so important that some officers reported coming into work that little bit early just to experience it because it sets them up for the day ahead.

Experienced officers are aware that their style of humour is, in some respects, 'profane'; it is a style of humour that is learnt on the job: 'In this job, cracking a joke when something bad happens becomes the norm. New officers have not yet been polluted by our warped sense of humour, or by this lot [the prisoners]' (senior officer, Garth).

As I have already suggested, the humour that prison officers use in their interactions with each other can be very hurtful and insulting. For example, one officer who stutters was called 'Klunk'. New recruits must be able to cope with such insults -- if they get angry or upset officers suspect that they will not be able to cope with the prisoners. Of course, this is arguably not the *sole* reason they engage in teasing; teasing also establishes the recruit's (low) status in the hierarchy of the group:

Because I'm the youngest and the newest, they take the piss out of me. Like nicknames – I've gone through more nicknames here than I got at high school. But you get better at doing it yourself as well ... I came out with a real corker the other day and I can't remember what it was now. And you know it's good 'cos they go 'Ooooh!' Its good though, 'cos some of them have taken me under their wing. (Probationer, Garth)

New recruits are almost always given a nickname, which may derive from the officer's surname, reflect his or her geographical roots (a Scouser or a Geordie) or the way in which the officer carries out his or her job. For example, 'Blister' is the name given to an officer who only 'comes out when the work's done', 'Wing-nut' to the officer whose ears stick out, 'Action Man' for the officer who bores his colleagues by his boasts of being in the SAS and for the laziest officer on the wing, the name of 'Barry, Half Man, Half Chair'! Officers usually 'try out' numerous nicknames on the new recruit until they find one that sticks.

The desire to attribute nicknames at the first opportunity suggests that officers feel the need to *place* new colleagues in the organisational hierarchy, *vis-à-vis* themselves. Putting someone 'in their place' with a nickname is a way of claiming intimacy and indicating that the person is 'one of us'. It is also a way of ordering social relations between colleagues. New recruits must be able to take all this in good part: if they meet these informal expectations of the job, as well as the formal expectations (ability to do basic key tasks, have an awareness of security issues and so on) then they will become accepted members of the wing.

Being accepted also involves learning both the formal Prison Rules and the informal, 'craft rules' of the job as well as the 'feeling rules' of the organisation. New recruits soon learn that the former are bent on a daily basis, but precisely how and when the rules can be bent is something that they only learn through time spent on the job. Rule-bending is problematic for inexperienced officers who are unsure of the prisoners, the staff, the routines and even the rules themselves. 'Doing things by the book' is thus seen as the safest strategy until one 'knows the ropes'. As one probationer put it: 'Until you know more it's best to stay with black and white.' (male officer, Garth). Similarly: 'I don't know ways of bending them [the rules] yet, 'cos you've got to do it in ways that don't compromise security' (male officer, Garth).

New recruits also learn, through observing experienced officers, how to interact with prisoners and the degree of social distance that they 'should' place between themselves and prisoners (as I shall show later, officers' views on these questions differ greatly). Over time, new recruits learn to develop their own work styles, and the degree of social distance they choose to place between themselves and prisoners may expand or contract accordingly.

The pressure to conform: group think

Every group exerts social pressure on its members to make them conform. Should the new recruit's behaviour and attitudes fail to correspond to group norms, he or she has four choices: to conform, to remain a deviant, to leave the group or to change the norms. Another choice rests with the other group members – removing the deviant member from the group (Herbert 1981: 312). Prison officers who attempt to resist the cultural values and expectations of their colleagues may find themselves in difficulties. When I asked an experienced, long-serving principal officer how easy it is for officers who disapprove of group norms to challenge or resist them, he replied that they would either be 'quickly put right' by their colleagues or they might even be 'ostracised'. When asked to elaborate on this, this principal officer was remarkably candid, drawing upon his work experiences at HMP Pentonville to make his point:

> Individually, prison officers are the salt of the earth. But as a *group* ... They can be evil. I certainly wouldn't want to cross them. When I [worked at Pentonville and] lived in Jebb Avenue, staff that *did* had their tyres slashed and paint stripper put on their cars.

The pressure to conform is strong. Most psychologists believe that all of us have basic psychological needs, one of which is the need for social approval, and that much of our behaviour is based on a desire to belong and identify with other persons or groups. The group provides, *inter alia*, emotional support. We all need to belong; thinking and acting along the same lines help us to do that. Unfortunately the pressure to conform to the values of the group can be so strong as to make people doubt the validity of their own experience. Asch's (1951) experiment is a good example of this; when shown cards with lines on that they 'knew' were the same length, some individuals simply did not like to say so, in the face of insistence that the lines were different. Others actually became uncertain of their own perceptions; they came to believe that, in the face of such opposition, they must be mistaken. Despite the cognitive functions that conformity may serve, there are dangers both for individuals and society at large of simply going along with the group (Janis 1983). Nowhere is this more evident than in Janis's identification of 'group think' as a feature of bad political decision-making. He notes that various blunders by US presidents – in particular J.F. Kennedy's (disastrous) decision to mount an invasion at the Bay of Pigs in Cuba despite serious reservations – arose because those who made them had conformed to the majority decision rather than voice an alternative opinion. The more consensual the group and the more isolate the individual (i.e. the less others agree with the deviant) the greater the power of the group to define reality and induce self-doubt in the deviant.

New staff are particularly unlikely to 'swim against the tide' (principal officer, Portland pers. comm.).

In the prison setting it is not only prisoners who form cliques, gangs and loosely knit groups to meet the need for social approval. Prison officers also coalesce into exclusive social groupings with shared interests, values and beliefs. Several officers confided that they were uncomfortable with certain aspects of the occupational culture, disliking particularly 'the macho side of the job'. Needing to 'fit in', however, they had found it difficult not to become ensnared. As one senior officer commented:

> I never cease to be amazed at how quickly the culture can grab somebody ... It's 'cos you're working in a very small, tight-knit community, and you need to exist in this community. And if you are seen to do something extraordinary, you will be excluded. And nobody likes to be excluded do they?

Individual prisons differ greatly both in terms of regime and 'ethos' or 'way', and officers who have to work in a prison where the ethos is contrary to their own values and preferred working styles will have to engage in a great deal of emotion work. Specifically, a prescribed norm of expressing irritation or lack of interest on the landings may go against the inner feelings of warmth and kindness an officer might feel towards co-operative and friendly prisoners. The following quotations, all from the same officer working at Lancaster Farms, illustrate this disjuncture particularly well. This long-serving officer, whose first posting had been to HMP Strangeways, found it extremely difficult to treat prisoners in the style that corresponded to the occupational norms of that prison, which at that time (the late 1970s) were hardly conducive to positive staff–prisoner relations. Part-time acting enabled him to cope:

> I felt that I had to put on an act. They expected you to shout and bawl. So in private I'd talk to prisoners in a very free and easy way, but when a senior officer walked past, I had to start shouting and bawling ... put on an act. I couldn't be myself.

Importantly, this officer believed that 'putting on an act' was essential if he was to retain his job: 'I felt that if I was my own self I wouldn't get through my probation. They were looking for the old hairy-arsed screw syndrome. Now, of course they want the opposite.' Once the officer had served his probationary year, however, what he described as his 'hairy-arsed screw' persona could be abandoned: The act stopped as soon as I got out of probation. As soon as I got my letter to say 'Welcome to the Club' I was invincible. I knew they couldn't get rid of me unless I did something really bad.'

To maintain the integrity of the group, prison officers engage in rituals. As I argued above, the most common rituals are the attribution of nicknames and the staging of pranks – both of which constitute important 'rites of passage' for recipients. Another widespread form of ritual is the use of technical language or jargon by which group members can more easily discuss work-related occurrences, objects and indeed people; in terms of the latter, new recruits quickly learn that talking about prisoners as 'scumbags', 'scroats' 'Scouse shits', Muppets and the like enables them to fit in with the culture. In the process, however, they learn that their own values must be submerged: 'Not only does jargon allow group members to communicate in a more concise and exact manner, but it sets them apart from those not belonging by the simple exclusion of others from the basic communication process' (Herbert 1981: 314).

Concluding comments: becoming and being

I have tried to demonstrate that the process of becoming a prison officer is a slow, challenging and complex one. The donning of the accoutrements of the position – the uniform, keys, chain and so forth – and the formal training which new recruits undergo are merely the start point of this process. It is not enough simply to put on the uniform; the officer must learn to *wear* it. Nor is it sufficient that new recruits learn the prison rules, the routines and working practices of the prison, the procedures for dealing with unco-operative prisoners, the norms of the occupational culture, the 'recipe' or 'craft' rules of the job and the 'feeling rules' of the prison. Rather, officers must both know them and *embody* them. In short, the new recruit must acquire the 'working personality' of the prison officer. This is not acquired through mere habituation and repetition; rather it involves *inhabiting a way of being*. It is in *this* sense that the prison officer himself, like the occupational culture to which he must subscribe, can be described an 'achievement' or 'process' produced over time.

In the chapters that follow, readers can see for themselves how the working personality of the prison officer 'plays out' in day-to-day interactions on the landings, not only between prison officers and prisoners but between prison officers themselves.

Notes

1 The May Committee (1979 paras 7.25–26) gave some thought to the possibility of lowering the minimum age for recruitment, but concluded that the officer's basic task, which is 'to detain, against their will, men and women of all ages, many of whom are devious and manipulative, and some of whom are on occasions violent ... requires a degree of maturity and experience that is unlikely to be found in anyone much below the age of 21'.

2 In submissions to the Wynn-Parry Commission (1958) the POA argued that a minimum of three O grade passes should be required for entry into the Prison Service. These submissions were rejected on the grounds that they would be a significant disincentive to recruitment.

3 There is a growing awareness amongst officers that this commonly used term, to describe the provision of meals to prisoners, is an inappropriate one, since it connotes the feeding of animals in a zoo.

4 In the 1970s, recruitment literature offers potential new recruits 'A New Job: A Brighter Future'. Women were told 'If you enjoy helping others, join me in the Modern Prison Service'.

Chapter 4

Them and us? How officers see prisoners

Throughout the complex process of 'becoming', prison officers necessarily have to consider their relationships with prisoners. It is, I think, worth restating here why an exploration of the character and quality of staff–prisoner relationships is important. First, as noted by the CRC in 1984, positive relationships between these two groups facilitate the efficient control of prisoners and (hence) the security of the prison. Secondly, positive staff–prisoner relations clearly make the prison a less painful place for prisoners. Thirdly, they generate a more congenial working environment for prison staff – the 'human service' variety at any rate. As we shall see, however, the development of positive relationships with prisoners is not a key concern for all officers; some (albeit a minority) refuse to recognise relationship-building as germane to their role. Officers who do, however, get to know the prisoners in their care, may come to recognise their virtues as well as their frailties and, in consequence, find that they get to like some of these prisoners too.

In the first part of this chapter I briefly outline the day-to-day work of prison officers. I then go on to discuss officers' perceptions of prisoners, and what they consider the 'right' staff–prisoner relationship to be. Prison officers hold widely differing views on this topic, and this can lead to staff conflicts (a topic I discuss in depth in Chapter 7). In the next part of this chapter I focus on the question of where power lies in prisons. As I shall demonstrate, this is of unceasing concern to prison officers, and it shapes, to a significant degree, their interactions with prisoners. Finally, I explore officers' perceptions of the 'good' officer and the question of whether the 'good' officer will challenge colleagues who 'get it wrong'.

What do prison officers *do*?

As I have already indicated, there is much more to being a prison officer than simply being there. In addition to their primarily custodial tasks – such as locking up and unlocking prisoners, providing meals, checking locks, bolts and bars, maintaining discipline, regulating visits and the flow of prisoners to and from work – the modern prison officer is also expected to change prisoners' behaviours and outlooks and to provide him or her with care. Prison work also demands a range of interactional skills, including an ability to communicate, a willingness to negotiate and to engage in what Hay and Sparks (1991) call a 'creative use of the self'.

The moment that offenders step within the prison walls they will find that certain roles are lost to them by virtue of the barrier that separates them from the outside world (Goffman 1968: 24). Moreover, as Goffman notes, the process of entrance into the prison also typically brings with it other kinds of loss and mortification: finger-printing, the removal of personal effects, the issuing of prison clothing, the assigning of a number and a cell allows the prisoner 'to be shaped and coded into an object that can be fed into the administrative machinery of the establishment, to be worked on smoothly by routine operations' (*ibid.*: 26). Stripped of his identity kit, the prisoner will find it difficult to present his usual image of himself to others. Prison officers, however, must get to know these prisoners *as individuals*; they must learn their foibles, personal circumstances, dispositions and ability to deal with incarceration. This knowledge (the latter in particular) is necessary for the smooth running of the regime, for security purposes and for the safety of staff and other prisoners. In order to carry out their job effectively, prison officers should be able to assess, with a fair degree of accuracy, the prisoners in their charge.

Most of my interviewees were keen to emphasise the numerous (and varied) roles a prison officer might be required to perform on any one day. Their list included 'locus parentis' (parent role), mentor (role model), counsellor (in the event of bad news), teacher, social worker, comedian (every officer noted the importance of having a sense of humour), psychologist (recognising when a prisoner is not acting like his or her usual self), filing clerk, probation officer (officers are now involved in through-care), fire-fighter (some staff are trained to use breathing apparatus and fire-fighting equipment), tourist guide (giving guided tours of the prison to outside visitors), stock controller (ensuring an adequate supply of toilet rolls, plastic cutlery, laundry and so on), security guard and, finally, police officer (dealing with disciplinary actions). As we shall see, however, not all officers perform all these roles. On the contrary, some officers are prepared to do little more than the last three. I was, none the less, struck by the range of tasks that prison officers are *asked* to perform, and the sheer volume and variety of prisoner inquiries and requests. Some of these requests are extraordinary – or at least they are extraordinary given the context in which they are made – and they are illustrative both of the needs of individual prisoners and of the varied nature of the prison officer role. For example, one evening in the Vulnerable Prisoner (VP) Unit at HMP Wymott, a nurse from the hospital approached a senior officer to discuss a prisoner's request for a bra. It transpired that the prisoner, a man in his early thirties, was in the process of undergoing sex-change hormone treatment (which had begun prior to his sentence) and had complained to officers that he had 'leaking breasts'. In addition, the prisoner had requested that the upper part of his body should be searched by female officers and the bottom half by male officers (he had been denied permission to have his male genitalia removed surgically whilst still a prisoner). Although there was some incredulity about this state of affairs and, it must be said, a fair amount of ribaldry, on the whole the uniformed staff (the majority of whom were men) seemed to take this situation in their stride. Generally, however, much of the prison officer's day is taken up with more mundane matters (see Liebling and Price 2001 for a summary of a prison officer's 'typical day').

How do prison officers perceive prisoners?

In the main, prison officers are under no illusions that prison will deter prisoners from further crimes. On the contrary, they invariably acknowledge prisoners' resignations to a life punctuated by prison. In this regard, numerous officers recounted how often prisoners due for release had told them that they would be 'coming back'; they had no reason to think otherwise, given that they were returning to the same circumstances that they had left on entering prison. Indeed, many realised that a prison sentence was likely to have decreased their chances of honest employment. Unsurprisingly, such perceptions affect how much interest prisoners show in courses aimed at rehabilitation and, subsequently, the level of interest that officers show, and manage to maintain, in delivering them.

Much of the cynicism that prison officers feel derives from their perception that the prison's efforts to rehabilitate are impossible, either because inadequate staffing levels make it impossible to run courses effectively, because prisoners had to go out to the same socio-economic circumstances or because prisoners are simply uninterested in being rehabilitated:

> The sooner the goal of rehabilitation goes, the better. You might as well deep-freeze them for six months. We'd be better off just talking to them [than having all these courses]. All they want anyway is 'When's my parole date?' 'When's my visit?' 'When's my phone call?' They're not interested in the courses – they don't even turn up. Unless they get free tea and biscuits, and then they rob the tea boat and bugger off! [What do you mean, rob the tea boat?] They bring little jars along and nick the coffee and sugar. (Male officer, Garth)

And again:

> At a place like this, with career criminals, you know for a fact that they're not gonna change – whatever courses they go on. And you know they're just paying lip-service when they're doing sentence planning and that. They know all the right buttons to press to get out. So you know it's a waste of time really. (Senior officer, Garth)

While many of my interviewees were pessimistic about the possibility of rehabilitating prisoners, they none the less felt that doing *something* was better than doing nothing, even if both staff and prisoners recognised the futility of the exercise, given the structural difficulties that prisoners would face 'on the out'. During one of our (many) conversations about rehabilitation, this senior officer (Lancaster Farms) remarked:

> They're just weighting down prison officers with bits of paper. These lads *know* we're giving them bollocks; they *know* there's nothing for them [on the outside]. It's horrendous. You can talk about sentence planning and courses as much as you like, but ... [So does this not make you despondent?] Well to a certain extent, but the *alternative's* so awful. And being positive is better for morale than being negative. Obviously, we lack the one thing that'd make a difference, and that's a job for them all.

Although some officers believe that they can 'make progress' with some prisoners (in the sense of generating in them a desire to change their behaviour or lifestyle) they also realise that the majority of prisoners that have participated in the courses they have delivered will, sooner or later, return to prison. Prisoners could perhaps be forgiven for being less than enthusiastic about being 'rehabilitated' into leading a 'good and useful life' whilst in prison; many criminologists are also sceptical of the prison's capacity for rehabilitation. As King and Morgan (1980: 16) acidly remark, prisoners have always known that prisons are really about captivity rather than rehabilitation and, in their view, there is little to be gained from pretending otherwise. There is certainly little opportunity to rehabilitate prisoners in the 'transit camp' context of the busy local prison, where resources are likely to be stretched to the limit. Indeed, of the many metaphors that prison officers use to describe the prison (see the Appendix), those of prison as 'sausage machine', 'meat factory' and 'conveyor belt' are perhaps the most commonly used to describe local and remand prisons.

The officers who participated in this study held divergent views as to the motivations for criminal behaviour: whilst many framed the problem of crime at the level of the individual (some held distinctly Lombrosian beliefs about the existence of a 'criminal mind'), others perceived prisoners as individuals who had simply chosen (or fallen into) a life of crime. Many officers are acutely aware of the economic circumstances from which most young offenders come into prison. As one such officer observed: 'You've got a forgotten generation with teenagers. They can't even get dole money. And they're restless' (male officer, Lancaster Farms).

The cynicism felt by prison officers stems in large part from officers' resignation at seeing the 'same old faces' returning to prison again and again, and of prisoners' failures to take responsibility for their actions. This can have the effect of 'hardening' officers to the pains of prisoners:

> They come in here whinging and whining ... it's never their fault or they've been stitched up. Your sympathy goes. Mind you, there's always one – the odd sad case – but generally speaking you see the same faces coming through the gate. (Male officer, Wymott)

Prisoners were seen by many of the officers in this study as calculating, selfish individuals who would readily take advantage of any goodwill shown by staff. One of the most common remarks made by officers about prisoners casts the prisoner as manipulator: 'If you give inmates an inch they'll take three miles. Kindness is taken as a weakness by this lot' (senior officer, Lancaster Farms)

Prison officers have a tendency to speak of prisoners (and prisons) in terms of certain recurrent metaphors. The metaphors that officers use for prisoners are revealing of the contempt in which they are held i.e., 'vultures'; 'bodies'; 'animals' (as in 'feeding the animals'); 'scum'; 'toe-rags'; 'inadequates'; 'children'; 'dangerous children'. Many officers also characterise prisoners in stereotypical vein; prisoners from Liverpool, for example, are invariably seen as 'gobby (mouthy) Scousers' and perceived as the worst-behaved prisoners while black prisoners are often seen as 'quick to play the race card'. All this seems to suggest that prison officers have a very 'fixed' view of prisoners; in reality, however, relationships between officers and prisoners are much more complex. To take such (metaphorical) descriptions at their face value is to adopt a 'distal'[1] analysis of prison life. As we shall see, some officers do admit to liking certain prisoners and to being sympathetic to their feelings of frustration, anxiety and regret. Likewise some prisoners admit to liking certain officers, and understand that they are 'only doing their job' (numerous prisoners, all prisons pers. comms.). In all the prisons in this study there was some degree of friendly rapport between staff and prisoners (although the degree of rapport differed markedly across prisons and between wings). At Lancaster Farms, Garth and Wymott, some officers reported that their relationships with certain prisoners were closer than they ever imagined could be the case when they first started working in prisons. Indeed, one or two of these officers admitted that with certain prisoners they were 'almost friends' (see below). This should not, perhaps, strike us as surprising, given that many officers and prisoners have similar socio-economic backgrounds and share similar interests and experiences.

Generally speaking, whether an officer can 'identify with' a prisoner (in terms of sharing interests and values) depends, in part, on the kind of prison in which the officer works, and the age and background of the prisoner. Identification depends to a lesser extent on the nature of the prisoner's offence. That is not to say, however, that a prisoner's offence has no bearing on the relationship; while many officers are willing to maintain a low level of social distance with prisoners who have committed (what officers perceive to be) 'normal' crimes – theft, forgery, burglary, minor assault and so on – they often maintain a high social distance with those who have committed certain offences (particularly sexual offences against children), particularly those who then complain about prison life: 'you get the ones that have booted somebody and put him in a wheelchair, and then they're moaning if their chips are cold. It really pisses me off that does' (male officer, Garth).

Adults and young offenders

There is a marked difference between the ways that officers speak about adult prisoners and the ways they speak about young offenders. While adult prisoners are generally seen as wanting little to do with uniformed staff except with regard to prison-related issues, young offenders are often seen as 'needy' – as 'craving contact with staff':

> Working with YOs is a different ballgame altogether from working with adults. Adults generally get on with it, and then occasionally they blow – and then boy do they blow. But YOs, they don't *think*; they need to keep asking staff questions all the time, and they're always pitching for a quick fight – then it's all over Also, staff have to physically run round after YOs a lot more, so they're more tiring in that sense. (Senior officer, Lancaster Farms)

Working with young offenders can also be emotionally demanding: 'In an adult situation, threats have to be taken much more seriously. YOs on the other hand blow hot and cold all the time; they're up and down all the time and we go up and down with them' (officer, Lancaster Farms).

It was clear from my conversations with prison officers and from their written reports on individual prisoners that imprisonment can be particularly frightening, lonely and stressful for young offenders. Officers told me that many of the young men imprisoned at Lancaster Farms, Portland and Stoke Heath were often tearful and anxious as well as aggressive; on every wing, observation books were replete with comments about the distressed state of so-and-so, and on numerous pages staff had pinned notes from prisoners threatening self-harm or informing staff of threats they had received from other prisoners. Some young prisoners barely cope with imprisonment; as this officer observed: 'some of them cry on coming out of their cells in a morning until they are locked up in the evening. It's hard to know what to do about it really' (officer, Lancaster Farms).

Comments such as this highlight the fact that these prisoners are *children*. Officers' reflections on the day-to-day behaviour of prisoners barely into their teens make this glaringly apparent. Elaborating on his remark that the prisoners at Portland 'seem to be getting younger these days', an officer on night duty commented: 'I get a lot of little squirts in here now. At night, you can hear 'em downstairs. They're like a lot of little budgies fluttering about.'

The immaturity of many young prisoners is reflected in this officer's subsequent description of their behaviour at night; during one of his patrols of the wing, he had had to censure, in something of the style of a boarding school house master, two young men who were having a pillow fight: 'There they were whacking each other with pillows. One of the 'em said "He's messed my bed up Sir". I said to 'im "Well make it again and get back into it!"'

There is general agreement amongst officers that young offenders are noisier and more boisterous than adult prisoners, even at night when they are locked up. Throughout the evening, especially on long summer evenings, the grounds of each of the young offender institutions in this study resounded with the noise of prisoners calling to each other from cell windows. Some of it is general banter but much of it is offensive and abusive; there is bullying of other inmates and encouragement of others to bully. Even at Lancaster Farms, where officers made great efforts to stamp out bullying, I was told that prisoners regularly force weaker prisoners to sing nursery rhymes out of cell windows, and that those who refuse to do so are likely to be punished, i.e. assaulted later. During association, or on the way to gym and/or work, young offenders routinely shout obscene comments about other offenders' families and make arrangements as to who will 'get it' next. These were alien activities to officers used to working with adults. As this senior officer working at Lancaster Farms put it:

> YOs are a lot noisier and more hassle, especially at night. At Long Lartin, you could patrol around at night and its lovely and peaceful. Here it's like a rough blooming council estate! [At Long Lartin] You might get a buzz of conversation if you're lucky, early on, but here ...

Culture shock revisited

Officers transferring from adult prisons to young offender institutions (and vice versa) may experience a degree of culture shock similar to that experienced on joining the service. Officers who transfer from adult prisons (particularly dispersals) to young offender institutions may be dismayed by the relatively 'tame' nature of the young offender regime and the dent that they feel their new role has made in their occupational identity. They may also be exasperated by the demands of young prisoners:

> When I came here I hated it. [Why?] I hated running after inmates. You didn't do that with cons ... Compared to Long Lartin it's a toy jail. (Male officer, Lancaster Farms)

Others are taken aback by the school-like nature of young offender regimes. Recalling his first encounter with Lancaster Farm's version of the Incentives and Earned Privileges Scheme, whereby good behaviour and attitudes are rewarded with coloured stars, one senior officer remarked: 'I couldn't believe it when I saw them [the officers] sticking stars on things. It was just like being in blooming kindergarten!' Arguably, the use of stick-on stars to indicate achievement symbolises both the childlike status of prisoners and the expectation that officers will behave like teachers.

Some prison officers find they are simply unable to cope with young prisoners. During one of my visits to Stoke Heath, an ex-dispersal officer remarked that when he saw a juvenile prisoner sticking his tongue out at him through a cell window he was completely nonplussed. He knew that he would look ridiculous if he put the prisoner on report, but in his eyes, the prisoner *had* committed an act of indiscipline. He knew, however, that if he did resort to the formal disciplinary procedures, his colleagues would laugh at him and exclaim 'but he's just a kid!' The officer was exasperated – he had not expected this. This was 'not proper prison work'! Conversely, officers transferring *to* a dispersal *from* a YOI may be shocked at the relaxed nature of the regime (for example, staff and prisoners on first-name terms, less structure, less emphasis on relatively petty rules) and dismayed to find that the working style they have developed over the years of working with young offenders is challenged by high-security adult prisoners.

On the other hand, officers who had worked for many years in adult prisons were often greatly relieved to be working with young offenders, primarily because they felt safer and in greater control. According to this basic-grade officer working at Lancaster Farms: 'When I came here from Long Lartin I thought I'd gone to Heaven.' In a very similar vein:

> My first few days here [Lancaster Farms] were a shock to the system. I didn't think places like this existed; it was like coming from Hell into Heaven. [In what sense?] Well you're more in control here. And they [the staff] seem to know what direction they're going in. At Acklington you just turned up and looked forward to getting out as soon as possible. (Male officer)

Relatedly, officers tend to treat adult prisoners and young offenders very differently. For example, many officers will allow adult prisoners to be on first-name terms with them but will not usually allow young prisoners to do so. Officers working with young offenders may also be prepared to modify the regime to take account of the energies of youth. For example at Lancaster Farms some officers arranged 'run-around quizzes' at weekends when there were few formal activities:

We'll get everybody in the unit out, right, and ask them a question, 'Is it A, is it B, or is it C'? A's over there , B's over there, C's over there [pointing to different parts of the association area] and they all charge around. It is not rehabilitation, or education, its not even, technically, meaningful activity, *but* it breaks a mood. (Senior officer, Lancaster Farms)

Officers working with young prisoners try to enforce rules that they know would be unenforceable in adult prisons, particularly long-term prisons:

Its not like adult prisoners, we don't do all this bed-pack stuff with adult prisoners. Forget it! ... Really ... They will make their own minds up which way they're going ... I mean you *try*, but you can't do the pushing that we do with the youngsters. The youngsters still actually need authority figures. They don't need to like us, but they need us to be there. It's part of growing up. (Senior officer, Lancaster Farms)

Similarly:

There is no comparison between, say, Albany and Portland. YOs seem to need a lot more support from staff. Rules have to be interpreted differently at each type of jail; each establishment has a different set of rules. For example, the 'no shouting out of windows' rule would be unenforceable at Albany ... Long-term prisons are more self-managing; the level of house rules is much less. Another example, making bed-packs would be unenforceable at Albany. (Male officer, Portland)

Contrasts in treatment notwithstanding, there is a tendency for both adult prisoners and young offenders to be *seen* as childlike; when prisoners get angry and upset, officers often describe them as having 'temper tantrums' or as 'attention-seeking'. Arguably, this analysis of prisoners' behaviour is both insensitive and naive; it fails (perhaps wilfully) to take sufficient account of the painful nature of imprisonment; of the frustrations, anxieties and fears that accompany living in prison for long periods. Officers are, in short, aware of the dependent state of *all* prisoners. In turn they may acknowledge (albeit reluctantly) that their own role is rather a domestic one:

To me, sometimes, it's like being a glorified baby-sitter. Because that's, that's what you're doin', yeah. I mean you're just ... you're just looking after everything, because there's a lot of 'em [that] because they've been here a long time that's what they need, they just need, like, somebody to do everything. They have everything done for 'em. They don't have to think, some of 'em, at all. And then when they do have to think it's like panic stations, you know. What's basic to sort of you and me seems like really traumatic to them, you know. (Female officer, Garth)

Resentment of prisoners' rights

Amongst uniformed prison staff, questions about just desert and legitimate expectations are to the fore. That prisoners 'have too many rights' – indeed 'more rights than staff' – and 'get too much' (most officers hold fast to the principle of 'less eligibility'[2]) was a familiar refrain amongst officers working in every prison in this study. In terms of the former, officers' claims that management 'cares more about prisoners than they do staff' was well rehearsed; in terms of the latter, a significant proportion of uniformed staff were of the view that prisoners were being 'pandered to' whereas officers have to make do with what they are given. Food is a particular focus of attention in the discussion of prisoners' rights. That prisoners are allowed a choice of menu is a particular irritation for many officers. Take, for example, this remark from an officer who had recently returned from control and restraint[3] training: 'It's gone ridiculous now ... We went on a C&R Advanced and we just had a cold packed lunch. You had no choice of meals. *Inmates* get one though!' (Senior officer, Moorland). Similarly, this time from a senior officer at Lancaster Farms: 'Prisoners should only get two choices – take it or leave it!'

Most officers who hold such views believe that the general public shares their sentiments:

The prisoners here have got more rights than I have. They've got entitlements for everything ... In my opinion you've got a prison system that doesn't reflect the views of the majority; they reflect the views of do-gooders. Prison Reform Trust, Howard League and so on – pro-criminal groups ... Why *should* they have rights? They should have *privileges*, and they should *earn* them. (Senior officer, Lancaster Farms)

Such resentments are part of the more general and long-standing resentment, on the part of many officers, that prisoners are viewed more favourably than *they* are, not only by prison reformers and the courts but also by their own managers. Whether or not the latter is the case is, in a sense irrelevant; what is important is that most officers *believe* it to be the case (for a discussion of this in the American context, see, for example, Dilulio 1987). In short, what is important is how the officer (as social actor) defines the situation; as the American sociologist W.I. Thomas observes, 'if men define situations as real, they are real in their consequences'.

Generally speaking, officers feel that most prisoners do not appreciate their efforts; on the contrary, there is a common perception that any kindness they show is 'mistaken for weakness'. Officers may attempt to protect themselves by deliberately increasing social distance:

> I came into this job thinking of prison officers as rough, strict and treating everyone like dirt. I thought I'd be the one to treat prisoners well. But it didn't work out like that. They just thought I was soft. The only thing they responded to was [my] being hard. I was as cynical as the rest of them within twelve months.

Those who do make efforts for prisoners are often disappointed when prisoners let them down. One officer, for example, reported that he had spent a great of time trying to persuade a local builder to employ a young offender who was due for release. He was eventually successful and the prisoner accepted the job but on the first day failed to turn up. Unfortunately (but perhaps unsurprisingly) such disappointments foster further cynicism amongst officers, along the lines of 'I won't bother in future'.

Getting the staff–prisoner relationship 'right'

Prison officers vary significantly in terms of the social distance they place between themselves and prisoners. On the whole, staff–prisoner interactions are qualitatively different from those that took place in the 1970s and much of the 1980s. As we have seen, uniformed staffs' perception of the prison in that period was that it was a place *of* and *for* punishment, not that imprisonment was a punishment in its own right. Although, as we shall see below, there were pockets of positive interaction, on the whole the staff–prisoner relationship in many prisons was brusque and overweening; prisoners *dare not* speak to officers and officers *would not* speak to prisoners. At HMP Strangeways, for example:

you used to get a lot of ex-army into the job, an', erm, they were used to, erm, discipline. They'd go past the cons with their key chains trailing and with their Dartmoor heavies[4] and the cons wouldn't dare even look at 'em ... They used to turn their faces to the wall! The ex-army lot weren't willing to treat people as equals. You're *joking!* They were heavy-handed ... brutal in fact. (Long-serving male officer, Lancaster Farms)

Consequently, close relationships between prisoners and staff were never built up; they were simply *inappropriate*. Many prison officers would have preferred it to stay that way:

It's a working relationship, that's all. There has to be that line. Some officers will chat to inmates and even touch them. [How do you mean?] They'll pat them on the shoulder and they'll go 'Alright mate?' I don't. You've got to have that line. They're on that side and I'm on this. (Male officer, Garth)

As was noted in Chapter 1, the Home Office Control Review Committee (1984) proposed that prisons 'depend on staff having a firm, confident and humane approach that enables them to maintain close contact with prisoners without confrontation'. In short, much depends on getting the staff–prisoner relationship 'right'. As has already been noted, precisely what constitutes the 'right' relationship was not made clear. As is glaringly apparent from the comments of my interviewees, prison officers, as a group, are not clear about this either. Officers tend have their own preferred styles; some which involve enlisting the co-operation of prisoners and some which do not. The 'proper' staff–prisoner relationship – the appropriate degree of friendliness, flexibility, willingness to negotiate and so on – was a well rehearsed topic in all the prisons in this study. Officers differed markedly in terms of their inclination to develop positive (or indeed *any*) relationships with prisoners. To ask officers how they feel about prisoners (and, relatedly, how they feel about their work) is to ask cultural questions, and the answers they give relate (at least in part) to their experiences to date.

It is difficult to capture the complexities of staff–prisoner relations. As I have already suggested, it would certainly be inaccurate to argue that the character of the staff–prisoner relationship is solely a relationship of 'Them and Us' although this is a trope that is commonly employed by prison officers. In vivid and dramatic stories officers may recount, for example, how 'they' tried to take over 'our' prison; in more mundane, everyday accounts we are told that 'they' routinely try to 'get one over' on 'us'. Yet in the day-to-day life of the landings, staff–prisoner relations are far more nuanced than these accounts might suggest. As this senior officer working at Lancaster Farms observed:

> At the end of the day, both sides are stuck in here. It's much nicer being stuck in here if you actually get on to a certain degree. I'm not talking about being their *pals*, 'cos that's not right or proper, erm, but you don't have to be in two armed camps. It's not to the benefit of *either* side for us to be in two armed camps.

How officers interact with prisoners is dependent on a range of situational and social factors, including the type of prison in which these interactions take place, the category and type of inmate (sex offender, lifer or whatever), staffs' prior work experiences and the occupational cultures of particular prisons, to which every officer is expected to subscribe. For some officers, getting staff–inmate relationships 'right' means helping and supporting inmates (Rutherford's 1993 Credo Three) while for others it means keeping a distance between 'us and them', either for reasons of efficiency (Credo Two) or to express a view that prison is for the punitive degradation of offenders (Credo One). In the prison setting, working credos dictate both the quality of the staff–inmate relationship and the approach that officers take to the job itself:

> A lot of people come into the job and they've got this view of prisoners, and it doesn't help ... Some of them see inmates as the lowest of the low – as the scum of the earth. But you can't tar them all with the same brush ... Some of them *are* very dangerous people, but some of them are okay. You try and do what you can for them. (Senior officer, Garth)

Drawing the 'line': friendly but not friends

Virtually all the officers in this study referred to the 'line' that must exist between officers and prisoners, but there was a great deal of discrepancy about where that line should be drawn, even between officers working in the same prison. For example, according to one male officer working at Garth: 'He's a prisoner and I'm a screw. End of story.' In contrast, another observed: 'You can get to know them better than your family. I know it sounds stupid but ...' Numerous officers claimed that their relationships with inmates *were* friendly, and that they were glad of this. They were equally keen to stress, however, that this did not mean that officers and inmates were *friends*; on the contrary they made a sharp distinction between these two modes of emotional engagement and stressed the inappropriateness (and potential dangers to security) of the latter relationship. Being friendly with inmates assists in day-to-day order maintenance; it 'oils the wheels' of the system. Being friends, on the other hand, suggests equality of status between two individuals and a state of mutual obligation; in the prison setting, where power and authority are supposed to lie with the staff, officers must 'draw the line' at becoming too close to individual prisoners in case mutual obligation threatens both their authority and the security of the prison. Indeed, one of the central criticisms that male officers make of women working in men's prisons is their tendency to become intimate with the prisoners (that female officers 'get off with the cons' was a commonly made remark). The 'trick' was to develop a relationship whereby staff and inmates could recognise each other's predicament and 'rub along' on a day-to-day basis with the minimum of friction.

While it was a common refrain amongst officers that 'you can be friendly but you can't be friends' since to become friends with a prisoner is to 'leave yourself wide open to all sorts of things', several officers admitted that they *were* 'almost like friends' with prisoners or that they would have been friends had they met in different circumstances. As this (relatively young) senior officer reflected:

> I've known inmates that, if this hadn't been a prison, me and him would have been good friends [Talking about a lifer that he had got to know, he added] We had a lot in common. He was the same age as me, he had the same interests, we got on really well ... Yeah, you could say firm friends.

With certain prisoners and in certain circumstances, officers found that the placing of the 'line' was especially problematic, not least because they have to rely on the co-operation of inmates on a day-to-day basis. For example, 'trusty' or 'red band' prisoners given the job of cleaner tend to get numerous 'perks', such as extra association and extra food as informal 'payment' for doing certain helpful tasks. Getting these perks, however, can lull these prisoners into thinking that they have a different sort of relationship with staff than other prisoners do. While officers are often prepared to cajole trusted prisoners, they are unwilling for the line to be moved too far:

> Sometimes they have to be cajoled a bit ... given the benefit of the doubt. For example, if they are late out of bed in the morning, you'll just say come on, shake a leg but you won't put them on report or anything like that. But then sometimes you'll go in and they'll be

just lying in bed with their arms folded behind their head and treating you like a mate – *that's* when you've got to draw the line 'cos they're getting too familiar. (Senior officer, Lancaster Farms)

Power in prisons; negotiation and coercion

Most prison officers (particularly those working with long-termers) concede that control – and hence order – is achieved most successfully through positive staff–prisoner relationships. Not all staff are happy with this state of affairs, however; as I stated earlier, some officers do not desire a positive relationship and would prefer it if prisoners simply spent more time 'behind their doors'. In all the prisons in this study, a significant number of staff were of the view that order in their own establishment was being achieved only because management were 'appeasing' (or 'pandering to') prisoners. As I stated in Chapter 1, the issue of 'appeasing' prisoners is a contentious one amongst uniformed staff. Amongst many of the officers I spoke to there was a strong belief that prisoners were 'getting too much' simply because management was frightened to say no to them. It can be noted, however, that what counts as 'appeasement' for one officer is perfectly reasonable negotiation for another.

Who holds the power? Negotiation and appeasement

The question of where power resides, then, is one of perennial concern to prison officers. Some officers felt that in the prisons in which they are working, or in which they had worked in the past, 'the balance of power has tipped the wrong way'. Dispersal and high-security training prisons were a popular target in this respect:

It's all a balance [between keeping control through rules and encouraging the co-operation of inmates]; it's just that at long term prisons, the balance is very much in favour of the prisoner. The management will give in to the prisoners at every conceivable opportunity, because in their eyes, that is the best way of keeping things quiet. In the middle of it, you've got, normally, totally demoralised staff, because the criminal is treated as king. (Senior officer, Lancaster Farms)

The belief that the 'criminal is king' in such prisons is held by many prison officers, particularly those with experience of working in regimes that are necessarily more relaxed. Many officers feel that a liberal regime is more difficult to work in for two main reasons. First, officers in long-term prisons have much more *sustained* contact with prisoners (prisoners at Garth in particular spent a great deal of time out of cell). Secondly, long-term prisoners tend to be much more informal, and *more familiar with*, uniformed staff than are prisoners in other regimes. During my period of fieldwork at Garth, there was some debate amongst staff about whether the prison was controlled by staff or by prisoners. One morning, as I sat talking to a group of staff on one of the wings, an officer who had recently transferred from a dispersal remarked that his colleagues' claim to be 'in control' was mistaken, and that in his view the low level of confrontations between themselves and prisoners was due more to their lack of awareness of the true extent of rule-breaking than to their being in control. In short he felt that his new colleagues were being 'conned'. He went on to argue that if they *were* more aware of the extent of prisoners' rule-breaking there would be a higher level of staff–prisoner confrontation at Garth. The officers vigorously disagreed with this officer's assessment, and a (rather heated) discussion ensued. The new officer eventually conceded that he might be mistaken – that his definition of the situation might stem from 'dispersal paranoia' and his anxieties from Garth's combination of relatively relaxed regime, low staffing levels (relative to a dispersal) and high proportion of newly recruited staff. In addition, the officer claimed to have heard numerous horror stories (some true, some less so) still circulating about Garth. Up until fairly recently Garth had a reputation across the service as being a confrontational prison, where assaults on staff were common and staff morale, in consequence, was low. The officer remained concerned about Garth staff's reputation for 'wanting to get on with everybody' just to avoid trouble.

Working with long-term prisoners does place different demands on prison officers. On the whole (there were a few exceptions) Garth's uniformed staff were relatively relaxed, informal and friendly to prisoners (as the Chief Inspector of Prisons (HMCIP 1997) put it, they have 'a light and easy manner'). Indeed, they made particular efforts to maintain a relaxed regime because they realised that the prison was also *home* to the men serving their sentences there: 'A lot of these that are here, its like ten years, fifteen, lifers ... It's like livin' with 'em really. You've got to keep, er, some sort of decent atmosphere going.'

In common with staff working in many other long-term regimes, Garth officers were much less officious, less provocative and more accommodating than many of the officers working in the young offender institutions. A paragraph from fieldnotes I made at Garth serves to illustrate this:

At one point, there was play-fighting between some of the officers (basic and senior grade) and a couple of inmates in the wing office. They were throwing a board rubber at each other. The senior officer snatched an empty plastic bottle from one of the inmates and stamped on it. It made a hell of a bang when the top blew off! After a bit of a scuffle, the same inmate pulled the senior officer's tie off (they are the clip-on type) and pretended to bash him over the knees with a long perspex ruler he'd found on the desk. After a few minutes, the officers looked like they'd had enough and needed to 'pull back' a bit. The senior officer started talking to the other officers about various tasks that needed doing and the inmates, having got the message that the time for horseplay was over, wandered out of the office.

The 'good' officer

For some officers, the above scenario would have been unthinkable since the 'good' officer never lets the prisoner up close. When asked what skills they thought a 'good'[5] officer needs, officers listed, in no particular order, 1) confidence; 2) the powers of persuasion (having the ability to sell sand to an Arab is how one officer described herself); 3) calmness (interestingly, however, one officer commented that being *too* calm can actually provoke prisoners – he was thinking specifically of those officers who stare calmly ahead while reciting the rules); 4) being a good team-player (officers quickly get to know the officers who are afraid of confrontations and who cannot be relied upon when 'trouble' arises); 5) being a good communicator (being prepared to talk to prisoners and to explain things); 6) being assertive when necessary (and recognising when it *is* necessary); 7) being a good listener – 'You've got to be like a sponge really'; 8) being mentally tough (as opposed to being physically tough. An officer who is 'mentally weak' was regarded as being vulnerable to the pressures of both prisoners and fellow officers); 9) having patience; 10) being fair (most officers said that it is important to be fair in dealings with prisoners); 11) liking people; 12), having 'common sense'; and 13) having a sense of humour (the latter two skills were perceived as vital by virtually every officer in this study).

The personal qualities and skills of uniformed staff do, of course, impact upon the nature of staff–prisoner relations. Numerous officers commented on the need to strike a balance between friendliness and inflexibility; as one senior officer working at Wymott reflected:

> You have to be approachable, but it doesn't do to be too familiar. On the other hand, it does not do to be constantly nicking, or putting on

a basic regime, inadequate or awkward inmates. [You have to] nurture him, show him the way; you have to be able to lead the horse to water and make him drink. This takes skill.

Prison officers' views on what makes a good officer differ markedly, even within the same prison. Compare these responses from two male officers working at HMYOI Portland:

You've got to have good ears for a start, and be able to listen to a lad. And you've got to be fair, and if you promise to do something, you've got to get back to them. Sometimes they'll ask me to spell something – well I might not be able to spell it, but I'll go and get a dictionary …

In contrast: 'I think one of the best skills you can have is being able to look an inmate in the eye and say No.'

In the eyes of some officers, then, a 'good' officer is one who sees the prison world in purely 'black and white' terms and who maintains order through sticking to the rules. No *means* No, rules are there to be obeyed and the 'line' between 'Them and Us' is sharply drawn at a point which demands little prisoner–staff interaction and hence rarely entails negotiation. In the eyes of others, 'good' officers are those who are flexible and who apply the rules appropriately and at their own discretion. Retaining credibility in the eyes of prisoners involves being seen as someone who operates in a fair and professional[6] manner; who recognises prisoners' pains and their lack of autonomy to ameliorate them. There were difficulties, however, associated with being seen as the officer most likely to help prisoners:

One of the main rules is if an inmate asks you to do something, you sort it. 'Cos if you don't, there's your credibility gone. They'll say [to other inmates] 'Don't go to him he's fucking useless!' But it can go the other way as well; they'll only come to *you* and then you've got the fly-round-the-jam pot syndrome. (Male officer, Garth)

Being a good communicator was seen by many as crucially important for conflict prevention and reduction. According to this ex-dispersal officer: 'I've never been assaulted, even though I've dealt with big guys with fighting backgrounds. Your ability to survive is your ability to talk to inmates. It's all about communication.'

Interestingly, the vast majority of my interviewees were of the view that the skills of social interaction – being 'good with people' – are skills that cannot be learnt simply through a training course. On the contrary, they argued that being able to get on with people is not a learnable skill. This is one such comment:

[Can officers be trained in getting on with people, do you think?] The ability to get on with people is something that is natural. I would say that would be down to the person's *personality*. It's a difficult question is that. I would say, I would say it would be very hard to train somebody like that. (Male officer, Lancaster Farms)

Similarly, when I asked a principal officer (YOI) what, in his view, makes for a professional prison officer, he replied: 'The ability to relate to, and deal with difficult, truculent people. This can only be gained by experience of life and by working with prisoners. It cannot be taught.'

Negotiation is something that does not come easily to some prison officers. These officers, many of whom were recruited from the military, believe that *dictation* is more appropriate to the prison officer role. In contrast, some officers are willing to negotiate even with very young prisoners, and on significant issues such as wing transfers. Here is an extract from my fieldnotes (Lancaster Farms) to illustrate the point:

A female senior officer has just been asked if she will swap one of her prisoners with one from a different wing. After studying the roll board for a few minutes, she selected a prisoner's name and told another officer to instruct him to pack his things. A few minutes later the prisoner came to see her in the office, pleading to stay on the wing on the ground that he had a good cleaning job which he would lose if transferred. The inmate begged and pleaded – he promised 'to be good and to be a good cleaner – only please can I stay on this wing Miss?' The interaction between this officer and this young prisoner was fascinating: she eventually said 'Alright, I'll try to find somebody else but I'm not promising. I'll get back to you'. There was then some discussion between herself and two other officers, during which they consulted the roll board again. Some minutes later the senior officer had indeed found someone else to move instead, and the prisoner was called back in. On being told he could stay on the wing after all, the prisoner, thrilled to bits, punched the air. As he went out of the office, smiling broadly, the senior officer shouted after him 'But you'd better behave yourself!'

Many officers rely on their sense of humour, their skills of persuasion and their ability to communicate effectively and fairly with people who may feel angry, anxious or depressed. These officers are acutely aware that prisoner co-operation often depended upon their ability to persuade and cajole; indeed they could rely on very little else. As one female officer put it: 'You've got to be good at talking. At Styal you had one officer to twenty-three women, and all you had was your radio and your gob.'

Every officer has his or her own way of controlling prisoners. They have two ways of maintaining control on a routine basis – formal and informal. The informal way necessitates the officer using his or her individual personality; some use humour (Dilulio's 'clowns') while some command respect based on their reputation for being 'firm but fair' and calm under pressure (Dilulio's 'statesmen'). The formal way, in contrast, involves routinely 'nicking' prisoners for every infraction of the rules. Many officers prefer informal methods; not only does this obviate the need for 'paperwork', as the following remarks illustrate, but the ability to deal with infractions informally is a matter of honour and pride:

> I always think when I put somebody on report I've abdicated my responsibility to the governor – it means that I can't cope [with that particular inmate or situation] – I've given up. A younger, less experienced officer might say [of the inmate who's getting up his nose] 'Well I'll have him', and go out of his way to get him. Older staff will just 'clock it' and deal with him at a later point, perhaps to the officer's advantage. (Male senior officer, Wymott)

Similarly:

> Nicking a prisoner amounts to getting someone else [i.e. a governor] to do your work for you. The best officers are good at taking the inmate on one side and letting him know that he's been clocked. (Male principal officer, Portland)

And again:

> Some officers place every act of indiscipline on report. Basically, if you've got to put people on report all the time, you're not doing your job right. Some prisoners you threaten, some you kid along, and some you can just tell. Knowing which are which comes from experience. [In my view] The worst sort of person you can have on any wing is one that's nicking prisoners all the time. (Male senior officer, Garth)

Officer–prisoner negotiation is illustrated in the following extract from my fieldnotes. It describes a (rather amusing) incident that occurred as I was 'shadowing' an officer on the (low visibility) wings at Garth:

> During wing patrol, an officer was looking for a certain inmate in order to bang him up. He looked around on the wing, shouting for him, but to no avail. I accompanied the officer on his search; we looked in doorways, in various rooms, in empty cells, etc. Eventually we passed a toilet, and the officer said he would have a look to see if he was in there. To my amazement, as the officer walked in, the inmate jumped out. He'd been hiding behind the door. The inmate thought it was funny, but the officer didn't. He said to the inmate, 'I've got some good news for you – me and you are going to see the governor in the morning' [meaning at adjudication]. 'Oh no, fuck off!' moaned the inmate. 'No, I'm not being pissed about' said the officer, and locked him in his cell. Later on, when he had been unlocked, the inmate came into the office, 'cap-in-hand', to ask if he could 'have a word' with the officer. Pleadingly, he asked the officer he had annoyed if he could do some cleaning or something instead of getting nicked. He was apparently due for his Cat C board and appearing before the governor would spoil his chances of being recategorised. In reply to his request, the officer clearly wanted to make him stew a bit, and said he would 'see'. When the inmate had gone out, I asked the officer what he would do, and he replied that he would get him to polish his boots or something instead! Clearly there is power being performed here; while the officer clearly has the 'upper hand' in the negotiation, the inmate felt that negotiation was a possibility; that he might be able to persuade the officer to deal with the matter informally.

Young offenders, like adult prisoners, attempt to negotiate (and hence make less painful) their prison lives. They endeavour, on a day-to-day basis, to negotiate with staff as to what cell they will be in, how many phone calls they can make, whether they can have extra blankets, towels or whatever, whether they can be transferred (or stay where they are), whether they can have a different sort of diet, whether they can go on a course, whether they can have extra visits, whether they can have a particular job and so on. As I have already noted, officers differ markedly in terms of the extent to which they will enter into negotiations with prisoners, particularly young prisoners. As we shall see below, some refuse to enter into any negotiation whatsoever, prefering the 'You will' approach and relying largely on the word 'No'.

Clearly, however, young offenders' negotiations *are* sometimes successful, and this can cause resentment amongst (and between) uniformed staff. During the course of my fieldwork, officers on a particular wing were complaining that a 'difficult' young prisoner had been offered what they called 'sweeteners' to conform to the regime. In short, the prisoner was being 'given money to behave' (or at least that was how it was described to me). This was not, however, far from the truth; the officers allowed me to read a letter from a governor which stipulated the way that this particular prisoner was to be dealt with to encourage him to conform. The prisoner was to receive £5.50 wages (for cleaning) plus extra canteen if he was seen to co-operate. He was also to be moved on a weekly basis between this establishment and one other, to give staff a break. Staff raised a number of issues about this arrangement; put more graphically they wanted to know 'what the hell is going on?' First, they were incensed that a governor was 'appeasing' a prisoner – 'and a kid at that'. They wanted to know why a prisoner should be 'rewarded' with extra privileges when he refused to conform, despite having signed a 'compact'[7] when prisoners on the other wings must, under the conditions of the Incentives and Privileges Scheme (IEPS), conform to receive privileges. Secondly, they were concerned that if other prisoners found out that non-conformity could gain rewards, they might follow suit.[8] In relation to the latter, this was probably never very likely; arguably, most prisoners do not want to serve their sentence in such a manner. This diminutive prisoner, who had spent a lot of time in segregation was described by segregation staff as 'very demanding' of staff time when he was on normal location; he was constantly ringing his cell bell for what staff saw as 'petty' reasons, such as when he wanted a light for his cigarette. As an officer observed, however, 'He's just a kid, and kids need attention'. The inmate certainly *looked* like a child; he was 17 years old but roughly four feet ten in height and weighing approximately six stones. Another officer agreed – 'yes, he is just a kid'. Unfortunately, staff on normal location found him a pest, and got so fed up with him that whenever he was unco-operative they sent him back to the block.

Staff–prisoner conflict

Although such negotiations can and do take place, officers do wield a significant amount of power over prisoners on a day-to-day basis, and that power may be abused. Abuse of power may involve deliberate unfairness, the making of false allegations against prisoners and, on occasion, physical assault. Officers themselves often find abuse of power deeply troubling. During an interview with one such officer, the officer remarked that power 'can sometimes go to an officer's head'. Although my discussion of staff conflict is largely confined to the next chapter, I include here a brief extract of this officer's subsequent comments since it indicates officers' disapproval of abusive staff:

> Some of 'em, put 'em in a white shirt and put a couple of Hot Meat Pies [HMP epaulettes] on their shoulders and they think they're God. [Really?] There are some that are on a power trip, believe me. [How does this sort of officer get on with other officers?) The sensible ones amongst us keep away from them. [Why?] 'Cos they can get you into trouble. If you get into the habit of turning a blind eye you could end up being charged in court as an accomplice in the assault of an inmate ... Some people are just on power trips, and its best to just keep away from 'em.

Other officers also acknowledged the problems caused by such staff. They claimed that officers were often reluctant to work with them, not least because they put their own physical health and job security in jeopardy. Reflecting on the trouble caused by aggressive, confrontational staff a female officer commented:

> At Belmarsh we had these gobby little scousers working with us and when they came on the shift it'd be horrible. They'd come in for a fight and – unsurprisingly – they'd have one! [What proportion of Belmarsh staff would be looking for a fight?] Those under thirty and inexperienced; especially new staff, who had to get notches on their belt if you like ... say 30–40 percent of the staff. [So how would officers go about getting a fight?] They'd target a con.

Illicit use of force

The tendency of some officers to 'target a con' is arguably a significant factor in the loss of control both at the individual and collective level. I was wary of asking officers about staff assaults on prisoners, partly because this is a very sensitive issue (and hence not one that I thought officers would be likely to discuss readily with outsiders) and partly because I did not wish officers to think I was only interested in the negative aspects of staff–prisoner interactions (as they claim that the media and general public are). I *did*, however, wish to understand *why* such violence occurs and *in what circumstances*. Just as I was wary of asking the questions, many officers were wary of telling me the answers. When most officers responded it was usually in vague terms, such as so-and-so used to happen, and so-and-so used to do this or that, and in such-and-such a prison. A small number of officers were, however, more forthcoming and it is on the revelations of these officers that the following discussion is based. Using extracts from our conversations, I focus on 1) the role of peer pressure and machismo in such assaults; 2) the likelihood of whistle-blowing; and 3) informal modes of 'paying back' unco-operative prisoners.

Many officers perceive unco-operative prisoners as 'fair game' and some sort of informal 'pay back' is thus commonplace. Officers told me that in the past, this frequently involved violence; assaults on prisoners often took place in prisoners' cells but staff also seized the opportunity to 'pay back' the prisoner during, for example, his removal to the segregation unit (see below). Several officers admitted that they had, in the past, assaulted unco-operative prisoners, explaining their actions as stemming directly from the (widely shared) staff perceptions of the time that 1) prisoners in general were 'the enemy'; and 2) prison was for punishment. Today the norm of prisoner-as-enemy is less pronounced (though it is still adhered to by some) but in the 1970s to challenge these perceptions was to risk stigmatisation by one's peers:

> I've seen inmates dragged down five landings – five flights of stairs – and then given a hammering. One inmate off the B wing for nutters was used as a battering ram [to open a gate when being moved off a landing]. He ended up with a broken shoulder and a broken arm ... [Why do some officers think it's okay to assault inmates?] Because its Us and Them isn't it? Some officers are happy to interact with inmates, but they draw the line at supporting them for fear of attracting negative attention towards themselves. When it comes to the crunch, they're the enemy, and if you stand back [when they present staff with problems] you're a black sheep. (Male officer, ex-Strangeways)

Peer pressure to engage in violence towards prisoners, and a strong reluctance to report fellow officers, were evident in Lord Justice Woolf's (1991) report of the Strangeways riot. It was clear to Lord Woolf that a minority of unprofessional, aggressive staff were spoiling the work of the majority; when I asked one officer who had worked at Strangeways whether he agreed with this interpretation, he replied:

> Yes, I'd agree with that. You get that in every single prison. You've got, erm, I wouldn't say it's as bad as it was, 'cos you used to get a lot more ex-army into the job, and erm, they were used to, erm, discipline ... they wanted a more disciplined attitude. Instead of

trying to solve a problem by negotiation, it'd just be a straight forward shouting match. [Right, right.] And, erm, some people in the army were used to that attitude. They weren't willing to negotiate, or they weren't willing to treat people as equals ... Actually they were brutal. (Male officer, ex-Strangeways)

To illustrate this, he described the usual style of removal to the segregation unit, in which officers 'used the inmate as a punch-bag'. He attributed such behaviour to 'the macho image that was very prevalent in Strangeways at that time. Staff felt that they had to live up to it'. Macho peer pressure encourages officers to put on an aggressive front with their colleagues, even those officers to whom aggression does not come easily. In this regard, the same officer remarked that: 'some officers – who'd no more think of hitting an inmate than committing suicide – once they get with certain company start talking about "giving him a good hiding" and so on.'

These officers admitted that for a variety of reasons, staff assaults (verbal and physical) on prisoners do still take place, either as a means of 'nipping things in the bud' – 'the breaking of little rules is jumped on immediately to make sure that bigger rules aren't broken'[9] – or to discipline unco-operative prisoners. At least one officer at Portland was prepared to admit that the treatment of young offenders in the prison was often abusive: 'If I'm honest, we treat 'em like dirt.'

During a somewhat scathing commentary on the social control methods preferred by Lancaster Farms (the reputations of individual establishments are well known and a source of both pride and resentment across the service), this same officer remarked that at Portland, 'we do it by fear!' Abusive treatment was seen as just desert. Recognising that illicit violence is more likely than it once was to end in disciplinary proceedings, this officer claimed that sanctioned techniques for managing dissent could be employed to inflict injury instead. From the same Portland officer:

It [inmate assault] still goes on but its more controlled now. [In what sense?] Well if an inmate's injured [though an assault by staff] officers might say he's been injured resisting control and restraint.

Challenges to solidarity: will officers blow the whistle?

I was interested to know the extent to which officers were prepared to support colleagues – i.e. subscribe to norm three – even if they knew those colleagues to be abusive. Officers found my question 'Would you report an officer's assault on a prisoner?' a very difficult one to answer, for a number of important (and conflicting) reasons. While they are supposed to treat inmates with humanity and fairness, prison officers are also supposed to act as a team. Although a staff assault on a prisoner is a serious disciplinary offence (which can result in dismissal), before an officer decides to report a colleague to higher-ranking officers he will take account of a number of things, including 1) the character of the victim (is he a trouble-maker or pest?); 2) relatedly, whether the prisoner 'deserved' it; 3) the severity of the assault (just a slap across the head or a beating); 4) how staff generally perceive the assailant (was his action 'out of character'? Whether the officer in question is a 'good bloke really' and this episode a 'one-off'?); and so on. These factors interact to enable closure (closing of ranks) to take place. Given officers' shared under-standings about the pressures and demands of the job, the perception that the offending officer is 'a good bloke really' is likely to mean that colleagues will 'turn a blind eye' or 'rally round' if such actions are exposed. There is, of course, as I have already noted, evidence that officers may also fail to report assaults because they are afraid of reprisals from colleagues.

When pressed, most of my interviewees said that they doubted they would 'blow the whistle' on a fellow officer, the primary reason being the cultural expectation of solidarity and trust between officers. Moreover, officers knew the pressures their fellow officers were under: 'I'd make it clear that I wouldn't want to work with them but I doubt if I could report them. I mean we're on the same side aren't we?' (Male officer, Garth) Similarly, from an officer working at Lancaster Farms:

[What do you do if you're faced with unprofessional staff who 'go over the top' with inmates. How do you deal with that?] There's a problem with that ... erm, we've got discipline guidelines, in here, for officers, that the officer's got to follow otherwise they end up in bother ... but, erm, I might know an officer is a bad officer, and he's doing things he shouldn't, but you're expected to work as a team, you're expected to have camaraderie, you're expected to support each other, and I might know that he does one or two things in a particularly unprofessional manner, but most of the time, he's okay. You don't wanna grass 'im up. That is the attitude. Because, basically, you understand he's okay. But, the fact is, erm, if I don't grass 'im up, and it's found out that I knew that he was doin' something unprofessional, I could be out of the job as well. It's, it's, a dodgy situation! ... I mean I always say in this job there's some officers you don't get on with. You can't ... you can't always get on with everybody. Its like typists in a typing pool; they're all doin' the same job but they won't get on with everybody. But at the end of the day, you'll all be there supporting each other, because if the shit hits the fan ... if you like me or not, you will support me. You know, if an inmate was assaulting me, the officer would come to help, and I would do the same. So it's a difficult situation. When you're in an aggressive environment you don't want to be seen to be grassin' somebody up, you know, so that people say 'Oh, you can't trust 'im'. It's a dodgy situation.

There's more than one way to skin a cat: cheating, riding and pay back

Today, pay back is more likely to be non-violent, not least because, as I suggested above, prison officers know that illicit violence towards prisoners may result in dismissal. A vengeful officer may choose other modes of pay back, for example writing, with the help of one or two like-minded officers, a fraudulent security information report (SIR) on the prisoner in the hope that this will trigger formal disciplinary pro-ceedings:

> If you're having a bad time with an inmate, your colleagues will help you out. [In what way?] Well there's more than one way to skin a cat ... We get together and put in an SIR[10] about the inmate, stating the source of the information as 'unknown'. You try to drop him in the shit. Basically, you cheat. (Male officer, Garth)

A number of my male interviewees alleged that officers, including them-selves, sometimes deliberately provoked prisoners so that they could remove them from the wing. This often involved the employment of strategies to cast the inmate as the villain. The following quotations are illustrative of this: 'Some officers will look for trouble. They'll goad inmates in the hope that they'll "bite".' (male officer, Lancaster Farms) Similarly, as one officer remarked when discussing a prisoner he did not like:

> There's nothing wrong with him that a good hiding wouldn't sort out. [Yes, but you can't do that any more can you?] No, we can't, but we can get up his nose so that he loses it and then we can bend him. (Senior officer, Lancaster Farms)

And again:

> We don't assault them, we just manipulate them so they end up going to the block under C&R ... This can really hurt them. [How do officers manipulate such inmates? Do you mean by goading them?] Yes, kind of. And riding them [dominating and oppressing] till they go for you. (Male officer, Portland)

These comments are particularly disturbing given that they were all made by officers working with young offenders. Despite the latter officer's claim that he and his colleagues did not assault prisoners, he subsequently unashamedly recalled an incident at Portland in which he deliberately injured a prisoner during a cell removal. As he told it, this prisoner had previously engaged in a dirty protest. On this occasion (a cell barricade) he and a number of other officers (wearing full riot gear) entered the cell and flattened the prisoner against the wall with their shields. Once the prisoner was pinioned, my informant head-butted the prisoner with his helmet. When asked by a nursing officer and a governor (both of whom were waiting outside on the landing) to explain the prisoner's injury (a broken nose) my informant simply announced 'Sorry, clash of heads Sir!' He then asked me 'How can they prove otherwise?' For this officer, such actions amount to 'rough justice' rather than assault. To other uniformed staff, however, these are the actions of a 'dangerous'[11] officer (this is a point I shall return to later). New officers tend to have 'dangerous' officers pointed out to them by more experienced colleagues, and such officers are given a wide berth. Unsurprisingly, such officers are also given a wide berth by prisoners.

That many prisoners *do* appreciate the patience and kindness often showed them by 'human service' officers is illustrated by the fact that officers sometimes receive 'thank-you cards' from prisoners about to be released and from ex-prisoners. These officers appreciate such gestures; others are less positive. When a senior officer working at Lancaster Farms proudly showed me a card addressed to several officers on the wing (thanking them for letting him have extra showers and such like) an officer who was opening the post hastily pointed out that his name was not on it. When the senior officer asked him if he should add his name, the officer replied: 'No thanks. I'd think I wasn't doing my job right if *my* name was on it!' This comment suggests that he did not want to be liked by prisoners; on the contrary he felt that doing the job 'right' and being a 'good' officer entailed keeping one's distance. Many officers, however, are acutely aware of the narrowness of the socio-economic (and moral) divide between themselves and prisoners; they understand that in many respects, prisoners are not very different from themselves:

> It's a very thin line between wearing a blue-and-white shirt [i.e. prison issue] and wearing a white shirt ... I think if you keep that at the back of your mind you can relate to them better ... You understand them better. (Senior officer, Garth)

Similarly:

> I can relate to these [prisoners] ... I've had scrapes [with the law] myself – nothing serious but I had to declare it. And I can see where they're coming from ... I was just on *this* side of the line instead of that side of the line. (Male officer, Garth)

A calming influence? Female officers

The ways in which women officers working in men's prisons view and carry out their work, and the ways in which they are seen by the men with whom they work is discussed more fully in Chapter 7. I intend here only to make a very brief comment on female officers' relationships with male prisoners. Before I do so, however, I want to comment briefly on the claim, made by some male officers, that a man's prison is simply 'no place for a woman'. The perceived vulnerability of female officers to the overtures of male prisoners was raised by these officers as sufficient justification for keeping the former away from the latter. As one male officer put it, 'Women are vulnerable to smooth talking'. This was cited as a potential threat both to the security of the prison and to the safety of the women themselves. Several officers claimed to have heard stories about, or claimed knowledge of, women officers 'running off with cons'. It is interesting to note, however, from my observations of staff–prisoner interactions, that when a male prisoner is sexually attracted to a male officer, and even when the prisoner makes this explicit, male officers are unlikely to be perceived as 'vulnerable' in the same way that women officers are. On the contrary, such overtures can give rise to much hilarity. For example, at Garth, a male probationer in his mid-twenties was rather taken aback by the attentions of a young, openly homosexual prisoner, and by the reaction of his colleagues when they found out about them. This officer's conversation with me ran as follows:

> He's told all the officers that he fancies me. He said to 'em all 'He's got a nice arse!' [So what did your colleagues say?] They take the mickey out of me about it. They ask me 'How's Shirley?' and the cons say to me 'Shirley's been asking about you!'

As we shall see in the following chapter, there are conflicting views amongst (male and female) officers as to whether women officers are 1) less confrontational than their male colleagues; and 2) able to develop more positive relationships with male prisoners as a result. The view that women officers exert a 'calming' influence in men's prisons (a claim that is made by many male and female officers) is a contentious one. With regard to the first claim, at least one female officer I interviewed introduced the concept of respect into the equation; she felt that if women officers do have more positive relationships it is because they treat prisoners with consideration. With regard to the second claim, numerous officers – male and female – argued that some women officers are 'as fond of a bit of aggro' as some of their male colleagues are. These female officers were seen as 1) enjoying using physical force on prisoners, for example being deliberately rough when applying control and restraint holds; and 2) 'wanting to be part of the shouting and bawling' that goes on between staff and prisoners (male officer, Garth pers. comm.). Moreover, numerous male officers claimed that far from being a source of calmness and equanimity, some of their female colleagues (usually the younger less experienced ones) 'employ the same kinds of "wind up" tactics that some of the blokes do' (male officer, Garth pers. comm.). Arguably, like their male counterparts, female officers who behave in this way do so either because they believe that this is the 'proper' way to treat prisoners or because of (male) peer pressure to conform to dominant occupational norms. This is an issue that I return to in the following chapter.

It's all about what an officer thinks an officer should do or be

Officers' working styles impact, of course, on the nature of the regime itself. The character of the regime on a particular wing is dependent on a variety of components, not least the working credos of senior officers. The atmosphere or 'tone' of a wing can change from day to day, depending cn which senior officer is on duty, and this can be extremely irritating for ordinary-grade staff who have to (to some extent at least) adjust their working styles and practices accordingly. It is interesting to note, also, that prison wings get distinctive reputations in the eyes of uniformed staff. At Lancaster Farms, for example, one wing had the reputation for having the scruffiest prisoners (because senior officers allowed them to go to work wearing prison-issue track suits when they were supposed to wear jeans and T-shirts) and for running a relatively liberal regime. The senior officers working on this wing were well aware that they were 'slagged off by the rest of the jail for giving the prisoners too much'. For example, one was in the habit of bringing videos from home so that the young prisoners could watch them during association, and when weather permitted he was in the habit of taking them outside for a game of volleyball. He did these things partly to relieve the boredom of the 'youngsters' on the wing and partly because he felt that such efforts 'paid off' in terms of creating better staff–prisoner relations. He was aware, though, that many of his own officers did not wish to make such efforts; whether they did or not depended largely on how they perceived their role. As the senior officer put it: 'It's all about what an officer thinks an officer should do or be.'

It is easier to run what officers call a 'tight ship' on some types of wing than on others. For example, it is easier for staff to run a tight ship on induction wings than a residential unit because the prisoners on the former know that they only have to put up with the restricted regime for a limited period of time (this may also explain why it is easier for staff in large busy locals, where there is a high proportion of remands, to get away with restrictive practices).

Control can of course be enhanced by various technologies. Garth was the only prison in this study where prisoners had in-cell television, and most officers were in favour of it, because 1) it 'domesticises' and 'normalises' the evening association period (many prisoners prefer to stay in their cells either alone or with a couple of friends rather than wander about on the landings); 2) it is a useful mechanism of control (prisoners are less likely to get into arguments over who watches what when they have their own TV set and more likely to conform to avoid losing this privilege); 3) TV helps prisoners to keep in touch with the outside world; and 4) as a former Chief Inspector of Prisons has noted, in-cell TV provides a proper excuse for a prisoner to remain in his cell and avoid the predators on the unit (HMCIP 1997: para.1.19). Finally, regimes which allow in-cell television can run with fewer evening staff. At Garth, even officers who were initially resistant to the idea of prisoners having televisions in their cells had come to the conclusion that it was a good idea, primarily because it kept prisoners quiet.

In one important respect, televisions are not out of place in prisons. As we shall see in the next chapter, prisons actually have many domestic features, precisely because they are places in which people have to live.

Notes

1   The distinction between 'distal' and 'proximal' thinking has a long history in intellectual inquiry. Distal thinking privileges results and outcomes, the apparently 'finished' and 'complete' things or objects of thought or action.

The distal is what is preconceived, what appears already constituted and known, what is simplified and distilled. 'Proximal' thinking, in contrast, deals in the continuous and unfinished (see Cooper and Law 1995 for a fascinating discussion of the distal/proximal debate). The distal approach to social inquiry is analogous to the view from a telescope; one can see far-away places and things but only in a certain degree of (fixed) detail. The proximal approach is analogous to what can be seen beneath a microscope. Here we find that fixed, biological structures are not fixed at all; rather they move, divide and merge. We see, in short, the structures of biological life *in process*. In the same way, a proximal approach allows the sociologist of the prison to see prison structures, relations and interactions as they develop, change and reproduce.

2   The principle of 'less eligibility' transformed penal policy (and hence prison conditions) in the mid-nineteenth century. Essentially, prison officials came to believe that the prisoner – (re)constructed as feckless, incorrigible (and hence dangerous) – should not be so well looked after that his circumstances corresponded to his non-criminal counterparts. He was, in fact, deemed 'less eligible' for warmth, food, clothing and rest than the 'deserving poor'.

3   Control and restraint (C&R) is a *defensive* method of physically dealing with prisoners. It uses controlled actions aimed at minimising physical injury, according to laid-down rules of authority and accountability (Barclay *et al.* 1994: 161).

4   'Dartmoor heavies' was the prison officers' name for heavy, highly polished, steel toe-capped boots.

5   An interesting discussion of officers 'at their best' can be found in Liebling and Price 2001).

6   Numerous officers mentioned being 'professional' but none really knew what they meant by it. They found it easier to discuss what made an officer *unprofessional*, i.e. 1) discussing inmates' offences in front of other inmates; 2) writing adverse reports because you don't like somebody; 3) always being late; and 4) offending against the discipline code.

7   One strand of the Woolf Report (1991 para. 12.129) was the introduction of the idea of a 'compact' (sometimes termed a 'contract') that should be made between prisoner and prison. Under such a compact the prisoner would receive, in return for his or her promises with regard to behaviour and 'performance', certain regime benefits.

8   It transpired that at this particular YOI, 'problem' inmates, i.e. those who are repeatedly charged with offences against good order and discipline, are allocated a personal governor who attempts to arrange a further 'compact' with the prisoner. It occurred to me that this scenario is a very good example of the dialectic of control as it occurs in the prison setting.

9   Some prison officers adopt what Sparks *et al.* (1996) term a a 'slippery slope' view of prisoners, which envisages a direct line between the tiniest infraction of discipline and anarchy unleashed.

10   An SIR is a security information report. These are passed from the wings to security staff who will act upon the information obtained. They may, for

example, bring the sniffer dog into the prisoner's cell and search the prisoners' visitors particularly thoroughly.

11 Officers perceived as 'dangerous' by fellow officers include those who use unnecessary force when dealing with prisoners and those suspected of bringing alcohol and drugs in for prisoners.

Chapter 5

Emotion and performance: the presentation of self in prisons

The domestic character of prisons

In addition to being a 'community', each prison is, quite literally, *home* to the prisoner for the period of his or her sentence, sometimes for extended periods of time. It would thus be unsurprising if elements of domesticity were absent. In prisons, therefore, we find family photographs, gossip and rumour, shopping lists for canteen purchases, football talk, argu-ments over TV programmes, over personal possessions, over lack of privacy and so on. In young offender institutions, as we have seen, we can even find rule-bending activities such as 'run-around quizzes' (prisoners are never supposed to run anywhere) laid on by staff to relieve the boredom and frustrations of institutional life.

Prisoners, especially long-term prisoners, try to make what is usually a bleak and comfortless environment more homely. At every prison in this study, photographs of family and friends were carefully placed on bedside cabinets and posters and photographs were stuck to walls. At Garth, where a greater range of personal possessions was allowed than in the other prisons in this study, and where prisoners were relatively free to decorate their cells as they wished, prisoners had also draped decorative wall hangings over institutional furniture and hung curtains at the windows. Some prisoners also kept caged birds; during one of my visits, a pet cockatiel escaped and began to fly around the wing. The bird's owner, several other prisoners and myself tried to get the bird back; for the next twenty minutes or so we whistled and cooed, ooooh'd and aaaah'd whenever the bird flew perilously close to open windows and we made lunges whenever it was close enough to catch. The officers calmly offered suggestions throughout. After the bird had flown around the wing several times, collided with walls, perched briefly on various window-sills and flown with a thump into a closed window (losing a few feathers in the process) one of the prisoners caught the bird and handed it back to its owner. We all breathed a sigh of relief. For a few minutes I almost forgot we were in a prison.

The degree of domesticity in prisons is striking. As I 'hung around' with staff on one of the wings at Garth, several prisoners wandered around the wings in flip-flops, jogging bottoms or shorts whilst eating bowls of corn flakes. One or two others wandered back from the showers with towels wrapped round their waists. On one of the wings of Wymott's Vulnerable Prisoner Unit, elderly prisoners sat around reading newspapers, pottered around in the kitchen, made matchstick models and drank endless cups of tea. During evening association in the young offender institutions, teenage prisoners smoked cigarettes with individual officers, played video games or pool, waited for their turn in the shower or watched TV. Every evening before 'bang-up' at Lancaster Farms, an officer and a young 'red band' (a trusted prisoner) trundled a tea urn along the landing, delivering a hot drink and a bun to each cell (what one officer called 'the sticky bun run').

Although prison officers have a tendency to present their role as a very masculine one (for a discussion of this in the American prison context see, for example, Martin and Jurik 1996) much of the prison officer's working week is taken up with 'housekeeping' – with tasks that are traditionally seen as 'women's work' (on this see also Toch 1994). Many of these housekeeping jobs 'are normally associated with the (typically female) role of parenting young children' (King and McDermott 1990: 63) and include supervising the spending of private 'cash',[1] ensuring that there is an adequate supply of toilet paper and clean laundry, that prisoners are receiving the meals they requested (as in hospitals, prisoners must complete a menu preference sheet) and the correct 'canteen' order (at Lancaster Farms the latter required that once a week, officers tip out the contents of literally dozens of carrier bags on to the pool table in order to count and check that orders of toiletries, birthday cards, packets of biscuits, chocolate bars, air fresheners, books of stamps, bottles of cordial, penny chews, etc. were correct) and that cells are being kept clean and tidy (this seems to have become of enormous importance since the introduction of the 'Incentives and Earned Privileges Scheme', especially in young offender institutions). Indeed I noticed that officers working in young offender regimes tend to have what Hockey (1986), writing of the experiences of army recruits, calls 'a near pathological concern for cleanliness, neatness and uniformity'. Yet this aspect of prison work is often downplayed, probably because telling others (and indeed themselves) that their work is risky and potentially dangerous sounds better to officers than saying they spend their days handing out toilet rolls and laundry (again see Toch 1994 on this). The contrast between officers' 'war stories' and the mundane realities of their everyday lives on the landings is marked: for example within minutes of an officer recounting how he had grappled with notoriously violent prisoners and fought his way through smoke and flying missiles at the Strangeways riot he was supervising prisoners behind the servery, wearing a catering hat and ladling out gravy and custard.

Domestic settings tend to be emotionally charged. In common with the home, where familiarity and boredom often degenerate into bickering and squabbles, I found that day-to-day interactions between prisoners and staff, and indeed between officers, are punctuated by sulks, rows, fall-outs and minor disagreements. In the process of settling these disputes, officers and prisoners cajole, flatter, take offence, get angry, offer advice, placate, tease each other and so on – this is as much a part of the complex business of living together in a prison as it is elsewhere. Indeed, wherever human beings spend long periods of time together in intimate settings they are drawn into emotional engagement with each other. Arguably, much of what happens in the daily life of prisons is explicable once the prison is recognised as a quasi-domestic sphere.

The prison as an emotional arena

Prisons are also, then, emotional places. Yet the performance and management of emotion in prisons, like the domestic nature of the prison setting, is a topic that has largely escaped academic attention. The emotional life of prisons is, of course, a topic of much discussion from all quarters when things 'go wrong'. This is especially true when prison disturbances occur; on such occasions there is usually a great deal of debate about the (largely negative) emotions experienced by all those involved, including the anger of prisoners regarding their conditions of confinement, the disgust of prison officers at the apparently wanton destruction of the prison fabric and the degree of confusion and fear experienced during the disturbance itself (see, e.g., Fitzgerald 1977; Woolf 1991). In contrast, the emotional life of prisons *on a day-to-day basis* – on the days when prisons are not beset by trouble and when nothing (much) goes wrong – has attracted much less interest. Yet the day-to-day emotional life of prisons is actually of greater theoretical importance because it is through the day-to-day performance and management of emotion that the prison itself is accomplished.

Prisons are emotional places for a number of reasons, the first and most obvious reason being that they are places in which large numbers of people are held captive against their will. We know that the prison is an emotionally painful place for prisoners and that prisoners are infantilised in most prison regimes. Unsurprisingly, feelings of powerless and frustration often give rise to resentment on the part of prisoners, particularly when formal power is abused. Similarly, attempts by prisoners to ameliorate the pains of imprisonment are often met with hostility and resentment by prison staff. In other words, staff–prisoner interactions and relationships are often emotionally charged, not least because the degree of intimacy involved in working with prisoners is relatively high. As I suggested in Chapter 1, prison officers – unlike police officers whose relationships with offenders are relatively fleeting – often spend sustained periods of time with the same prisoners, many of whom will have suffered a variety of personal traumas, difficulties and disappointments both before and during their sentences. The latter is likely to be especially true in the context of long-term prisons. In consequence, working in prisons is emotionally demanding and the emotions generated by prison work are many and varied. During my fieldwork, officers confided that they were fearful of certain prisoners, that they were jealous of colleagues who were able to do 'quality work' while they pounded the landings, that they were disappointed that their prison had 'gone downhill', that they were frustrated by their managers (who are widely perceived as unsympathetic to the needs of uniformed staff and ignorant of the day-to-day realities of life at the 'sharp end'), that they were bewildered (and disgusted) that some of their fellow officers actually wanted to work with sex offenders (some of whom had committed the most heinous offences against children) and that they were bored working on a wing that was 'more like an old folks' home than a prison' because it was inhabited by elderly prisoners. Others ridiculed colleagues who worked in a therapeutic community, new recruits derided 'old dinosaurs' and 'dinosaurs' grumbled about new recruits. In the quietness of the interview room, new recruits disclosed that they felt bullied by other officers and female officers said they were fed up with sexist behaviour.

Managing emotion

On a day-to-day basis, however, these emotions are not freely expressed. Rather, prison officers try to ensure that when they perform emotion they do so in the 'right' circumstances and settings. In short, prison officers are obliged to manage their own emotions as well as those of prisoners. This chapter, then, focuses specifically on the relationship between emotional expression and emotion management and the *performance* of prison work. I do not use the word performance lightly; on the contrary, prison officers are acutely aware that they must play parts and stage-manage their actions if they are to control the impressions they convey to prisoners and, just as importantly, to fellow staff. As we have seen, new recruits must learn the organisation's 'emotional map'; as Hochschild (1993) puts it in her observations of organisations more generally, recruits must learn, for example, where laughter begins in different areas of the organisation (and where it ends) and where, along an accelerating array of insults, it is acceptable to take offence without too much counter-offence.

The management of prisoners' emotions is attempted at both the level of the institution and at the level of the individual officer. In terms of the former, emotion management programmes are now instituted in a number of prisons, on the grounds that the inability to control emotions – particularly anger – is what brings many prisoners into prison in the first place. Anger management and enhanced thinking skills classes, for example, aim to show prisoners how to respond more rationally and less emotionally to stressful situations. Similarly, one of the aims of the therapeutic regime (see Chapter 7) is to encourage the 'difficult' prisoner to interact in a more reflexive and considered way.

At the level of individual officers, emotion management has two dimensions. First, as I have already suggested, they must deal, on a day-to-day basis, with the emotions expressed by prisoners. The ability to do so varies from officer to officer; while most are confident that they can deal with prisoners' anger (officers always have the option of the segregation unit) many are ill-equipped to deal with emotions that require a tender and patient response. Secondly, prison officers must, as I suggested above, manage the emotions that the prison generates within *them*. This is an important issue. How officers *feel* about the work they do, and how they feel about prisoners and fellow officers, has significant implications not only for the routine practices of prisons (and hence the nature and quality of imprisonment itself) but also for relationships with fellow staff.

Through an examination of the occupational norms of prison officers we begin to understand the need for, and the significance of, emotion work in prisons. As in police work, the occupational culture of the prison officer stresses, amongst other things, the importance of 'machismo' for successful job performance. There is a (long-standing) cultural expectation that prison officers will be courageous, resilient, authoritative and fearless in all situations and that they will manage those emotions thought to be 'non-masculine' (for example anxiety, fear, stress and depression). Similarly, male officers tend to be particularly careful, in their interactions with prisoners, not to show *qualities* they regard as traditionally female, e.g. sensitivity, understanding and compassion. Many female officers, in contrast, deliberately employ these qualities with prisoners in order to prevent and manage conflictual situations. None the less, when women officers start work in male prisons they are usually aware that to some extent, the occupational norms apply to them too. They are certainly aware that their performance *as officers* will be judged according to their ability to conform to these norms. Consequently, they attempt to dismantle female stereotypes – of women as passive, helpless, manipulative and so on. As I suggested earlier, they achieve this in different ways; like many of their male counterparts, most female officers, having little interest in confrontations with prisoners, strive simply to be fair, dispassionate and professional, but others, particularly some of the younger female officers, prefer to present a 'hard' front (see Chapter 7).

Which emotions, then, can prison officers legitimately feel and display to colleagues and to prisoners, and which emotions do they feel the most need to manage? Certainly most officers understand the need to manage emotion at work since there are risks associated with the expression of emotions deemed 'inappropriate' to the prison officer role. As I suggested earlier in this book, prisons, like other organisations, have their own 'feeling rules' about the kinds of emotions it is appropriate for officers to express (and to indeed feel) at work, and it is imperative that prison officers learn them. Those who transgress them are unlikely to be trusted.

Stress and anxiety

As I suggested in Chapter 1, the Prison Service has, in recent years, formally acknowledged the stressful nature of prison work. Although disclosures of personal distress at work are uncommon (see below), a large number of my interviewees acknowledged that the job could be extremely stressful. Some of these officers confided that they had, on occasion, felt too stressed and anxious to go to work, or that they knew colleagues who felt that way. Reflecting on his feelings about Wymott prior to the most recent riot, this senior officer said simply: 'It was horrible. I used to sit on the edge of the bed in a morning and say "Oh God, I can't face it" but you just had to go in and try to cope.' In a similar vein, this senior officer recalled the daily mental struggle of going to work in Long Lartin: 'I was retching on my way to work ... I just couldn't face going in. When I got to the gate, I had to fight off wanting to go home … I was fighting all the way. One day, I broke down in tears at work and they sent me home.'

The degree of emotion work that officers are forced to engage in when suffering these levels of anxiety and stress is intense. Officers who feel that they have lost control over prisoners are likely to be particularly stressed; those who worked at Wymott immediately prior to the 1993 riot described, in graphic detail how, on the night shift, prisoners had removed florescent lighting tubes and hurled them – along with heavy PP9 batteries – at officers as they patrolled the wings. These prison officers felt – knew – that the prisoners were out of their control; consequently, many of the officers were afraid to go on to the prison spurs. When I asked one officer how he and his colleagues had coped with this, he replied:

> We didn't; we had the highest sick-rate in the service. Some staff lost it through stress. One chap went home, and the house was empty, his wife and kids were out, and he cut up his uniform with a pair of scissors. And when his wife came home, his uniform was in shreds. His head had gone. We had a riot soon after that, and that was the best thing that happened to us.

Similarly, this time from a senior officer still working at Wymott:

> It was hell on earth. It was confrontation all the time. [Night staff] Had to go on a spur with twenty-eight drug-crazed inmates who could be doing anything. And some staff didn't want to go on the spurs … You had to force yourself to do it. It was very stressful.

The emotional battering that staff experience in such circumstances was highlighted by another officer working in Wymott, a prison that had also experienced, in the past, a number of prisoner suicides:

> Stress is increased when the atmosphere rapidly goes from nothing to fighting [i.e. from sitting in the office to responding to an alarm bell]. Pre-riot this happened four or five times a day … When this happens, your adrenalin levels go rapidly up and down, and this is even worse for night staff who's bodies are winding down during the course of the night. The shock of finding somebody slashing-up or hanging plays havoc with the system. (Male officer, Wymott)

Several officers drew my attention to a newspaper report (based on a survey carried out by Cooper in 1997) which rated a variety of occupations according to the degrees of stress to which each placed on its employees. The officers were quick to point out that, according to Cooper's survey, the job of the prison officer is one of the most stressful (perhaps *the* most stressful) occupation in Britain today. A subsequent report by Kent (1998) argued that prison officers consistently come out top for stress at work. Such reports are welcomed by prison officers precisely because they emphasise that stress is a structural problem; that stress inheres in the nature of the job itself and is not a reflection of a particular weakness within individuals. As I indicated in Chapter 1, what is often ignored by managers is the role of the organisation in the production of stress. Thus we find, for example, systems of stress 'management' reinforcing the notion of stress and anxiety as 'personal problems' to be dealt with.

Sources of stress

Numerous officers commented on the insidious nature of stress at work; on how it 'crept up' on staff without them realising it until it was too late. They were aware that, at root, it was the *unpredictability* of the job that created anxiety, and that unpredictability was exacerbated by poor prison architecture:

> There's an underlying stress the minute you walk through the gate. That's mainly 'cos of the layout and the unpredictability of the job. To me, just being aware of something all the time [i.e. the possibility of harm] is stress itself. Officers know that at any time they can get a smack in the face opening a cell door. (Male officer, Garth)

Stress is not only generated by disturbing events; for many officers the fact of 'never knowing who or what to believe' is the most stressful and wearing aspect of the job. Different grades of prison officer tend to identify different sources of stress. Generally speaking, principle officers[2] (and to some extent senior officers) are less likely than ordinary-grade staff to identify 'difficult' prisoner behaviour and a conflict of work styles as principal stressors, and more likely to identify shortages of staff, the subsequent 'nightmare' of working out the staff detail and the 'piling up of paperwork'. Ordinary-grade officers, however, identified a variety of routine stressors, including 1) the unpredictability of the job itself (constant policy change and decreasing job security); 2) 'difficult' inmates (officers reported that they were being asked to deal with increasing numbers of confrontational prisoners from other establishments); 3) the shift system and long hours; 4); working with staff who were lazy and unreliable; 5) finding oneself on the same shift as the 'wing psychopaths' (i.e. those officers who deliberately provoke prisoners); 6) working in a prison with a poor physical layout and hence poor sight-lines; 7) working with staff who hold opposing philosophies; 8) lack of leadership from superior officers (this can result in the fragmentation of staff into cliques, loss of morale and irregular working practices); 9) working with 'strangers' (officers from other wings) rather than one's regular and trusted colleagues; and 10) management bullying.

A bullying management style was identified by several officers as a significant factor in the generation of workplace stress. These officers all felt that they were subject to, or had at some time been subjected to, management bullying. Some told stories of being verbally abused (this was the case for both male and female officers); others spoke of how individual officers (particularly probationers) were pressurised to work overtime, to change shifts or work to unsafe manning levels. In one of the prisons in this study, several principal officers claimed that there was 'a bullying culture', whereby those who fell out of favour with a particular governor were picked on and humiliated in front of other staff. One of these officers, now a governor himself, recounted an occasion on which a colleague had been 'reduced to tears' by such treatment – a remark suggestive of an officer belittled, humiliated and (in consequence) unable to cope. Bullying can have a devastating effect on staff morale; at the time of my fieldwork in this particular prison, one principal officer was off work suffering from stress and three more felt that they were 'on the brink' (pers. comm.).

Stress may also, of course, generate tension between prisoners and staff. Although stress does not, of course, excuse intolerance and aggression towards prisoners, it partly explains why officers who are generally tolerant of prisoners sometimes resort to the well worn order to 'get behind your door'.

Spoiled identity: the dangers of disclosure

While most officers were prepared to acknowledge that certain aspects of the job *can* be stressful, they were quick to emphasise that this did not necessarily mean that they themselves were 'stressed'. Indeed, despite the prevalence of care teams[3] in prisons, admitting to feeling stressed is still perceived by many officers as an admission of mental weakness – one which amounts to saying one can no longer do the job, that one's 'bottle's gone' (numerous officers pers. comms.). As such, admitting to stress is to risk acquiring what Goffman (1963) terms a 'spoiled identity'; in the prison setting this amounts to the officer being constructed – and ultimately stigmatised – as a prison officer no longer able to cope in a prison. The widely held perception that the job is less secure than it was has significant implications for disclosure of feelings of stress; fears about redundancy may encourage stressed staff simply to engage in more emotion management:

It's especially difficult to admit now, because the job is less secure. Before, you'd have to shoot the governor before you lost your job. You don't like to let too many people know that you're under pressure. (Male officer, Garth)

I do not know what proportion of officers use the services of care teams; what I do know is that many officers mistrust the motives of care team members, are scathing about the suitability of some care team members for the task and doubt the confidentiality of care team support. According to one senior officer, this is perhaps unsurprising: 'It's the nature of the job – prison officers are very wary people.' Concerns about breaches of confidentiality, in an environment where gossip is rife and the value placed on machismo high, were, for many officers, sufficient reason to give the care team a wide berth: 'I wouldn't use them if I had a problem ... I use them if I want a rumour spreading! And the trouble with this job is mud sticks' (female officer, Garth). Similarly:

You tend not to go to the care team. It's usually the busy-bodies of the service that do that sort of job, and you wouldn't want to tell them anything anyway – it'd be all round the jail! ... In the prison, its like a rumour factory; things get blown out of all proportion. So if anybody saw you going to one of them ... if they didn't know anything they'd make it up! (Senior officer, Garth)

Most officers are simply reluctant to be seen as needing help (see, e.g., Thomas 2000). While they might prefer to share their problems with their partners rather than work colleagues, this is also problematic. Many officers believe that their partners – like all 'outsiders' – do not understand the job and, moreover, have no wish to do so:

I'm not very into blinkin', er, goin' to people with my problems anyway ... I've gotta sort 'em out for myself. But I understand it's a different age ... er, um, Certainly, I mean I was Manchester trained, Strangeways trained. You didn't go looking for help. You sorted it out yourself. [So would you prefer to find help via more informal channels, such as talking to your wife?] Yeah, well ... they always say a problem shared is a problem halved, like – but certainly the problem with the Prison Service is you can't talk about the finer points of it [to anybody outside the service] because it doesn't *mean* anything to anybody who doesn't work in it! [Oh I see what you mean]. And it would be unreasonable of me to expect my wife to actually understand the ins and outs of it. (Senior officer, Lancaster Farms)

One officer made an interesting point in relation to the reluctance of staff to seek help – a point made to me on an earlier occasion by a prison governor: '[Uniformed staff] need to be educated to feel that it's okay to speak to people about their problems' (senior officer, Garth). What this remark suggests is that discussions about the stresses of prison work, and the ways in which stress can be kept to a minimum, should be an in-built part of basic training. In other words, recruits should perhaps be made aware at the outset that they were joining an occupation that, by its very nature, was likely to generate problems for which they were *expected*, at one time or another, to seek help. At present, there are practical reasons for officers to deny they are suffering from stress; long-serving officers have certainly not yet forgotten the service's traditional attitude to such complaints: 'I was told "Don't ever get nervous debility on your sick note" because it would affect my career chances' (principal officer, Stoke Heath). Moreover, some of those who had suffered from stress, and who had taken sick leave to recover, found that they were the object of ridicule when they returned: 'When I got back [to work] some took the piss … they called me "Wibble" and "Bouncy Castle" – stuff like that' (male officer, Garth).

Managing emotion: anxiety, sympathy and fear

Anxiety is a commonly felt, ongoing emotion, in the sense that most prison officers experience some degree of anxiety whenever they are at work. Anxiety arises from the unpredictability of prison life; although much of prison life is mundane and routine, the officer is always conscious that a prisoner *may* assault him, that a prisoner *may* try to escape, that a prisoner *may* try to take him hostage, etc. New recruits experience anxiety particularly keenly. Not only do they lack experience of dealing with prisoners (and indeed, other prison officers) they are expected to look competent, even though they are performing to an unfamiliar script. Like their more experienced colleagues they learn, over time, to reduce their anxieties by enveloping themselves in the 'cloak of competence' pertinent to the prison officer role.

As we shall see in a moment, neither is it easy, in this occupational climate, for prisoner officers to admit to feeling afraid. As I indicated in Chapter 1, the expression of anger, in contrast, does not carry the same stigma as the expression of anxiety and fear. It is much easier for officers to admit to feeling angry, since anger is generally seen a 'manly' emotion[4] (and as writers such as Scraton *et al.* (1991) have noted, masculinity is celebrated in prisons). Nonetheless, anger must also be managed, since its expression can lead to staff–prisoner confrontations and antagonise both prisoners and staff.[5] Nonetheless for some officers, anger – along with irritation and frustration – are the emotions experienced most often. According to this officer: 'You have to force yourself to stop shouting at 'em, 'cos they're that stupid. I'm not kidding. I might as well stand and talk to this wall ... You get sick of it. Sometimes you feel like giving them a slap.' The feeling rules of the prison also make it difficult for officers, particularly male officers, to display empathy towards prisoners, even towards young prisoners in distress. The following comment (from a long-serving, principal officer working with young offenders) illustrates this beyond doubt:

> You could have an inmate who's family ... whose had a member of their family that's died, and its hard for men to show, sort of show concern. Well you can show concern but ... erm, sort of whereas it wouldn't be wrong – apparently it goes on in female prisons, you know you can put your arm round a female prisoner and give them your condolences sort of thing – but its harder in a, in a male prison, you know ... But whilst not giving them a hug, you're able to sort of pat them on the shoulder ... [You see] it's still a macho culture – you just don't express yourself. Officers wouldn't dare to cuddle anybody – even if the inmate was depressed or suicidal – in case staff thought he was queer or soft. But like I say some officers *will* pat the inmate on the shoulder or the back, if they can see that he's upset.

This officer's comment allows us a glimpse into the painful, isolating character of imprisonment; to see that prisons are places where emotions run high but where the constraints on emotional expression (placed on both prisoners and staff) are strong. A prisoner who expresses anger may find himself in the segregation unit; if he expresses distress or depression he may be laughed at or preyed upon by other prisoners. Similarly, staff who express anger may find themselves in confrontations with prisoners; if they express anxiety or fear they are likely to be seen as a 'wimp' by colleagues and by prisoners as a 'soft touch'. As we shall see, however, all these emotions are *felt*, at some point, by most prison officers.

Face work

In the prison setting, the construction of an authoritative, confident and dispassionate persona can, perhaps unsurprisingly, entail an intense degree of 'face work'[6] and a number of emotion work strategies. Like others whose work entails intimate interactions with distressed individuals and the carrying out of unpleasant and sometimes frightening tasks (in Chapter 1 I compared prison officers to medical staff, ambulance crews and fire-fighters), prison officers employ certain coping strategies. These include humour, strategies of depersonalisation (prisoners are 'bodies' to be counted) and a rhetoric of coping and detachment (that officers should not get too close to prisoners is an occupational norm – one that has acquired even greater significance in the post-Woodcock and Learmont contexts)[7] to get through the working day. Like those in the medical profession, officers find that the wearing of a uniform makes certain acts more permissible. This is not simply because of what the uniform symbolises to the prisoner but also because the uniform provides psychological protection for the officer. The uniform signifies mental preparation for the task at hand; without it the individual may feel exposed and vulnerable (as I shall elaborate in Chapter 8, the uniform also functions as a decontamination suit which is quickly abandoned after work). The uniform alone, however, is not sufficient to bestow a context of control on an encounter with a prisoner; officers must also acquire the correct 'manner' (or at least some version of it) – a particular way of walking, talking, of *being* a prison officer.

An important and qualifying point must be made at this point. Prisons are concerned primarily with the delivery of *custody* while medical and rescue services are primarily concerned with the delivery of *care*. Consequently the emotion work that medical staff and rescue workers engage in is primarily carried out in the context of alleviating the distress of worthy individuals, i.e. individuals who, as blameless patients, are seen as worthy of sympathy and compassion. Prison officers' emotion work, on the other hand, is more problematic, since it emerges in interactions with individuals who are often perceived as *unworthy* of such emotions (this applies to sex offenders in particular). Even officers who strive to work closely and positively with such prisoners often find it difficult to manage feelings of anger and disgust; similarly officers who normally maintain high social distance from prisoners may feel guilty or distressed when feelings of sympathy *do* emerge (these conflicting feelings are not ameliorated by the 'nonce-bashing' attitudes of some fellow staff). As we shall see, emotion management strategies with all types of prisoner are difficult to achieve and may occasionally fail.

Performing emotion: courage and indifference

As I suggested in Chapter 1, most officers try not to think about the potential dangers of their workplace. This does not mean, however, that they do not, on occasion, feel fearful. On the contrary, fear (e.g. of certain situations and certain prisoners) is not uncommon, but prison officers generally manage their fear, refusing to articulate it (or even think about it), especially at work. One might say, then, that prison officers must be aware of potential dangers but they cannot afford to dwell on them. To dwell on what may happen, for example, as the officer proceeds (sometimes alone) along a blind spur to lock up two or three dozen prisoners – some of whom may have committed extremely violent crimes – would, as numerous officers noted, be 'crippling'. Stated simply:

> I think when you sit down and think that you're on a landing on your own with forty-eight inmates, including rapists and murderers, and you have to go down the spur and lock them up ... If you thought about it, you'd never get off the chair. The fear is not always there, but you have to be aware. (Male officer, Garth)

Even very experienced officers can feel anxious at work. A senior officer working at Lancaster Farms told me that every morning when he arrived at the gate, he had 'butterflies in my stomach ... an air of expectancy about what the day will bring'. It is not until late morning that he has settled into the day; that is the point at which he can tell whether the regime is running smoothly (or not). By then, prisoners have been unlocked, breakfasted, applications have been taken, those going to work, education or the gym have left the wing and some of the office paperwork is underway. When I asked this ('human service') officer what he was apprehensive *about* on a day-to-day basis he replied that it was 'mainly the threat of physical assault'.

Clearly, to manage one's emotions in order to give a social audience (whether it be prisoners or colleagues) the impression that one is emotionally unaffected by specific attitudes, behaviours and/or settings is to engage in impression management. Thus in the prison setting (as in other settings where danger and harm must be dealt with) emotion management and impression management are inextricably intertwined. Time and time again, officers commented on the need to 'put on an act', and on the importance of masking how they *really* feel during certain types of interactions and with certain prisoners. The following quotations illustrate officers' need to develop and maintain a credible persona of fearlessness, and the contexts in which this mask has to be maintained:

There's a lot of bravado. You've got to put a barrier up 'cos they're looking for chinks in your armour. You become a good actor ... keeping a particular expression on your face. Sometimes you feel you're going red and fidgeting, so you learn to keep a [dead]pan face. If you're seen to be a soft touch, it'd be round the jail in no time. (Male officer, Garth)

Similarly, from an officer still in his probationary year at Garth:'I had one inmate block me in the boot room. He stood against the door and said that I'd called him a fucking liar. I was shitting it, but you can't stand there blurting your eyes out. You've got to do something.' That they are engaging in a public 'performance' every time they come to work is not lost on prison officers:

I put my uniform on and the minute I've put on my belt and chain, and I've put my hair up, I'm no longer Jane. I think it's like a staged performance ... [Do you?] Yeah. When it's roll call in a morning, it's like 'Lights, Camera, Action!' At work I'm not Jane. [Who are you?] I don't know – this big bad wolf comes out of me ... And I'm quite docile and dippy at home. At work, I won't allow my dippiness to come through. You've got to perform. (Female officer, Garth)

What stands out in these quotations is the extent to which courage, confidence and indifference are performed on a day-to-day basis.

As I suggested earlier, sometimes officers do not manage to manage their fear. During my fieldwork, a principal officer told me that he had spent most of the morning talking to an officer who had become so fearful of certain prisoners that he was unable to go into work. On the last occasion the officer had tried, he had driven into the car park but had been unable to get out of his car. I had some idea of the anxiety that this officer must have been experiencing during my own first day at Garth. Having carried out fieldwork for several years and in a variety of prisons, at one point I suddenly felt slightly anxious for my safety. As I stood on one of the spurs, I realised that myself and one officer were surrounded by dozens of prisoners, and that the rest of the staff were down the corridor and out of sight of both of us. I found myself trying to locate the alarm bell 'just in case', but tried to look nonchalant and carefree. I recognised that it does take courage to walk down a spur alone; on the occasions I did so whist shadowing an officer (to unlock a prisoner for the gym) I felt vulnerable and rather foolish. As other prisoners hung around, I tried to look relaxed – as if I did this every day of the week. I am not sure they were convinced.

At Garth, the fear of being taken hostage – many officers' greatest unspoken fear – was not lessened by the fact that, contrary to one of the formal rules of the organisation (that in the interests of security and staff safety officers should not lock and unlock alone), many officers were apparently having to do precisely that, on the ground that 'the job wouldn't get done otherwise' (it appeared that there is often a general informal expectation that officers will work alone whenever there is a shortage of staff on the shift). Such working arrangements have important implications for staff–prisoner relations. That prison officers are greatly outnumbered by prisoners has already been noted; because of this fact prison officers in this situation generally understand that their day-to-day safety is crucially dependent on positive relations between the prisoners and themselves: 'You never really know what each day will bring. You just hope that, at the end of it, you've done nice for them, and they'll let you out' (male officer, Garth).

The impact of architecture on emotions

Foucault (1979) has illustrated, with persuasive clarity, the importance of architecture for the surveillance (and hence discipline) of individuals. Architecture which allows maximum surveillance makes it possible for those in power in a particular setting – whether it be the factory, school, hospital or the prison – to regulate and discipline subservient others. In the prison context it is interesting to note that architecture which permits a high level of surveillance of prisoners by staff also permits a high level of surveillance of staff by their managers. I noticed, for example, that if senior officers on a new wing at Garth (see below) observed that officers were spending too much time congregating on one part of the landing to chat, they knocked on the office window and gestured to the officers to move around or to go and stand somewhere else.

The architecture of a prison is a significant factor in the control of prisoners and the maintenance of order; as Dilulio (1987: 84) notes it can be either a great ally or a great adversary in any attempt to establish and maintain orderly institutions. The physical layout of a prison has implications both for officers' perceptions of their own safety and for the safety of prisoners. Garth prison was of particular interest in that it comprises two architectural extremes; the old part of the prison (four out of the five wings) has numerous hard-to-monitor areas – 'blind' spurs and corners where sight-lines are extremely poor. On these wings not only were the prisoners out of view of staff for much of the time, staff were also out of view of each other. As I have already indicated, the result was that some officers felt unsafe and relied very much on their positive relations with prisoners to maintain control.

The newly built E wing, in contrast (the fifth wing of the prison), had galleried landings where sight-lines were extremely good. Whenever prisoners were out of their cells, they were in full view of staff. Surveillance was enhanced by CCTV cameras located at various points. The positive benefits of the layout of the wing were mentioned by every member of E wing staff; not only did all officers say they felt safe, they were also able to take advantage of a 'back stage' area where they could spend time completely free from prisoners. On this wing, all the spaces into which prisoners had, on other wings, some degree of access – for example the tea-making room and the senior officer's office – were out of bounds to prisoners. A barred gate separated the front and back-stage areas. This was of great significance to E wing staff. In contrast, prisoners, once unlocked, could roam relatively freely on the old wings, and officers were allocated to different landings, each with their own blind corners. Moreover, on these wings, staffing levels dictated that at certain points in the day, there might be only one officer working on each landing, i.e. one officer on the 'ones', one officer on the 'twos' and one officer on the 'threes'. As a result, all three officers felt isolated. As one of them (a young male officer) put it: 'All you've got for company is the alarm bell.' Unsurprisingly, these staff felt anxious: 'It's very, very unsafe for staff. The staff on the three's landing are almost invisible to other staff. The design is appalling but we can't do anything about it' (male senior officer). Similarly: 'It can be frightening on these wings. You get used to it but it doesn't go away' (male officer).

A female officer recently out of her probationary year also commented on her anxieties about the layout of the old wings:

> Very intimidating at first it was. It didn't take me too long to, erm, get over that feeling, but when I first came on here … it's just not what I envisaged at all. I mean if you go down to the new wing, well they've done that in the Victorian style again because it's the open landings and things you see, and it's totally different. But when I first came on here, I thought Oh no! and when I had to go … when they once sent me down there [on the spur] to go and get somebody, I thought Oh my God! But you do get used to it, and you do, you know … there's only been may be once that I've been concerned, but the rest of the time … There's usually other people about, and you've usually got a radio … You've got a radio, and they give you personal alarms and things. But, at the end of the day, I think that if you worry about it *too* much, then you can't do it. And that's why they give you that observation week you see … to show you that

this is where you're gonna be working, and that *these* are who you're gonna be working with.

In contrast, those who had transferred over *to* E wing from the old wings commented on the extent to which the new layout had improved their morale:

On the other wings, it was like an asylum. [Why?] It's not built right; you're ill-at-ease – it was bloody depressing actually. But here, it's like a barrel of fun to me, all day. It's great. I feel sorry for the staff on the other wings, but they've not been on here so I suppose they don't know what they're missing. (Male officer)

Similarly:

I used to dread going onto A and B wings, especially the muster area. When you work there you're on your own a lot of the time – like when you're on the landing dishing out the mail and the news-papers … and you're not supposed to leave the mail unattended but then you'd have to go let somebody in his cell … go off wandering down the spur. It was a nightmare. (Male officer)

Officers transferring to E wing quickly became unused to working out of sight of colleagues; indeed they so disliked being cross-deployed to other wings (this happened when other wings were short-staffed) that one officer – a man in his early fifties – had told the senior officer that he would do all the domestic chores in the wing kitchen and rest room on the condition that he was never sent to other wings. Officers who had worked in a variety of prisons were in no doubt as to which type of prison design made them feel safest. According to this senior officer:

The Victorian radial design is still the most effective way of man-ning a prison, because you've got a centre point to control the movement, your support for each of the groups is close by, and it keeps quite a large number of people in a manageable area. You can't improve on it.

The degree of stress experienced by staff on E wing was relatively low, and the sense of camaraderie between officers pronounced:

The camaraderie's great. I've never gone home stressed from here. In fact, some days I don't want to go home! On Sunday, it was like being on holiday; I'd cooked the breakfast [for all the staff] and then at lunch time we went off to the club, and we came back and we had wine gums and the telly was on. It was great! On the other wings, they'll [the inmates] come in the office all the time and sit on the SO's desk, for no other reason than they want to cause mischief. (Male officer)

Compared to the other wings, E wing had a relatively low level of staff–prisoner contact. Indeed, one of the wing's potentially negative aspects was that officers might begin to rely on surveillance to control prisoners rather than on social interaction and the positive relationships that can develop in the process. In contrast, it was clear that officers working on the old wings compensated for poor sight-lines by spending time developing good relationships with prisoners. It was also interesting to note that on E wing, in contrast to elsewhere, relations between uniformed staff seemed comparatively close. Indeed, several officers perceived their relationships with fellow officers as 'like a family'. Elaborating on the closeness of this relationship, one female officer remarked: 'We're very tactile too. We often give each other a hug.'

These officers socialised out of work hours, shared lifts to work and swapped shifts. Some even went on holiday together. It was interesting to note that familial feelings towards work colleagues seemed in large part to depend on *where* prison officers worked. Those who felt that they were part of a family at work tended to be those who worked on wings that had a large proportion of newly recruited staff, a number of female officers, supportive senior officers, inmate-free zones, good working conditions (comfortable rest room, adequately equipped kitchen, adequate changing facilities) and where the physical layout enabled staff to feel safe. Those who saw their work group as 'like a family' felt emotional attachment to the group as a whole but also attached familial roles to particular individuals within it. As in non-prison settings, however, being part of a family has certain implications:

In here there's officers that could be your mother, your son, your brother … there's that closeness there. It's not *intimate* as such, but you're *with* this lot, and you *need* each other. And if you have a fall-out, it's like a domestic. And you have to work hard to get it right.

The perception of colleagues as 'like family' is not, however, universal. When I asked officers on other wings, and in other prisons, whether they saw their colleagues in this way, many were adamant that they did not.

For them, family was wives and children, mothers, brothers and sisters. Fellow officers were simply people they worked with.

Emotional detachment?

I have suggested that prison officers engage in a significant degree of impression management in order to appear authoritative and confident in their day-to-day dealings with prisoners, and that like nurses, they are expected to remain emotionally detached. As I indicated in Chapter 3, the need for detachment is formally impressed upon officers during basic training on the grounds that friendliness and familiarity can lead to manipulation by prisoners and ultimately compromises of security. An occupational ethos in which strategies of depersonalisation and emotional detachment are deemed to be important is therefore present in most prisons (as we shall see, therapeutic communities, which place particular emphasis on the development of positive relationships between prisoners and staff, are an exception).

As I suggested earlier, that prisoners 'mistake kindness for weakness' is a comment often made by prison officers. New recruits learn to manage feelings of sympathy and their natural inclinations to help prisoners in their efforts to avoid being manipulated or 'conditioned' by prisoners. These fears arise from being continuously told – first at training college and then by mentors – that in their dealings with prisoners, they should 'never trust the bastards'. Fears of being seen as a 'soft touch' thus invade all aspects of officers' interactions with prisoners, even with regard to easily granted requests: 'An inmate might ask for a phone call 'cos his wife's chucked him, but if you said yes he'd tell all his mates and so you have to go against the grain. Some find it hard at first but you've just got to do it' (basic-grade officer, Garth).

Staff expressions of sympathy *per se* are not forbidden however; under certain circumstances, such as when a prisoner has had bad news (e.g. parole 'knock backs', family and relationship problems, bereavements, etc.) many officers can and often do express sympathy towards prisoners. What are not appropriate, however, are expressions of sympathy that have an uneasy fit with occupational norms. Hence officers are less likely to express sympathy towards 'difficult' prisoners who have problems (particularly those who have offered violence to staff) than to co-operative ones. They are also less likely to display sympathy in the presence of other officers; this is particularly true during the probationary year, when officers are afraid of being seen as 'soft' (better to be perceived as 'hard'). The degree of sympathy it is appropriate to feel and display is also significant; while an officer can, as I have already suggested, legitimately pat a distressed prisoner on the back or express dismay at the suicide of a well liked prisoner, it is less acceptable to hug a distressed prisoner, or to cry openly after a prison death. Displays of emotion are thus generally kept under wraps or displayed in specific emotional zones.

The spatial structuring of emotional language: emotion zones

Like all organisations, prisons have emotional zones – places and settings that become understood in terms of particular emotions. In the prison, specific emotional zones permit officers legitimately to (in the terms of the feeling rules of the organisation) perform anger and 'blow off steam' while other zones may be selected by officers wishing to express sadness and grief (e.g. two women officers told me that this was their selected zone 'for a cry' upon hearing of the death of a well liked prisoner; in other spaces within the prison – in particular the gatehouse – emotional reticence is the norm). On a day-to-day basis, of course, the officer will emote somewhere between these two extremes. Just as the officer who is always angry or fearful is likely to be given a wide berth by his colleagues, the officer who is overly sympathetic and friendly is viewed with suspicion. Both may be viewed as posing a threat to the security of the prison or to the occupational identity of the prison officer.

There are settings and occasions, however, when the ritualised expression of emotion is appropriate; indeed it is expected. As an emotional zone understood in terms of anger and disgust, the debriefing room used by SOTP tutors is a particular case in point. Here, it is legitimate to perform (often intense) anger and disgust towards the disclosures of sex offenders. It is important to note, however, that the debriefing room also *produces* these emotions. This is not to say that emotional performances in this setting (or any setting for that matter) are superficial or calculating; on the contrary in performing anger (or any other emotion) we may be fully engaged 'doing what comes naturally', even if the emotion is a product of cultural history and intelligible only by virtue of the rules it obeys (Gergen 1999). Rather, I want to argue that SOTP tutors know that it is very important to emote 'properly' in this setting; they know that not only is the display of anger and disgust fitting, the failure to display any sign of these emotions is to risk being judged personally deficient or deviant (along the lines of 'Are you a pervert too?'). As I have noted elsewhere, in the context of the SOTP, this scenario is a very real possibility (see Crawley 2000b).

The emotion zone of the debriefing room is an interesting one for a number of reasons. First, it is a space highly charged with emotion. Secondly, those who use it are required to engage in an (appropriate) emotional performance for the benefit of other officers ('See, I find sex offenders disgusting, just like you'). Thirdly, officers engage in an emotional performance for their own reassurance; as we shall see in Chapter 7, those who do SOTP work may experience feelings that threaten their sense of self, namely that they been 'contaminated' by their contact with sex offenders. In other words that they have 'caught' perverted thoughts from those they are trying to treat (again see Crawley *ibid.*). Through the collective performance of disgust and anger these anxieties may be ameliorated. On a day-to-day basis, of course, tutors must manage their feelings of anger and disgust in order to deliver the programme in a positive manner.

When emotions are performed in parts of the prison not normally understood in terms of emotional expression, the performance may startle both the recipients of the performance – the audience – and the actor himself. On one occasion during my fieldwork, one of my key contact's feelings of frustration, resentment, disappointment and anger at what he felt to be unfair treatment (he was consistently passed over for promotion) got the better of him. On discovering, immediately after learning that he had failed a promotion board for the fourth time, that he was being expected to extend his shift (a fellow officer had phoned in sick) he tore the large bunch of keys from his belt and, close to tears, threw them across the control room – where they narrowly missed another officer – before storming out of the room in his frustration and anger at being 'mucked about'. This officer's emotional performance was intended to communicate his distress and to encourage his managers to treat him more thoughtfully in the future. The performance lost some of its potency, however, when he had to return for his keys in order to get back through the gate. As a result of his outburst, this officer subsequently had to go before the governor. A few days after the incident, and still visibly distressed by it, the officer told me that his emotional explosion had shocked *him* as well as those who had witnessed it. He admitted that he was 'stressed out'; he was also frightened of what the outcome of his disciplinary hearing would be. He knew that if he was dismissed he would forfeit much of his pension, and he was afraid to tell his wife about the incident 'cos it'll just worry her'. He never did tell her; the final outcome of the disciplinary hearing was the receipt of a final warning. It is notable that in *these* circumstances, officers *are* willing to call upon stress to explain their behaviour. Is it acceptable to admit that managers are causing stress, because this does not reflect on officers' ability to deal with prisoners. On the contrary, it suggests that managers are preventing officers from doing their job. It is much less acceptable for an officer to admit that prisoners are causing stress, because controlling prisoners is one of the officer's core functions.

Although prison officers pride themselves on being able convincingly to hide their feelings over time and under pressure, emotion work can take its toll. The act can go stale, and private feelings can leak through the mask – in irritation, anger, rebellion or distress. Moreover, as we shall see in Chapter 8, difficulties occur when work-related performances stick; that is, when they become situationally unspecific. As I indicated in Chapter 1, an important – and often unwanted – consequence of routinely managing emotion is that in the process of doing so it is possible to become estranged from one's 'real' feelings. In other words, routine emotion work can result in prison officers being unable to feel certain emotions at all, even outside the prison setting. This is the process that prison officers are referring to when they say that the job has 'changed' them (an issue that I return to in Chapter 7). That is not to say that emotional detachment in prisons is always easy; on the contrary for some officers it is very difficult to achieve. Even experienced officers may find that occasionally the 'front' falls, and unanticipated emotions are exposed, overwhelming them. As we shall see in a moment, this can be a great shock.

Emotion mis-management – the intrusive script

I want now to describe one officer's unexpected failure to manage the emotion that is potentially most in conflict with the occupational norms of prisons – sympathy for the prisoner – in an emotion zone generally understood in terms of anger and contempt. During a particularly long interview (just over three hours), a very experienced officer (who had worked for the Prison Service for over twenty years and in a variety of prisons) recalled an occasion on which he 'froze' mid-performance, precisely because the strategy of depersonalisation he had relied upon for so long failed him. In theatrical parlance this is known as 'corpsing' – a term used to refer to what happens when an actor loses his or her place in the script, dries, is unable to continue, no longer believes in the play and, seeing the audience watching and waiting, freezes to the spot, unable to continue with the 'performance'. When an actor 'corpses', the entire performance is put in jeopardy and the other actors must find ways to improvise around the corpse (Hopfl and Linstead 1993: 90). As Hopfl and Linstead note, what is happening is that the 'corpsing' actor has seen the play for what it is, and has experienced the 'shock of recognition'. Corpsing is thus not a failure of technique, but a failure of the mask itself.

During our conversation, in which my interviewee was explaining the emotional hardening that inevitably takes place amongst uniformed staff, this officer suddenly changed tack; he went on to describe a scenario which had caused him to experience feelings of shock on seeing the distress of a youth he had himself helped remove to segregation. The following account, in the officer's own words, describes both the change of direction our conversation took and the officer's feelings of shock and bewilderment at the unanticipated rush of sympathy he felt for this young prisoner – an explosion of emotion that was generated by the fact that the prisoner physically resembled his own son:

It's like the army and killing; your emotions get hardened really … Having said that, though … when you're bending them, and they're crying [long pause] Just recently, I 'saw' my son when I was doing it and it gave me a terrible feeling. When I saw that little con in that cell, stripped and crying, I froze inside … [Did you? How do you mean?] I can't really describe the feeling … I feel funny even thinking about it now. It makes the hairs on the back of my neck stand up … [Did you … did your colleagues, the other officers, did they know?] [shakes his head]. [Did you ever tell them?] [shakes his head again]. [Have you ever told them?] [shakes his head again] ['Cos I was wondering if other officers have felt this?] Apart from my missus, you're the only person that knows. [So you don't know if other officers have experienced it as well?] No, because I suppose it's that macho thing as well that comes into it, erm … You don't wanna let on. [Mmm] Good point, I don't know. I don't know anybody else has experienced or not. I'd be interested to know … *very* interested to know. (Senior officer, Lancaster Farms)

What happened to this officer was not just that he experienced un-expected feelings of sympathy; rather he experienced a profound surge of human empathy and compassion for this *person* – a person who reminded him of his son. He had suddenly found himself in an unfamiliar emotional terrain and performing from an intrusive script from elsewhere – from home. His feelings did not correspond to his perceptions of himself as a prison officer; they were involuntary, he was unprepared for them and hence shocked by their appearance. Three responses were available to this officer: 1) to perform according to the new script and comfort the distressed prisoner; 2) to ignore the new script and make a rapid readjustment to the familiar one; and 3) to fail to respond to either script and 'freeze'. In the event, the officer simply froze; he was unable to respond either to the old script or the new one, so was unable to do anything at all. His feelings caused him to question his perception of young offenders:

erm, it didn't have the effect on me am I in the right job, or should I not be in this job, … erm … I suppose being in for so long, that thought never crossed my mind … I think it just re-emphasized the fact that they're *kids* … That incident down there, it pulled me up if you like. It said 'Whoah! What are you doing?'

Moreover, he was afraid that these emotions would surface again. To protect himself, he had since developed a strategy of avoidance to ensure that they would not. Basically, he determined to keep a low profile whenever prisoners were being removed to the segregation unit, because there are social costs if the mask is *seen* to slip. Corpsing is likely to have serious consequences in the prison setting – particularly *this* setting – since every officer, as a member of a 'performance team' (Goffman 1971: 85) is expected to act in concert with his colleagues to present a concerted 'front' while hiding from view the 'backstage' of social relations. As Goffman notes:

> while a team-performance is in progress, any member of the team has the power to give the show away or to disrupt it by inappropriate conduct. Each team-mate is forced to rely on the good conduct and behaviour of his fellows, and they, in turn, are forced to rely on him. (*Ibid.*: 88)

It is through such co-operation that the team is able to maintain a particular definition of the situation; if an actor fails in his performance, this both demystifies the performance and calls for 'repair work' from other actors if the social or corporate show is to go on (see Goffman 1959). Should anyone present a signal that he or she is not invested in the part that he or she is proferring – by forgetting his or her 'lines', falling over, bursting into tears and so on – the theatrical reality is shattered. In such circumstances, as in the theatre, others present 'are made aware of the actor *as such*, the person behind the role; the appearance of Joe, or whoever, as planner, personnel manager [or prison officer] fails to be an imposing one and we glimpse the actor behind the part' (Mangham and Overington 1987: 102). Not to support each others' performance or 'face' is to disrupt the entire scene because no one can continue in performance when others are embarrassed or shamed (i.e. 'out of face'). In the prison setting, where officers rely heavily on teamwork, particularly when they perceive themselves or their colleagues to be in danger, the officer who corpses is likely to lose the confidence and trust of his or her colleagues.

Perhaps the most significant aspect of this episode I have just described is that the officer was more likely to 'corpse' in this setting (where there is a deliberate indifference to the prisoners' distress) than in any other part of the prison. This is because the discrepancy between the emotion script he was expecting to perform and the script that he found himself performing was so great.

As we can see from this officer's comments, prison officers are often afraid to acknowledge their emotions – despite the impossibility of doing the job without emotion. Consequently, as we have seen, levels of emotion management are high. Moreover, the officer's comments make clear the significance of 'depersonalisation' in the prison setting; when asked to consider why he had never 'frozen' before, this officer remarked that generally speaking: 'you don't *think* ... don't put the human aspect on it. You're doin' a job. Finished. And to suddenly have that ... that feeling jump into your head that your lad is there, it was like touching a hot iron ... I felt myself beginning to ... lose it.'

In prisons, strategies of depersonalisation are firmly in place. Officers speak routinely about the number of 'bodies' that must be fed, brought from reception, got ready for court and so on; arguably this language of 'emotional distancing' enables officers to deal with large numbers of prisoners with the minimum of emotional involvement. As the same officer commented: 'Although you don't see these as people, they are. But you can keep them in separate boxes ... they're different people to people outside.'

The routine, bureaucratic denial of humanity in prisons, such as the use of a 'Body Book' (see Liebling 1998) which officers sign when handing over prisoners, and the tendency to construct prisoners as 'Other' through the use of descriptive terms such as 'scum', 'cons', 'scroats', 'shits', 'toe-rags' and 'nonces' creates a space in which in-humane treatment may occur (for an excellent discussion of how modernity and its attendant bureaucratic institutions distance 'Other' individuals in a way that makes brutality possible or even inevitable, see Kelman 1973; Bauman 1989). As both authors note in their analyses of Nazi violence, moral inhibitions tend to be eroded if actions are routinised and if victims are dehumanised by ideological definitions and indoctrinations. In short, it is easier to hurt people that we do not identify with and that we see as numbers or bodies rather than human beings. When this officer 'froze' it was precisely because depersonalisation failed and the *prisoner as person* emerged.

Notes

1   Prisoners are not allowed access to cash; all earnings and any money sent to the prisoner from outside go directly to the prisoner's account and is held in the prison's finance department. The only way that prisoners can confirm what is in this account is to ask officers to find out for them.

2   Principal officers now spend much more time engaged in managerial activities than on the landings.

3   Each Prison Service establishment now has a 'care team' whose role is to provide emotional and practical support for prison staff. Care teams are multidisciplinary; members (all of whom give their services voluntarily) are drawn from a variety of departments, such as the chaplaincy, psychology, probation, health care and of course from the discipline grades. The first care teams were set up in 1991, following the separation of the Prison Service Staff Care and Welfare Service (PSSCWS) from the Home Office. The date is significant; it follows the serious prison disturbances of 1990, after which many staff – particularly those working at Strangeways – were traumatised by their experiences. Many officers reported suffering nightmares, flash-backs and anxiety attacks following the disturbance at the prison.

4   As I shall elaborate below, not all men see anger as manly. For some men, the ability to keep control of one's anger – to keep one's cool – is a more manly response to challenging situations (on this see Jefferson 1998).

5   Several officers spoke with disdain of 'psycho' officers, individuals whom they perceive as putting *them* at risk by their aggressive, confrontational behaviour with prisoners.

6   In contemporary communication theories (see especially the work of Goffman) the term 'face' refers to the positive social value we effectively claim for ourselves – an image of self delineated in terms of approved social attributes, an image others may share. The term 'face work' refers to the actions we take to make whatever we are doing consistent with face. These actions become habitualised and standard; each person, occupational group and society has its own characteristic repertoire of face-saving practices.

7   In the Prison Service generally it is understood that relaxed relations between staff and prisoners can 'condition' staff into being less vigilant on security matters. This concern became of particular significance in the context of recent escapes from two high-security prisons, namely HMP Whitemoor (see Home Office 1994) and HMP Parkhurst (Home Office 1995).

Chapter 6

When things go wrong: suicide and conflict

Perhaps unsurprisingly, given the growing numbers of people in prison, the painful and emotional nature of imprisonment, the domestic and claustrophobic nature of the prison setting and the limits on available resources, prisons do not always run smoothly. On the contrary, a variety of problems and difficulties arise on a day-to-day basis, but these are generally settled (or at least die down) relatively quickly. Occasionally serious problems arise, and these are more difficult to solve. Sometimes, for example, in the case of a prison suicide, they are impossible to solve, and prison officers must simply deal with the situation as it stands. In this chapter I want to discuss two types of prison incident that have the potential to impact significantly on staff emotions. The first of these is prisoner suicide and the second is prisoner dissent – particularly dissent at the collective level. Later in the chapter I focus on (formal and informal) staff responses to the dissent, and highlight the ways in which such responses maintain the more 'traditional' occupational cultures of prison and raise staff morale.

Suicides in prison

The suicide of a prisoner can be very distressing for prison staff, particularly for those who are unfortunate enough to find the prisoner's body (usually the night staff since most suicides take place at night). Like many of us, officers finding a suicide may never have seen a dead body before. During my fieldwork, a number of young men took, or attempted to take, their own lives in their cells. The suicide of one prisoner, a young man of seventeen, had a significant impact on the officer who found his body – a man who up until nine months earlier had been employed as a carpenter. The young man's body, discovered during his night duty, was the first dead body he had ever seen; his comments, in response to my questions about how the experience had affected him, are illustrative of both the immediate and delayed impact that prison suicides can have on officers' emotions. Although this officer initially claimed to have felt 'okay' since finding the body, he subsequently admitted that he had found the experience upsetting: 'He looked awful. I had to take his weight so that the other officer could cut him down, and then we laid him on the bed. The smell was awful 'cos he had fouled himself. It was terrible' (male officer, YOI). The distress experienced on such occasions is not an issue that prison officers are inclined to talk to their colleagues about, in case their emotions are seen as inappropriate because 'it's only a con'. Officers who have had to deal with suicides in prison, however, often challenge claims of indifference: 'Staff who find suicides are *always* upset by the experience. Anybody who says they're not moved by it has got to be lying' (male officer, Stoke Heath).

The following comments provide insights into 1) the distress that prisoner suicides can generate amongst prison officers; 2) the emotional labour officers feel they must engage in such circumstances in order to match their emotions and emotional displays to the feeling rules of the prison; and 3) the impact of prisoner suicides on staff's perceptions of their job:

> A successful suicide is the worst scenario we could have on nights … it's the worst scenario. At the time you deal with it; you sort stuff out, someone might even manage to make a joke … but when it's over, that's when the shock sets in. You never get over it; I think it's the sense of failure. (Male officer, Portland)

Similarly:

> I had a lad that hung himself. I found the lad by his bed, and it looked like he had tried to hang himself and then thought better of it, 'cos he was on one knee as if trying to get up again. He was stone cold when I found him. Phew … That was very upsetting that was. (Long-serving male officer, Portland)

And again: 'I can remember that incident of three or four years ago as clearly as I could then. It was horrific. I questioned my job, the service, and everything' (officer, Portland).

There is a considerable literature on death and dying but very little of it explores how sudden death is managed, or the anomaly of the newly dead body (Meerabeau and Page 1998). The newly dead body, though literally an inanimate object, has a marginal, ambiguous status: for example nurses may continue to see the newly dead body not as a body, but as the person they looked after. It is not surprising that prison officers report similar feelings; describing his emotions in the hours and days after the suicide, a middle-aged, newly recruited officer who had found a prisoner's body found it difficult even to go past the scene of death. The ambiguous status of both the cell and the body is apparent in the following comment: 'At first I tried to avert my eyes when going past the cell, but I *made* myself look in – and it was just an empty cell.'

As Leibling (1992) has also noted, the impact of suicide on prison officers can be great. Many report feelings of shock, guilt, disappointment, depression and anxiety both at the time of the death and during the time surrounding inquest proceedings. When a suicide occurs, prison officers initially respond in very different ways. Some officers laugh and joke about what has happened (the 'That's one less for dinner'/'There's an extra portion of chips going spare now'/'Hope it's not stew on the menu today' approach). Others simply shrug their shoulders – theirs is the 'This is a prison, he's a prisoner, so what?' approach. Yet others tell 'dead body stories' (these officers recount the details of the scene of death over and over again) or take a 'good riddance' attitude (the 'That's one less to mug a granny' approach). In contrast, other officers – particularly those who discover the body or had a particularly good relationship with the deceased – may be visibly shocked and upset. Despite these feelings, these officers may also prefer not to talk to the care team, even though debriefings after events such as suicide, hostage and riots are intended to enable people to create a meaningful narrative of what happened to them and hence 'move on'. Several officers, for example, said they preferred to talk to their wives and partners, yet they had been approached on numerous occasions by members of the care team, who advised that they should also talk to *them*. These approaches were often resented; as one of the officers put it: 'I felt that they almost wanted me not to cope so that they would have some caring to do.' This 'sheep dip' approach to counselling (Tehrani 1999) – the blanket use of post-trauma intervention 'just in case' – is indeed a controversial one (see McFarlane 1988; Raphael *et al.* 1995; Bourne and Oliver 1998).

Given concerns from various quarters (see, e.g., Liebling 1992; HMCIP 1999; about the growing numbers of suicides in prisons, I want to make, at this point, a comment on what I shall (hesitatingly) term a 'culture of staff carelessness' that was evident, albeit to significantly varying degrees, in all the prisons of this study. There have been numerous accounts, in the literature and reports on prisons, of the tendency of some officers to behave in a blasé manner towards the prisoners in their care – i.e. ignoring or jamming cell bells (on the presumption that the prisoner simply wants a light for his cigarette or such like) and claiming that potentially suicidal prisoners are just 'trying it on' or 'just trying to get attention'. Indeed I heard and saw this for myself throughout the course of my research. Clearly, such attitudes and behaviour can never be justified, not least because prison officers have a legal 'duty of care' towards prisoners. None the less, as Liebling (1998: 76) notes, such attitudes may (at least to some extent) be *understandable*. She observes that officers who *as a group* feel unvalued and uncared-for, and who often have more prisoners than cells, are likely to deny and minimise prisoners' problems and to express frustration and other negative attitudes towards prisoners requesting attention. In short, unsupported staff may be more likely to leave prisoners unsupported. Arguably officers' common and long-standing refrain that 'prisoners get more than we do' is extremely pertinent here.

Prisoner dissent

As we have seen, control is achieved, in the main, through positive staff–prisoner relations. Sometimes, however, control is lost, both at the collective or (more usually) the individual level. When prisoners do not conform, and control breaks down, officers have a number of responses at their disposal to try to regain it. The first, and most obvious, response is for the officer simply to talk to the prisoner, since unco-operative behaviour often stems from feelings of anxiety, from fall-outs with other prisoners or from receiving bad news. Another response available to the officer is to put the prisoner 'behind his door' until he quietens down. If such measures fail, more formal, reactive mechanisms are set in train. Methods of controlling resistant prisoners have changed somewhat over the years; the formal reactive response used throughout the 1960s and 1970s – what some officers called the 'mêlée of fist, staves and feet' – has been replaced by a 'technology of the body' known as 'control and restraint' (see below) – a reactive response which is (or is supposed to be), clinical, methodical and strategic. Abusive and inappropriate methods for dealing with prisoners do, however, still exist and as we have seen are still put into practice.

Dissent[1] in prison may present itself in a variety of forms; everyday dissent includes 1) prisoner-on-staff assaults (some serious, others less so); and 2) prisoner-on-prisoner assaults. When dissent takes place, the prisoner (or prisoners) is usually removed to the segregation unit, either under 'control and restraint' or, if the prisoner is calm, by allowing him to walk there, escorted but under his own steam. Attempts have increasingly been made to deal with dissent proactively through good prison management. Proactive management of dissent depends on forward planning and introducing consistency and predictability into the regime (Barclay *et al.* 1994). As Barclay *et al.* note, two Reports – Dunbar's (1987) *Sense of Direction* and the Woolf Report (1991) – envisaged concepts which are applicable to the management of dissent. The former pointed to the need to achieve 'dynamic security'[2] while the latter emphasised the need to strike a balance between security, control and justice. Both are concerned with the management of dissent on a day-to-day basis. Sometimes, however, proactive strategies to manage dissent are ineffective and staff must resort to reactive strategies. As we have already seen from the comments of long-serving officers, the removal of prisoners to the punishment block was often a brutal affair. Although most long-serving officers are glad that they had 'got past the days of blood and snot on the landings' (male officer, Lancaster Farms pers. comm.), apocryphal stories (illustrative but not necessarily entirely accurate) about old methods of subduing unco-operative inmates still survive and are retold on the landings. They tell of groups of staff protecting themselves with old mattresses and using whatever means they could to restrain prisoners. Before the development of C&R the removal of unco-operative prisoners from their cells was carried out in a 'chaotic' as well as brutal fashion, as illustrated by the following comments (all ranks, all six prisons pers. comm.):

Before C and R, we were mob-handed. We all piled in. I remember during one scuffle the SO shouted 'whoever's got hold of my leg will they let go?' (Male officer, Stoke Heath)

There was much more rough-and-tumble before C&R. The methods of subduing an inmate have changed; all you could rely on before was numbers. You just all piled on! (Senior officer, Wymott)

There were no set guidelines for dealing with violent inmates before C&R came in. You just gave inmates a hammering. (Senior officer, Lancaster Farms)

C and R put an end to a lot of staff-on-inmate violence ... All you had before, basically, was a mattress and about ten officers [each] with a stick. (Senior officer, Stoke Heath)

> Previously, we had no strategy for dealing with it ['trouble' from inmates]. It was just a mass fight. (Male officer, Wymott)

Officers told me that in these circumstances, injuries to prisoners were often deliberately inflicted. For example, officers attempting to remove an unco-operative prisoner from a cell simply: 'used a mattress and just splattered the inmate against the back wall' (principal officer and C&R trainer). As I suggested earlier, the removal of a prisoner to the segregation unit was often an opportunity for other officers to 'settle old scores'; as one senior officer recalled: 'In the old days, if an inmate played up on the wing, you'd get an officer run in and give him a kick and then disappear into the background.' Dissent was also managed medically. According to an ex-Parkhurst officer:

> It was a case of jump on where you could ... and we used the wicker suit and large doses of muscle relaxant.

Following the creation of minimum use of force tactical intervention squads (MUFTI) in the 1970s (such squads were developed and used to break up demonstrations and disturbances) prisons began routinely to employ MUFTI techniques when dealing with disruptive individuals. On such occasions, teams of officers, wearing hard building-site hats, thick gloves and carrying batons and perspex shields, would enter cells and remove the prisoner to the segregation unit. The only real difference from what went before was that they had abandoned the old mattress and acquired a perspex shield, gloves and a hat; according to numerous officers, the 'minimum use of force' part was somewhat inaccurate. As they recall, 'staff still just piled in and did as much damage as possible to the inmate'.

Those of my interviewees who had worked in the Prison Service in the 1970s commented that offering violence to prisoners was never questioned – it was simply what one *did*: 'Risley was a brutal regime. We'd beat them up and throw them in the corner of the cell, and if they looked at you, you'd beat them up a bit more. We didn't know any different then.' However, even when they did 'know different', many staff simply carried on, sometimes with the full knowledge of their managers:

> [When I worked at Strangeways], some officers went further than shouting and bawling; they used physical force on a fairly regular basis. [How did they get away with this?] They got away with it 'cos those in charge turned a blind eye. (Male officer, Lancaster Farms)

The regime in place at Strangeways up until 1990 has, of course, been discussed a great deal (see especially Woolf 1991). It was a regime in which antagonism between staff and prisoners was intense, and where 'pay back' was commonplace. Describing the occupational culture of Strangeways in that period, this same officer commented:

> If an alarm went off, a mêlée ensued — you'd get officers running 300 yards just to get a punch in! [Really? Why?] Oh yeah. Cos they had this macho image they wanted to live up to. I've never seen that in the whole of the five years I've been at Lancaster Farms. You get physical force, but not brutalising of inmates for the sake of it.

The following quotation illustrates the *communicative* quality of staff violence; it is intended as an individual and general deterrent:

> Hand on heart, I've never seen un-called-for violence in *this* jail, but traditionally, if a prisoner performed, you bounced him off every wall on the way to the block! That was to show *others*, as well as him, that officers wouldn't put up with that. (Senior officer, Lancaster Farms)

Similarly:

> At Manchester, the, the heavy mob – which was just a collective term for whoever was free at the time – was quite impressive. And they sent out a very clear message: 'If you behave yourselves, you've got nothing to fear from us, but if you come on strong, this lot will come for you.'

Aggressive displays such as these are iconic and indexical (Pierce 1940). Weaponry, costume (in this case riot gear) and the thudding of running feet demonstrate the threat posed to those who refuse to conform in prisons. This threat is signalled both to the rule-breaker and the potential rule-breaker; it sends out a message to all that rule-breakers will be dealt with.

Technologies of the body: control and restraint

It was not until 1983 that C&R procedures were developed. C&R is a reactive, but defensive method of physically dealing with prisoners. It uses controlled actions aimed at minimising physical injury, according to laid-down rules of authority and accountability (Barclay *et al.* 1994: 161). The basis of C&R is a team of three officers; two officers restrain the prisoner by the application of wrist-locks and the third officer holds the prisoner's head. C&R procedures are carried out at three different levels. Level 1 is restricted to the use of arm locks, cell removals and breakaway techniques. All uniformed staff are trained to this level. Level 2 involves training in the correct use of staves and shields. Staff trained to Level 3 (C&R advanced) are taught riot control techniques and strategies for barricade removal; only staff trained to advanced level are permitted to attend an 'Operation Tornado', i.e. engage in riot control (see below). These officers do not only work in riot situations; they can also be put on stand-by if, say, the drug dogs are brought in to search cells and staff suspect they will face resistance from prisoners.

Generally speaking, the introduction of C&R has reduced the level of injuries to both staff and prisoners, but on occasion C&R techniques *have* caused injuries to prisoners, usually because specific holds have been applied incorrectly or for too long. Annual refresher training is now mandatory (see IG 90/1996) following an increasing number of formal complaints from prisoners that they had been injured by inadequately trained staff.

Collective dissent: riots and riot control

Much less common than day-to-day altercations between prisoners, and between prisoners and staff, are incidents of hostage-taking and collective disturbances. Clearly, the Prison Service must be prepared for incidents of serious conflict with prisoners and it is for this reason that the Prison Service ensures that a certain number of officers are trained in C&R techniques to an advanced standard.

When a collective disturbance takes place at a prison, three-man teams trained to an advanced standard are combined together. When the disturbance occurs elsewhere, i.e. in another prison, six teams of three (eighteen officers) are initially sent from establishments nearest the one in difficulty. If the disturbance worsens, officers are drawn from prisons further afield. These Operation Tornado staff wear protective clothing comprising a helmet with visor (some with radio headsets), boots, shin guards, a 'box' to protect genitals, a stout leather belt, fire-proof overall and heavy-duty gloves. They carry side-handled batons and transparent short or long shields that can withstand repeated poundings and stabbings by make-shift weapons such as scaffolding poles, and protect officers from a variety of projectiles that may be hurled by prisoners as the teams advance forward (length of shield determines the position in team, i.e long shields in front, short shields behind).

Riot training

Riot training is noisy and dirty and officers are often hurt in the process. It is, however, a spectacular sight for the observer; as I stood on a gantry I was able to observe scores of officers form serried ranks which move forward, act, split, move forward, act, split and so on, removing 'barricades' as they advance into the 'prison'[3] itself. Even during riot training the noise and the smoke are intense and the 'conflict' is extremely realistic.[4] As I watched, officers held on to each other's belts as they progressed through the smoke, while 'prisoners' (trainers kitted out in orange boiler suits) hurled obscenities and lumps of wood (which rained down on helmets and visors) and delivered blows with scaffolding poles. As I watched, one male officer was hit in the mouth by a block of wood (he had forgotten to lower his visor) and another two officers (both of them men) fell down a flight of stairs.

C&R advanced training is strenuous and, despite the protective clothing, entails a relatively high risk of some degree of physical injury (sprains and cuts are commonplace). The course is, none the less, a very popular one amongst uniformed staff, especially younger officers taking part in the course. All the latter told me they had found it 'exhilarating' and 'exciting' but also 'scary'. The riot scenario proceeds in as realistic a manner as possible; realism is certainly achieved, given the comments from this Lancaster Farms officer who had taken part in it:

> It's very heavy on your arms holding up the shields for hours. Your visor's all steamed up, you're dripping with sweat ... you're knackered. The first day it's blocks of wood, then it's bricks bouncing off your helmet and it hurts sometimes 'cos it jars your head ... The adrenalin kicks in though, and when you do the arrest [of the 'prisoners'] – even though they're your colleagues – you really do have to stop and think about what you're doing. The 'red mist' descends, it really does ...

It is common for officers to get emotionally 'carried away' with the excitement of riot training. One of the trainers commented that officers sometimes get so involved in what they are doing that they 'switch off' and are no longer able to respond to trainers' instructions. As the trainer put it: 'Somebody's in but the bloody lights are out! They nod [when you tell them to do something] but then they go and do something different.'

Several officers admitted to having succumbed to an overwhelming feeling of anger during the 'riot'. This is one such comment: 'You get carried away doing the training ... You'd make a pact with your mate not to hurt each other but you do. You can't help it' (male officer, Lindholme Training Unit).

Given the physical intensity of the training, it helps if the officers are physically fit; unfortunately not all officers are: as one officer put it 'For fit lads, it was okay but my arms were trembling like hell with holding the shield up above my head for so long.'

Discussing the poor levels of fitness of some of the officers taking part in the course, one trainer remarked that although the criterion for attendance was that the officer should be fit physically and mentally, many were neither. He remarked that in terms of physical fitness: 'I've seen some that have come in here and they couldn't blow a bloody candle out!'

At the time of my observations, officers did not have to produce a medical certificate to show that they were physically fit to gain a place on the course. However, the trainers understood that the Prison Service was aiming to have mandatory certification in place by the year 2000. Neither, at the time of my observations, was the service fully geared up for women officers to engage in riot training. The protective clothing was too big for most of the female officers; as a result they had to roll up their overalls, wear foam in their helmets to make them smaller and make do with shin-pads so long that they came up to their knees. The trainers told me that this problem was also being addressed.

On each training course there are, perhaps inevitably, usually one or two 'loose canons' – officers who are 'out of control' during the scenarios (C&R trainers pers. comm.). These officers act over-aggressively. In contrast, some officers 'freeze' when they are confronted by an angry group of 'prisoners' who are screaming and shouting. In real-life situations, the intensity of prison disturbances – the noise (the banging of scaffolding poles on metal gates, the shouting, swearing and threats from prisoners), the darkness (all lights on the landings and stairways may be extinguished) and the smoke from burning buildings – sometimes proves too much for officers to cope with, particularly if they have arrived at the disturbance with ongoing personal problems of their own. These officers may suffer from post-traumatic stress syndrome and have to retire from the service (PSSCWS pers. comm.).

Riots as repair work

In some circumstances, however, riots can be beneficial to the morale of both uniformed staff and governors. When staff feel that staff–prisoner relations are no longer 'right' (i.e. when they feel that the prisoners are outside their control) they may wish for a riot, because that will put an end to the status quo and create a space for change. When the then governor of one of the prisons in this study commented that he thought staff stress levels had fallen since the most recent riot at his establishment, I asked him, hesitantly, if that meant that the riot had had some positive results. He agreed that this was indeed the case: 'We felt so fed up about the place we felt like giving the inmates a box of matches. But in the end, they got their own matches [and the prison was much better afterwards].' Similarly, from a male officer working in the same prison at the same time: 'The riot was the best thing that happened to us.'

Riots are also significant events for the reaffirming of staff solidarity and for the identification of 'suspect' staff:

> If things go well, staff feel they can rely on each other again in similar situations. They're very quick to make derogatory remarks about their colleagues though … For example, if they are asking for staff to go to a riot [at another prison], and one declines, some officers will be very quick to claim he has 'bottled out'.

Prison riots generate a mixture of emotions. Although acutely aware of the anxieties which grip their families when riots take place (see Chapter 8) many officers find riots exciting – good fun even:

> Riots are very stressful for wives, but brilliant for male officers … In riots, you *know* that you can't lose. If there's a chance of that, you wait for reinforcements. Basically you're a highly organised and trained team versus a rabble.

Prison riots, then, can both generate and rekindle staff solidarity: as one officer put it 'this is what it's all about … [During riots] All past differences go out the window' (male officer, Portland). Several officers also commented on the polarising effect of riots – in such circumstances the staff–prisoner relationship becomes explicitly one of 'Them and Us'. Relatedly, many officers commented on the more positive effects of disturbances on staff morale, especially the reaffirming of comradeship. The following comment from a principal officer is illustrative of all these issues: '[When there's a riot] It's "Them and Us" without any doubt then … [afterwards] there's a good buzz about the place … [with sandwiches and that.] Also, disturbances allow officers to "get a bit of venom out".' 'Getting a bit of venom out' relates to 'pay back' (see above), but it also indicates the extent of officers' routine management of resentment, anger and frustration.

Concluding comments

The most exhilarating form of action available to prison officers is responding to a riot situation. A major disturbance is, for prison officers, both a highly symbolic and functional event. It makes (dramatically) explicit the notion of 'Us' and 'Them' and in so doing coalesces a staff group that may be demoralised and fragmented into a cohesive force with a communal aim – that of overpowering 'the enemy'. In such situations, petty squabbles and rivalries are forgotten and teamwork is to the fore; whatever their earlier differences with colleagues, prison officers are ready to do whatever it takes to regain the establishment and look after each other. Officers' tales about their feelings *before* ('When you're on the bus going to the prison you're shitting yourself 'cos you don't know what to expect'), *during* ('at Strangeways you could hear the helicopters overhead and see the spotlights flashing by the windows ... it was like being in Vietnam') and *after* the operation to retake a prison are important for the maintenance of the occupational culture and for raising morale. In attempting to theorise the significance of the riot for achieving as well as maintaining solidarity, it may be fruitful to borrow, from anthropology, the concept of the 'ceremony of aggregation', whereby the riot becomes a ceremony 'in which social relations that have been interrupted are about to be renewed' (Radcliffe-Brown 1952: 243 but see also Kuper 1983).

As I indicated earlier, riots are not, of course, everyday occurrences. Rather, many prisons usually manage to 'go on' from week to week, from month to month and from year to year with relatively few serious conflicts between prisoners and staff. When conflict does occur, it is usually at the individual rather than the collective level. Moreover, conflicts in prisons are not solely prisoner–staff conflicts. On the contrary, disagreements between individual officers, groups of officers and between officers and their managers constituted a significant degree of conflict in every prison in this study, and these divisions are rooted in the ideologies and working practices and styles of individual members of uniformed staff. It is to these issues that I turn in the next chapter.

Notes

1   Dissent in prisons can broadly be conceived as any episode or expression of non-conformity to generally accepted and established rules or practices. Although dissent may start at a simple level as verbal attacks, it often spirals into more complex conflict situations that are difficult to manage (Barclay *et al.* 1994: 158).

2   'Dynamic security' (i.e. security resulting from well developed staff–prisoner relationships and an active regime) is recognised by many prison managers as more important than physical security in the maintenance of control. Dynamic security is characterised by strong visible leadership and good communication; control depends upon staff knowing what is going on (Dunbar 1985).

3   At HMP Lindholme, where these observations took place, the training 'scenarios' were carried out in and around the 'landings' of mock prison wings located inside a large aircraft hanger. Each 'wing' was built to a different design; for example one was designed like a Victorian galleried wing (where sight-lines were relatively good) and another as a 'spurred' wing where sight-lines were extremely poor.

4   Because of new health and safety guidelines, the C&R scenario has had to be 'toned down'. According to C&R trainers, the scenario 'used to be like a pub room brawl … We used to use concrete blocks and that'.

Chapter 7

How prison officers see their work, themselves and each other

Prison officers, then, are a diverse group, and they defend distinctly different visions and versions of the prison officer role. They differ significantly in their attitudes towards (and subsequently their treatment of) prisoners; these differences derive, in part, from officers' views on 1) the causes of crime; and 2) the purpose of imprisonment and how this purpose can be best achieved. As I suggested earlier, these competing views can generate (often significant) tensions, resentments and conflicts between prison officers.

In the first part of this chapter I describe how officers working in the 'mainstream' regimes of the six prisons in this study see their work. In the next two parts I consider how officers see themselves and each other while in part four I consider how officers see the prison. As we shall see, inter-staff conflicts as to what the prison officer role should consist of, how the job should be done and who should be doing it, are often intense. For officers working in 'specialist' regimes such as the thera-peutic community (TC) and on programmes such as the Sex Offender Treatment Programme (SOTP), conflicts with fellow officers may be pronounced, and they must develop coping strategies to deal with them. There is a methodological point to be made here. To identify the dominant cultural norms of prison officers, I found it valuable to be present when these norms were challenged. At such times and in such contexts, officers were often put under pressure to defend their values and beliefs to 'mainstream' colleagues. Prison work such as SOTP tutoring and therapeutic counselling clearly stretches the boundaries of what the prison officer role *can* be, but officers each have their own views as to what that role *should* be. This tension can foster (sometimes extremely strong) feelings of resentment and frustration. By way of illustration, the final part of this chapter draws upon empirical data from two 'specialist' regimes.

How prison officers see their work

In the early stages of my research I was rather puzzled at the disparity in responses to the question 'How do you see your role?' Despite the many changes that have taken place within the service, numerous officers claimed that their role had shrunk. They argued that a variety of jobs, including those entailing the supervision of prisoners in prison gardens and farms, had previously kept them armed with a range of skills, but now that these jobs were gone,[1] they were 'back to square one'. These officers reflected on how, prior to the mid-1990s, one of the tasks of the prison officer was to escort prisoners to court and to act as 'dock man' until prisoners had been dealt with. The job of dock officer had been a popular one; it represented a day away from the wings and allowed the officer the opportunity to mix with different people, such as court professionals, police officers and prison officers from other prisons. This role, along with that of gate officer and communications officer, provided variety, got people off the wings and provided some respite from prisoners. Unable to get involved in rehabilitative work (there is a finite amount of such work available, and anyway, *somebody* has got to work on the landings) and with no access to prison duties that might take them outside the prison or away from prisoners (court and escort duties have now been contracted out and operational-support-grade staff (OSGs) have taken over many of the inmate-free tasks previously available in the communications room and the gatehouse), these officers are restricted to tasks that are primarily custodial. The loss of inmate-free jobs is regretted, especially by older, long-serving prison officers and by officers who work in particularly demanding environments. Many of these officers would welcome the chance to leave the 'coal face' and be inmate-free occasionally:

> You're at the cutting edge all day long now. Before you could go up to the cutting edge and then go away from it, but now you're condemning a man to nose-to-nose confrontation because prison auxiliaries [now operational support grade] are taking all these cushy jobs.

Similarly:

> Budgetting restraints etcetera have de-skilled staff. All the variety
> has been given away [to save money]. Even those that are doing the
> courses will probably find they're soon being run by contracted-out
> people from the local college, or scout groups or whatever!? (Male
> officer, Garth)

In contrast, other officers claimed that they had had the opportunity to
become involved in a variety of interesting, rehabilitative work with
prisoners, such as the delivery (and in some cases development of)
courses oriented towards drug awareness and good parenting. As a
result these officers felt that they had acquired additional valuable skills.
One explanation for the stark contrast in the views of these two groups
was suggested to me by a senior officer working at Lancaster Farms:

> [I'm a bit confused because I can see officers running courses, and
> doing things that get them more involved with inmates, but on the
> other hand, I keep hearing other officers say that they are being
> reduced to turnkeys again. So there seems to be some contradiction
> here.] Right. Well there is a view, held by some staff, that they don't
> get a fair crack of the whip *vis-à-vis* more rewarding jobs. People do
> not like spending their time unlocking doors for people – the
> hospital want this, visits want that – which is what I spend most of
> my time doing. They all accept that lockin' 'em up is what the job is
> really about, but when it comes to the more, er, interesting
> activities, some people get the chance to get into all that sort of stuff
> and some people don't. Mind you, they don't all *want* to get into
> these sort of jobs, but they still get a little bit hacked off when
> they're doin' all the runnin' around for somebody else to get all the
> brownie points, er, and I understand that. That's why on this wing
> my objective, my ideal, my aim, is to have every officer on [here]
> able to do any session of the induction – for *their* benefit, so that
> they feel confident, that on any day they can do anything they're
> asked to do on induction. He can do Anti-bullying One, he can do
> Anti-bullying Two, and I want him to be able to do the HIV session,
> I want him to do the Coping session, I want everyone to do that,
> 'cos it's better jobs for them. That's my aim. But its a lot harder than
> you might think. You have to accept the fact that not all prison
> officers are gonna make teachers. Not all prison officers want to be.
> But most of the other interesting jobs they could have done have
> gone.

The examples I have provided above are at two ends of a spectrum, and relate primarily to job *content*. In between are various other viewpoints on the job that relate more to the *context* in which the job gets done – for example that the job is 'unpredictable' – or to the emotions that the job generates – for example that the job is 'stressful' (see Chapter 5).

Much of prison life *is* mundane, routine and boring for both staff and prisoners, especially at weekends when there is no work or education and few other activities for prisoners to get involved in. Weekend boredom for prison officers is particularly pronounced at adult prisons such as Garth, where prisoners tend to seek officers' company much less than young offenders do. Because Garth prisoners were allowed to enter the cells of other prisoners (provided of course that they have been invited to do so) to chat, smoke, play cards, watch television and so on, they tended not to need the company of uniformed staff, for whom weekends are thus rather tedious: 'After you've read all the papers and that, there's nothing else to do' (male officer, Garth).

Numerous officers in all the prisons in this study said that they found the job boring. By and large, these officers were those who, for one reason or another, were not involved to any degree in the delivery of courses. When asked to sum up his job, this long-serving officer working at Wymott offered the following, rather bleak description:

> It's like standing at a bus stop waiting for a bus that never comes. You spend a bit of time looking around when you're waiting for the bus, looking at the different people in the queue, and the posters and that, but after a bit you get fed up looking at it. To me, that's what this job is. For me, the bus comes when it's time to go home. Others think it's wonderful, but for me, the job satisfaction is nil. When you're talking to the same dead-beats every day, with the same questions … Its like asking a road-sweeper if he finds his job interesting and stimulating. You're not here to enjoy yourself. You're here to earn money.

It is clear that 'the pay' was the primary reason for this officer's continuing employment in the Prison Service. Similarly, when asked whether or not he found his job rewarding, a senior officer working at Portland YOI replied: 'No. Boys come and go. They're of no significance really … to the vast majority of staff anyway. It's like working in any factory really. The staff make the job.'

Despite current expectations (see in particular the current recruitment literature) that prison officers will think of themselves as professionals, and that they will engage with the goals and vision of the Prison Service, the perception that prisoners are 'of no significance' is actually fairly common. As we saw in Chapter 5, prisoners are often seen by officers as merely 'bodies' to be processed. Officers who had, in the past, worked in large local prisons which have relatively few resources to draw upon to put the Prison Service Statement of Purpose[2] into practice (particularly the second part), noted that in such prisons uniformed staff were often able to do little more than ensure that every prisoner was counted, fed and bathed. For this reason, officers working in such prisons were often described by officers working in more stimulating regimes as 'just sheep-herders' (male officer, Lancaster Farms pers. comm.).

As I suggested earlier, however, many of my interviewees were acutely aware that 'getting involved' and 'getting skills' was a way of improving their chances of 'survival' in an age in which a 'job for life' can no longer be guaranteed – not even in the Prison Service:

> [Attending training courses and running classes] ... gives you a feather in your cap. And you need that to *survive* – to guarantee yourself a job ... VERSE got rid of a lot of the older ones; now *they've* gone, who'll be next [in the next round of job cuts]? (Male officer, Garth)

Many officers get a great deal of satisfaction from 'human services' work such as running inmate development courses. Indeed, some of these officers think that they could, and should, be allowed to take on much more of this type of work, on the grounds that they are as competent as the professional teachers whose services are bought in from the local colleges: 'Why pay teachers' wages to run an evening class for example, when we could do it just as well?' (male officer, Lancaster Farms). The belief that prison officers are just as capable as many specialist staff is commonplace in prisons. Indeed, prison officers have, over the years, insisted that they were better placed to do human services work than 'outsiders' because they, more than anybody, understand prisoners (on this see, e.g., Thomas 1972; May 1979). The presence of prison specialists has also long been resented by officers because specialists are seen as restricting the scope of officers' own employment. From my observations, prison psychologists seem to be particularly begrudged. They were regarded by the majority of my interviewees as a high-profile occupational group who, in the current treatment/risk-oriented climate, got a disproportionately high level of their prison's available financial resources and a status that was undeservedly influential. Employing psychologists in the prison at all was also seen by some officers as yet another indication of the Prison Service's tendency to treat prisoners better than staff. According to this officer working at Lancaster Farms:

> Having a psychology department is a good example of giving everything to inmates and nothing to staff. They're bringing more inmates in and putting them all on courses, and then they're cutting staff and then sending them on courses to see if they're getting stressed or not. It's fucking stupid isn't it?

Resentment may stem partly from the fact that prison officers often perceive themselves as psychologists all bar the training; as people who are good at 'reading' other people (prisoners in particular) and predicting what prisoners will (or will not) do. One officer, for example, claimed that: 'Prison officers are the most experienced, untrained and unpaid psychologists in the Prison Service.'

I'm a prison officer, not a teacher!

While all officers wish to be seen (by both colleagues and prisoners) as competent in the tasks oriented towards custody, not all officers wish to be seen as good teachers. On the contrary, there is a certain amount of stigma attached to (what prison officers describe as) 'teaching',[3] not least because teaching often entails sustained interaction with prisoners. Officers who teach are in a minority; not simply because there is not enough of this kind of work to go around, but because officers who would like to try it may be dissuaded from doing so by other uniformed staff: 'you get a lot of peer pressure not to do it. [Why?] I don't know. Jealousy or whatever' (male officer, Garth).

This officer pointed out that prison officers who volunteer to extend their role beyond the basic custodial one are often the subject of adverse comments from their peers, along the lines that they are 'arse-creepers' or 'empire-builders'. As a result, many officers emphatically refuse to run classes with prisoners. As I suggested above, refusal to teach may be rooted in a firm belief that 'teaching' is not a proper part of the prison officer role. An officer with almost a quarter of a century in the service put it this way: 'I'm used to being a prison officer, not a teacher. It'd be like telling a teacher to come and be a prison officer.'

On the other hand, a refusal to teach may stem from neither ideological principles nor social conformity. Rather, it may reflect officers' fear of failure, or more specifically officers' awareness that they do not have the ability or confidence to teach. As such, officers' apparent lack of interest in teaching may hide very real fears of looking incompetent in the classroom. According to one officer who was reluctant to get involved in the Inmate Development Programme: 'I wouldn't want to do the IDPR 'cos I haven't got the capability to do it ... It's a personality thing. It's probably a coward's way out. I just don't want to let anybody down – colleagues or inmates' (male officer, Garth).

Moreover, an officer's recognition that he has only a very superficial understanding of the course material can be extremely unnerving. As this male officer working at Garth reflected:

> I did a two-day course on anger management, and a presentation-skills course, also two days. And then I'm supposed to present a course with some very angry people! Packages that are put in place at a dispersal, by the time they get here they've been cut and hashed and bodged. If somebody [on the course] says to me 'Well how should you deal with so-and-so?', I'd have to say 'I'll look it up in the manual'.

An officer's refusal to teach may thus be a face-saving strategy:

> They refuse more out of trepidation than anything else. Basically, they don't think they will be *able* to do it and so they say they're not interested to save face. Once they've had some training though, and got a bit of confidence, and they've sat in with the others that are doing it, they love it. You can't keep them *out* then. (Senior officer, Lancaster Farms)

As we can see from the comments of this senior officer, loss of face in the classroom can be prevented simply by providing an officer with adequate training and support. Indeed, quite often those who have received proper training find that they prefer their classroom role to their custodial one. The following quotation from a senior officer, which I include in its entirety, summarises the range of officers' feelings about, and responses to, classroom work admirably:

> You have to accept the fact that not all prison officers are gonna make teachers. Not all prison officers *want* to be. Nobody joined the Prison Service 'cos they wanted to deliver anti-bullying sessions. Nobody. Nobody even thought about it when they joined; these are things that've come up. And some people take to it like a duck to water. Some people end up much rather doing that than anything else. Erm, some people – Danielle's an example – she's a very good unit officer, she works hard – diligent, good relationship with prisoners, [but] she can't deliver induction sessions. She can't do it.

The prospect of goin' in front of a class, er, of prisoners, and spieling to 'em … No … It's horses for courses. Some officers just cannot face the prospect of being a classroom teacher. Now Jack Bridges on the other hand, you try stoppin' 'im! Try stoppin' 'im! He *wants* to be up there. He loves it! 'Get the spotlight on me and watch me perform!' I'll bet you he opens his fridge at home and bursts into song, I'll bet he does! He loves it. Now you see he's always gonna want to do it. His problem is he *always* wants to be doin' that, and doesn't want to be cleaning officer. See that's the other side of the coin. But a lot of them do a bit of all sorts, which is fine.

Once bitten by the teaching bug, some officers are keen to be involved in developing courses as well as delivering them and, as I discovered, are often willing to do so at home in their own time and on their own computers. As the same senior officer notes, however, disappointment is often the reward for such efforts, because there is not enough teaching work to go around:

> Most of the people have picked it up from watching other people do it … Now, just as an example, Jack was involved with the anti-bullying package … they [he and a fellow officer] have put packages together and delivered them, so to a certain extent its their baby, er, Jack wants to develop it, but I mean I've had to put the brakes on Jack a little bit, he … he wants to develop it, and develop it, and develop it, and he says I've built eight new bits into the programme and I said but we only want two! I have to remind him that we're an induction unit.

Officers like Jack were in a minority. At the other extreme I met a small number of officers who resented even *speaking* to prisoners in any capacity other than to issue orders.

In-service training

Many of my interviewees claimed that they had limited access to in-service training, and that some of the training they had received was inadequate for the tasks they were being asked to perform. This was often a big disappointment, especially to those who had taken on extra 'human services' tasks in the prison in an attempt to make their job more interesting and/or to enhance career development. This was particularly true for many officers working as tutors on the Sex Offender Treatment Programme and for officer-counsellors working in the therapeutic community.

The majority of my interviewees said that access to specific training courses was problematic. Although a number of mandatory training hours for uniformed staff (six days per annum per officer at the time of my research) are built into the systems of attendance, staff sickness, leave and general staffing problems made even this difficult to achieve. According to one principal officer (YOI) in charge of training:

> It's easy enough to *arrange* training courses. The problem is getting management to release the staff to attend them. Management have their own priorities and agendas, such as making sure there are enough staff on their own wings.

Many of my interviewees were angry that they had been prevented from attending training sessions because of staff shortages on the wings. Some claimed that a significant amount of the training that *had* been delivered had been delivered via a 'Chinese whispers' approach. They claimed that sentence planning, through-care and even suicide awareness training were often delivered in the following way, i.e. a small number of officers (approximately half a dozen) attend a course, return to the prison and proceed to teach the rest of the staff. Thus the six newly trained staff became the 'experts'. However, these 'experts' said that they often found themselves having to cut corners when teaching others because of a lack of resources – in particular lack of time. In other words, they had to modify what they had learnt. Consequently, they felt that the officers they trained might not be trained in the way that the training manual intended. Rather worryingly, this principal officer in charge of training said that he even had difficulties putting training oriented towards security and suicide prevention into operation when both staff and hours were in short supply:

> For example, HQ comes up with a package – say suicide awareness. The length of time that officers are supposed to spend on this is eight hours. In practice, however, only the training officer has this long. Other officers only get two hours – just the key aspects of the package. Whatever the stated visions, values and goals, corners are cut. Security and suicide awareness are not supposed to be skimped on, because if failures occur here the Prison Service can be brought into disrepute. Put more bluntly, the shit hits the fan. In practice, however, sometimes they have to be skimped on.

He went on to say that in reality:

> The service cannot possibly deliver all of their [training] packages
> because there's not enough hours in a day. For example, the jail-
> craft package is a seven-day one, but that's had to be reduced to the
> bare bones so that it takes up only two days of staff time. This is
> because headquarters have just no idea of operations. They don't
> realise that staff can't *deliver* all these packages. They aren't aware
> of what can get in the way to hamper putting the package to
> everybody.

Several officers complained that it was difficult even to get training to
operate the prison computer system. As I sat with a group of officers in
Lancaster Farms, I was told by one of them that:

> Staff here have had no training on using the computer. They just
> install it and then you have to get on with it – word of mouth. It's
> ridiculous. You just play with the buttons till you find what you
> want. Or you ask somebody – and then we *all* play with the buttons!

The prison officer and the police officer

Readers will recall that in Chapter 1 I suggested that it is helpful to
compare prison work to policing, and that I argued for certain
similarities in the ways that police and prison officers think about their
work. While certain cognitive responses *are* common to both
occupations, as we have already seen, striking differences also exist
between these two occupational groups. While many prison officers
acknowledge that their role is to some extent one of law enforcement – in
the sense that they must ensure that prisoners conform to the Prison
Rules – they tend not to feel that their job is closer to policing than to
other occupations. On the contrary, numerous officers said that they felt
their job was closer to nursing and psychiatric work, not least because
they found themselves having to deal with increasing numbers of
emotionally disturbed or drug-dependent prisoners. As this principal
officer remarked when asked how he thought his job compared to that of
the police:

> Our job is closer to nursing. After the 1970s, the prison officer's role
> changed. It's now a caring profession, in which we go from gaoler
> to mummy. I see us as very much a part of the law enforcement

agency; I see us as a keeper – obviously we are a keeper of people who society and parliament and courts have deemed should be taken away – but, erm, I think we mustn't confuse our roles with those of the police. If there's any comparison, I believe its between us and nurses of mental illness …

Emotive tasks

Certain tasks that prison officers are expected to perform are particularly emotive. When I asked officers which aspects of the job had disturbed or troubled them during their employment in the Prison Service, I found that they varied greatly in terms of the sorts of behaviours, events, situations and types of prisoner they found most difficult to deal with. On the whole, officers who had previously worked in the armed forces, or who had done nursing at some point in their lives, claimed to be more able to cope with potentially embarrassing or distressing events and situations (such as strip-searching prisoners and dealing with suicide and self-harm) than officers who had not. In terms of type of task, a large number of my interviewees said that they found strip-searching unpleasant, and often embarrassing. Acutely aware of the emotions that strip-searching can generate in the prisoner, some officers said that they relied on banter in an effort to reduce the potential for embarrassment and/or conflict. According to this senior officer:

> The training actually reflects the fact that strip-searching is difficult for people. [Does it?] Yes. Yeah, you'd have to be extremely insensitive, not to find it difficult. I mean nobody likes – well, apart from a pervert – nobody likes strip-searching. Nobody likes it. But it's necessary. I mean I don't really want to be rubbin' 'em down, but I've gotta do it. It's part of my job, and, with the kids, you banter with 'em a lot. But I've always talked to prisoners when I'm searchin' 'em. All the time. As far as I'm concerned, er, you … I've always found that while you're chin-waggin' with somebody they find it very difficult to belt you. Very difficult indeed … I mean the minute somebody's got their knickers round their ankles, their dignity disappears. Erm, and certainly in *their* eyes, you've got so much *power* over them … they're there with their dangly bits floppin' in the breeze. They're vulnerable. Erm, it brings home to them the fact that they're in prison that you can do that. But I don't *wanna* see his dangly bits. I don't want, er, him squatting' so I can see if he's got anything rammed up his blinking arsehole but, that is the way it is. It's gotta be done. Fortunately as a senior officer I don't have to do an awful lot of that now.

Several long-serving officers said that they had disliked working with mentally disordered prisoners,[4] particularly since the prisons in which most of these prisoners had been housed had inadequate resources and facilities to meet their needs. Reflecting on the problems of some of the mentally disordered men who had been imprisoned in HMP Strangeways in the 1980s, the same senior officer reflected: 'Oh, God. They'd do stuff like ... they'd be walking along the landing and there'd be turds falling out of their trouser bottoms! Christ it was awful'. Strangeways was, according to this officer and numerous other officers who had worked at the prison throughout the 1970s and 1980s, a place where people with widely differing needs were simply thrown together. They recalled that the prison stank of urine and faeces (as did their own uniforms at the end of the working day), that it was grossly overcrowded, that they regularly ran out of beds and that there was little for prisoners to do. They also reflected that they and other officers were often bored, often brutal, and that they had since felt shocked and dismayed by what they had heard and seen, and what they themselves had done to prisoners. All claimed that in a prison such as Strangeways it had been easy for officers to become insensitive and callous, and to carry out tasks that demeaned prisoners, and they had routinely done so. One officer recalled, for example, the common practice of stripping and scrubbing down rough sleepers who were particularly dirty and smelly with a yard brush. He recalled that he and his colleagues had done so with barely a second thought.

Officers who had worked in newer, less crowded prisons had also encountered tasks and routines that disturbed them. One young officer, who had previously worked in HMP Woodhill's special segregation unit, recalled being troubled by the treatment of disruptive prisoners housed there. Describing the unit, in which he said there was a padded cell with a spy hole in the ceiling through which staff could view the prisoner, he recalled feeling that the treatment of such prisoners was wrong:

> One time, I'd just come on duty, and I heard all this noise coming from the cell. I went to have a look and I saw the inmate, all dressed like in canvas, running about in the cell. He was like a beast in a cage ... it looked really Victorian. It shocked me that did.

This officer said he felt sure that there must be a better, more humane way of dealing with disruptive and disturbed prisoners than was practised in the unit. He had not felt able, however, to discuss his concerns with his colleagues. When I asked why not, he said that there was 'a lot of pressure to be macho, you know ... Those sort of concerns just aren't discussed.' Because he felt unable to discuss his feelings, he did not know if any of his colleagues felt the same way. He said he thought that if he had mentioned that he was upset by what he had seen, his colleagues would make fun of him. So he had kept his feelings to himself.

Some of the officers who were working in the young offender institutions in this study – particularly those with teenage children of their own – said that the sight of distressed young prisoners could be upsetting at times. They also observed, however, that the longer one worked in the job the more 'immune' to prisoners' distress one tended to become. When I asked one officer (a man in his mid-forties) what aspects of the job he found difficult, he replied:

> seeing some of the very young ones come in … and they're very vulnerable and they're frightened – peer pressure and that. And if you're a father with kids the same sort of age, which I am, it gets to you a bit. [So how do you deal with these feelings?] You get hardened to it after a while, sadly.

As we shall see in a moment, most experienced officers feel that they have become 'hardened' by prison work.

Neglected, unvalued, de-sensitised: how officers see themselves

There is a general understanding amongst prison officers that they are unvalued by the general public. Most believe that the general public do not regard prison officers as on a par with other 'public service' workers – a source of resentment and disappointment which is reflected in the following comment:

> We never get a mention on Christmas Day. [On the TV and radio] It's always 'Let's give a thought to the policemen, the nurses, the firemen and the ambulance-men who work on Christmas day.' They never mention prison officers. (Male officer, Lancaster Farms)

Arguably, negative media portrayals of prisons do little to generate admiration or gratitude for those who work in them. The majority of staff commented that they find the term 'warders' derogatory (although the term 'warder' went out of use in 1924 it is still used widely in the press) because it paints an inaccurate picture of what prison officers actually do. Prison officers in general resent stereotypical and skewed portrayals of them and their work, and largely blame the media for the stereotype that prevails:

> To the general public, we're all mindless morons. Everything about prisons is portrayed in a certain way. Even when you get a documentary that's supposed to be about real prison life, they want to make it look different. That Strangeways documentary they did when I was working there, that was a case in point. The producer wanted to portray a certain picture, so he did certain things ... he did one week's programme in the Block, and he portrayed ... he took the camera crew through this gloomy dungeon. The Block at Strangeways was as bright as day! [And] They wanted us to stage-manage alarm bells, and I said I'm not doing *that*. You say you want to do a documentary – show it like it is! 'Cos we didn't spend all day every day beating seven kinds o' muck out of 'em. Or running to alarm bells. Most days were as borin' as hell. (Senior officer, ex-Strangeways, now YOI)

All the officers who participated in my research believed that the public viewed them in a negative light. Given the general public's limited understanding of prisons, and the numerous (and sometimes horrendous) accounts of prison regimes to hit the headlines over the years, they could to some extent understand this. None the less they were still stung by disparaging attitudes towards them and the general lack of recognition for the positive work done by the majority. The following quotation, from a long-serving senior officer working at Lancaster Farms, is presented in its entirety as it reveals the intensity of many officers' feelings of hurt defiance:

> Public opinion has always looked at jailers a bit warily – 'they must be strange to be doin' a job like that'. But I mean that isn't the case at all, there's a wide variety of people from all walks of life doin' it. Er, but stereotypes rule okay. Always have done. [Mind you] When you get high profile, er, jailing, as goes on up there [Lancaster Farms] it undermines the stereotype, and that doesn't do us any harm at all. We'd all agree with that ... But the public are not sympathetic to prison officers; never have been, and as far as I can see, never will be. Whether that is purely through ignorance, erm, or an inbuilt unease about people who deprive other people of their freedom, I don't know. I mean my argument's always been [that] I don't deprive anybody of their freedom – the courts do that. But, you're not gonna get brownie points, erm, from anything to do with

jailers. We're not a sympathetic group ... *We* think we should get more [public approval] 'cos its a bloody shitty job, er, and Joe Public actually wants to be protected from these people ... But I don't think you will cure people's attitudes, overnight. I think it'll take a long long time, if ever. Because at the end of the day, however fancy your jail is, you're putting somebody into a cage. Basically. Erm, and people [think] 'Ooh, don't know about that ...' I think that's got to be behind it. But prison officers haven't helped themselves. In the past they've been reluctant to have people in; you get the group mentality of 'Nobody likes us, everybody hates us, we don't care. Form a circle, round go the wagons, we'll fight anybody'. Jailers have always done that, and always will. 'So you don't like us, so what?' ... And that's the way it's always worked. And we still tend to do it, even at a place like ours. We don't ... deep down, any of us that's been in a long time, don't really think Joe Public's attitude is gonna change ... radically. Some of the younger ones ... er ... may think it will. Some of 'em think that 'cos we're doing all this 'Hey, positive, inmate development, anti-bullying and what-have-you' that they'll get a better relationship with Joe Public ... they won't ... they won't. It doesn't make any difference. 'Cos no matter what they do, inside that jail, in the eyes of people outside, they're jailers, and there's somat not quite right about jailers.

The feelings of this officer, shared by many others like him, translate, on a day-to-day basis, into cautious interactions outside the prison setting. From the same officer:

[What is the attitude of outsiders to you?] Sometimes you get hostility, sometimes you don't. Er, once again it all depends on the area that you're in ... I mean where I live I never used to go there in my uniform at all if I could help it. Because it's a rough area. But I'll walk round town with my uniform on without a worry, I don't care. Like when I was working in London, you'd never see me outside the jail with my uniform on [Would that still apply if you worked down there now?] Yes. Even more so now. Even more so now, yeah. It all depends on the area, you get a feeling of where you are, erm, so yes, I mean, if you're talking to people in Preston, then yeah, I dare say 99.9% of them won't go outside the gate without a suit jacket on.

As I have already indicated, most of the prison officers I spoke to felt that their managers did not like them very much either. This perception can generate a great deal of resentment. It also generates despondency, and a great deal of cynicism about initiatives such as Investors in People. There was a common perception among my interviewees that senior managers within the Prison Service are more interested in 'playing about' with words such as 'excellence' and 'efficiency' than in actually leading, motivating and supporting uniformed prison staff. Whenever I asked officers (all ranks) about the Investors in People initiative, most simply burst out laughing, rolled their eyes to the ceiling or mumbled an expletive. Further questioning prompted the following (and many more, very similar) comments:

> It's a pile of crap. One minute they're telling you you're so important it hurts, the next, they're cutting your legs out from under you. I hear the words 'Investors in People' and my stomach goes queasy ... bilious. Like I'm at sea. (Senior officer, Wymott)

Similarly:

> Investors in People is the biggest load of garbage that the Department has ever put out! It's a numbers game, between staffing, inmates and money. They don't know what people *are*; they're not *interested* in people, let alone investing in them! (Long-serving senior officer, Stoke Heath)

The officers who did not feel this way about management tended to be those who were relatively new to the service. Very few of the officers I spoke to *felt* invested in by their managers; on the contrary, they felt as they always had – unsupported and undervalued. In short they felt – as one (usually mild-mannered) principal officer rather colourfully put it – that the Prison Service had simply placed 'a veneer of excellence over a bucket of shit!'

Although many of the officers I met were unhappy about management styles and decisions, about the relative lack of training available and about the lack of opportunities for promotion, it was also clear that publicly complaining about these sorts of issues made some officers uncomfortable. For these officers, complaining (or 'whingeing') is unmanly. One day when a group of officers working at Lancaster Farms were complaining to me about various aspects of the job, a young, relatively new officer turned to me and rolled his eyes to the ceiling. A little later, when the group had broken up, he insisted that *he* had nothing to complain about. The complaints of these officers were later commented upon by the senior officer who had overheard them; when handing me a cup of coffee he remarked sarcastically, 'Flipping heck. I almost ran in with a box of tissues!' He then jokingly gave us both a handful of tissues, and pretended to dab his eyes. On another occasion in the same office, an officer was complaining to me, at some length, about the lack of support for officers from the 'invisible' governor (that is, the governor that 'never seems to be in the prison'). As he did so, another officer stood behind him pretending to wind him up with a big key. The same senior officer suggested that the latter officer was, in fact:

> engaging in the sort of self-protection that all screws engage in. He actually probably agreed with what the officer was saying but didn't want to appear whiney. Better to appear macho – to appear to be able to cope with all eventualities.

Changed by the job

That they had been 'changed' by prison work was a common perception amongst officers in every prison in this study. Most felt that they had become 'harder' since joining the Prison Service, in the sense that they had become desensitised to the distress and suffering of others. Those who felt that they had started out as relatively sensitive individuals found that over the months and years they had become blasé and insensitive in their dealings with prisoners. They had found that this was particularly the case when they worked in prisons with a high turnover of prisoners with whom they had had relatively little contact, and where the cultural expectation to be 'hard' was relatively intense:

> Everyone's told me I've got harder. Having met death in a variety of ways – through seeing slashings up and so on – it becomes 'So what?' The first suicide we had here [Lancaster Farms] affected a lot of staff badly; if that had happened at Wandsworth when I worked there we'd have just chucked him on the stretcher and made some joke. The warped sense of humour keeps you going. It's a defence mechanism. You grieve privately, not publicly. You can't grieve in this job; people would think you were soft ... I was pleased at the attitude of the staff to the suicide we had here – people who found him talking to each other about how they felt. If I'd been at Wandsworth, I'd have thought 'What are you doing you big wuzzies?' (Senior officer)

Neither does situational violence affect every officer in the same way. As Kauffman (1988: 223) notes, men who have experienced violence before, particularly in military situations, are less affected by the violence they find in the prison than are officers who have not. They have 'seen it all before' and so come to the prison already inured to violence. For officers who have never been in military service, involvement in the prison world *over time* tends to have the same effect; what is at first bizarre and frightening becomes normal, routine. On the whole, people just accept it as being part of the job.

How prison officers see each other

There is (often intense) rivalry between prisons. As I have already suggested, large, Victorian local prisons were (and are) often seen as the 'best' prisons – as the only 'proper prisons' – by the prison officers who work in them. As I shall show in this section, there is also rivalry *within* prisons; between the staff working on different wings and between prison officers working on the same wing. These rivalries are rooted in beliefs about the 'right' working style, the 'proper' way to treat prisoners and the 'best' type of regime.

Group rivalry

The introduction of group working (with Fresh Start) resulted in officers being detailed to specific wings for sustained periods of time (rather than being allocated a wing and a role each morning) and during this time they may have relatively little contact with staff on other wings. Consequently, personal identities tend now to be wing, rather than establishment-based: 'Under Fresh Start, group-working was supposed to improve continuity [of tasks] and it does. But now there are four pictures of the prison, not one general picture ... 'cos each wing does its own thing' (principal officer).

On the one hand, group working can create a greater level of solidarity – at least between the members of each group. On the other hand, group working can impede solidarity within the prison as a whole, because each group has a tendency to put its own interests above those of the other uniformed groups. According to one senior officer at Garth, group working:

> works well, as long as staff have integrity. But what tends to happen is that staff get devious. [Because of the fear of being short-staffed] They start hiding people and gobbling up extra staff when they don't need them. Central detailing gives management more control ... with group-working you can wheel and deal amongst yourselves.

Competition between wings is not entirely new; before group working, prisons had 'subdivisions'. According to the same senior officer, 'one subdivision was always better than another in the eyes of the staff'. Since Fresh Start, competition is simply more pronounced:

> What Fresh Start did was inject gaps; there's a vacuum, er, the group-working system started to split the corporate identity, and you've got one group working against another group. Er, which didn't happen before. At Manchester you worked at the boys' prison or you worked at the main prison, and that was it. But you weren't ... I mean with Fresh Start and the group working – you drew into each other, stopped helping each other, and [and hiding staff?] and hiding *prisoners*! [How do you mean?] Well when you wanted a decent prisoner for working in the canteen, you couldn't get 'em 'cos people would say 'Oh we want him, he's our tea-boy, you're not havin' him'. It was 'No, this is our group, we won't help'. No, everything's gone downhill [since Fresh Start]; morale-wise, control-wise, er, it's all gone. It's all gone.

In short, uniformed work groups tend to 'consume their own smoke', and are often reluctant to help out other wings, even if they know other wings are short staffed. As we have seen from the above quotation, there is also a tendency to 'hide' staff so that other wings will not know how well staffed the wing is.

Wing rivalry (our wing's the best)

Prison wings each have their own distinctive identities. The identity of a particular wing (which is generally rooted in its ethos) as identified by officers who work on it may, or may not, correspond to the identity ascribed to it by officers working on other wings. At Lancaster Farms, for example, Derwent wing ran a relatively relaxed regime, in part because the majority of prisoners on this wing were remand prisoners. This is a comparatively 'difficult' population to control precisely because of their status; many are anxious about impending trials and having difficulty coping with the possibility of a custodial sentence, yet staff working there feel that staff–prisoner relations are relatively positive, largely because officers are flexible and relatively liberal. Amongst staff on other wings, however, the wing was known as 'Darkest Derwent' – a name suggestive of a place that was seen (particularly by those who resented the work of human service staff) as uncivilised and disorderly. Similarly, Garth's C wing was known by staff on other wings as 'The Bronx', because it housed some of the most confrontational prisoners in the prison and because of the apparent heavy drug use amongst prisoners on that wing (one officer claimed that only a fraction of C wing prisoners were *not* using drugs and that virtually all MDT tests were positive). Wymott's I wing, in contrast, was described by some officers as 'like an old folks' home' because a significant proportion of its prisoner population (all of them vulnerable prisoners) were elderly. For officers subscribing to the Punishment credo, the therapeutic community at Portland was the 'bean-bag wing' because officers working there necessarily spent much of their time talking, on a fairly informal basis, to prisoners. The character of a particular wing may be radically different from other wings in the same prison, in terms of the working credos of officers employed there, the nature of the regime and (perhaps in consequence) the attitudes and behaviours of prisoners living there: '[So how does D wing compare to E wing?] It's like going up Park Avenue, and then going up the Bronx. [Why?] 'Cos at the moment all the shits on D wing' (male officer, Garth).

Whatever the wing is like, officers tend to claim that their own wing is the 'best' one to work on, and tell each other cautionary tales about other wings. They recount, for example, how on some wings, prisoners 'do as they like' or 'get too much'. In relation to the latter, officers working on one wing at Lancaster Farms criticised staff on another wing for being too generous with regard to incentives and earned privileges: 'On here, if you look on the board, you'll be hard-pressed to find someone on Gold. On Derwent, they give them out like Smarties (male officer, Windermere wing).

Prison officers also engage in various rituals to assert the superiority of 'their' wing. In at least two of the prisons in this study, officers on different wings competed with each other to see which wing could 'bang up' prisoners the quickest. At HMP Moorland, one wing prided itself on being able to achieve 'bang-up' within a minute of the bell sounding (a brass bell was rung as a final warning to prisoners to get behind their doors). One officer insisted on taking me to see this ritual in operation so that I could to compare it with the speed of 'bang-up' on other wings. It is a source of pride to some officers that their wing can achieve 'bang-up' the quickest, since this is seen as demonstrating to others that officers on this wing are more 'on top of things' than staff on other wings. Perhaps unsurprisingly, however, a reputation for being the wing with the fastest bang-up is not achieved without effort: 'Basically, you've got to keep at it. Visiting and new staff disrupt it a bit' (senior officer, Moorland).

Wings have reputations for being 'too soft' or for being 'lax', for 'running a tight ship' or for being 'hairy' (i.e. intimidating). At Garth, the days I spent on D wing were certainly more eventful than those I spent on E wing. Here are two contrasting extracts from my fieldnotes: 'I'm in the SO's office on D wing, and I've just looked at the clock. It's only eleven o'clock, and so far they've had a fight, a removal to the block and an escaped cockatiel!' On E wing in contrast: 'I'm sitting in the SO's office on E wing. It's 1.30 pm and I haven't even *seen* an inmate. This is very much a back-stage area.'

No shared sense of direction: bean-bags, carrots and big sticks

As an occupational group, prison officers are conscious that they have different attitudes, values and visions, and that in consequence, that they are often pulling in different directions. As one officer from Garth put it: 'Some believe in the balaclava and the big stick. Some believe in talking to cons.' While most officers were of the view that it 'takes all sorts' to run a prison, and that it would be unhelpful if all staff subscribed to the same working credo (most officers agreed that prisons need a 'blend' of staff), they were at the same time frustrated and irritated by the actions (and inactions) of officers who subscribed to different credos from themselves and whom they saw, in consequence, as undermining their own efforts. Those who work hard to develop positive relationships with prisoners complain about pettifogging and authoritarian officers, but perhaps particularly about lazy officers, whom they usually consider to be making their own jobs more difficult and the lives of prisoners more stressful. Lazy staff are those who pass on jobs to their colleagues, who 'hide' when undesirable jobs need doing, who go off 'sick' more often than others and who 'fob off' prisoners seeking help. Close relationships do, however, exist between like-minded groups of staff.

Subordinate resistance: the dilemma of the senior officer

When ordinary-grade officers achieve promotion to the rank of senior officer, they then have to find ways to *perform* that rank. Many officers find it difficult to make the transition to the senior grade because the role is, at least in part, a managerial one. Being promoted to senior officer whilst *in situ* (that is, to the same wing on which the officer is already working) is a particularly difficult transition to make because it requires that officers distances themselves from officers that were previously their peers. According to one principal officer: 'The most difficult transition to make is that from basic grade to SO, because you must divorce yourself from the lads.'

Newly promoted senior officers will also find that their role is an extremely full one. While principal officers have responsibility for the wing itself (principal officers set the policy of the wing or unit), senior officers are responsible for the everyday running of the wing. It is a busy and varied role. As the same principal officer put it: 'The SO is the choreographer. Everything revolves around him. He runs the unit on a day-to-day basis.'

In order for the wing to run smoothly, basic-grade officers must, of course, follow the instructions of their senior officers. However, at least one senior officer was prepared to admit that this does not always happen:

> It's actually fairer for a new SO to go to a different wing ... Having done what I did – working as acting SO on the wing where I was a basic grade, you know – you're acting SO amongst your own kind. I've never had a problem with it, and they accepted me, but it *can* be difficult for some people. You're suddenly giving orders to people who were your mates, and there *is* a subtle change ... your relationship changes. There are *some* SOs who will never actually make the transition. I mean we have one on our group, and, deep down, he wants to be one of the boys, and that makes it difficult to be an effective manager. 'Cos you ... you can't run with the hare and hunt with the hounds is the old saying, and it's right. You've got to be one or the other.

Newly promoted senior officers (and indeed more experienced senior officers transferring to different wings) may experience a great deal of resistance from ordinary grade officers. As one such officer told me, any newcomer questioning the quality and nature of the regime on the wing to which he has been promoted can cause resentment amongst the staff already working on that wing. 'Since I came on here I've had continual bombardment about how good the unit is, and why there's no need to change it.' This officer, who had recently transferred from the induction unit (which had a relatively 'disciplined' regime) to a remand wing, where the regime was relatively relaxed, had found the move both stressful and frustrating. He had encountered numerous difficulties trying to change the working practices (and ultimately the ethos of the wing) and was not at all sure that he could push through the changes he wished to make. On the contrary, he was acutely aware that he was dependent on the goodwill and support of his staff, and that his proposals to 'tighten up' the regime would only come about through co-operation from them: 'At the end of the day, an SO is only as good as his team. If they say No [to the changes you want to make] what are you gonna do?' To achieve regime changes without also antagonising his staff, he recognised that he had to proceed with caution: 'I've got to tread carefully; to spend the first week or two "seeing how the land lies" and *then* make proposals for change.'

Arguably, this process illustrates the two-way character of power between the lower ranks and middle management. Officers who 'act up' to the senior-officer rank for any length of time are in a particularly vulnerable position since the authority they hold is only temporary:

> The SO is probably the hardest job. If an SO bollocks a uniformed member one day, and the next day management say to him 'Well, you've done a good job but ...' and he's back at basic grade again, then the others are laughing at you. I, as PO, can hide away in my office [when things are going badly] but an SO can't. (Principal officer)

Newly promoted senior officers may also find that the management training they receive is barely adequate for the demands made upon them; although newly promoted senior officers attend a middle-management course, a number of senior officers claimed that this was rather limited. As a result: 'Basically you learn on the hoof, which is scary' (senior officer).

No place for a woman? The sexualised work environment

The claim, made by some male officers, that a male prison is simply 'no place for a woman' was discussed very briefly in Chapter 4. In this section I want to expand on that discussion, and to examine the ways in which women officers who do work in male prisons think about, and carry out, their work, and how they see their relationships with the men with whom they must interact (colleagues and prisoners).

Although women officers are welcomed into the service at the recruitment stage, some find that once on the landings of male prisons they are not fully accepted by some of their male colleagues. As we shall see, this lack of acceptance is often made explicit. Female officers may find themselves at the receiving end of sexist and degrading jokes and remarks; at the same time however they may find they are 'protected' by the male officers with whom they are working. Perhaps unsurprisingly, most women officers resent both these responses, not least because they indicate that as prison officers they are seen as less capable than men (for a discussion of this in relation to American prisons, see Martin and Jurik 1996; Pogrebin and Poole 1997).

As we saw in Chapter 3, becoming proficient in the art of repartee, story-telling and the ability to tell a good joke – often at the expense of a colleague – is in important part of the socialisation process, and new officers are *expected* to engage in it or at least not to take offence when insults and jokes are directed at them. Sometimes, however, officers *do* take offence. Female officers, for example, are likely to take offence when the banter is blatantly sexist, particularly when it also makes explicit the view that women should not work in male prisons. The behaviour of some male officers to female officers can be extremely hostile. Describing the negative experiences of a relatively inexperienced officer (a young woman in her early twenties) one female senior officer (a woman in her forties) stressed her belief that such behaviour was as much to do with bullying[5] – with the exertion of power over those perceived as vulnerable either through lack of experience or through youth – as it was to do with sexuality. She put it this way:

> Most men readily accept that women play a very important role in the prison setting, 'cos we can defuse situations, especially as the majority of inmates wouldn't dream of hitting a female and would probably go to a female officer's assistance instead. But you get the odd chauvinist pig who thinks a woman belongs in the kitchen, barefoot. And it's a form of bullying. [What sort of things does this kind of officer say?] They say 'You stay in the office, we'll go out on the landings. You're only a split-arse. You put the kettle on!' And funnily enough, its always the same terminology – 'split-arse'. To me, it's not just sexual harassment, it's bullying, 'cos they wouldn't do it with *me*. They pick their victims; they're a bit like lions aren't they? The ones you see on the telly stalking zebras and that. They pick out their prey … [They think] 'we'll pick *her*, she'll cry'.

Several female officers admitted that they had had to put up with sexist remarks from male colleagues. For example, a female officer working at Garth had:

> experienced a lot of sexist attitudes – mostly older staff. I've had an officer say that a woman who works in the Prison Service must be kinky, and some of the talk can be really nasty. People might say it doesn't happen – equal opportunities and that – but it does. I've even had a governor say to me that I'm a woman doing a man's job.

Similarly, from a female officer working at Lancaster Farms:

> When I first started here, there were nasty innuendoes from the blokes. I used to go home quite upset. (What sorts of comments did

they make?) In an office full of people, there'd be sexual innuendoes, and if you made a mistake, you were [told you were] a right silly cow. It's better now, but sometimes it's a bit OTT. I've become a bit more thick-skinned, but its been difficult 'cos I was brought up to respect older people, so I wasn't used to answering back. But all females get sexual innuendoes ... it's better to put up with it, not rock the boat, 'cos the blokes all stick together.

For this officer, the worst aspect of the job (a job which, overall, she found challenging but extremely rewarding) was the hostility of some of her male colleagues, and she was not alone in her reluctance to report their behaviour to higher-ranking staff. A female colleague had also decided not to complain about sexual harassment for fear of the consequences: 'If women complain, they tend to be ostracised, and the reputation as a trouble-maker follows you about – even to different prisons'.

The belief that they have to 'prove themselves' to be accepted is common amongst women officers, who often find that any mistakes made by themselves or their female colleagues are immediately seized upon as 'evidence' of the unsuitability of women for working in male prisons. Unsurprisingly, some women officers are cautious of expressing their opinions, or making assertions, and if they make mistakes they then feel they are 'letting the side down'. As a result, they tend to work especially hard: 'Female staff, being in a minority, have to work harder so that men can't accuse us of being incapable. Consequently there's lots of lazy men but no lazy women!' (female officer, Garth).

Some male officers simply do not want women officers in 'their' prisons. As this principal officer from Portland argued:

They're not accepted fully. I bet if you did a poll of staff attitudes that's what you'd find. Portland's ethos is one of discipline ... to be fair, though, the women working here are first class. Whether women can actually *do* the job seems irrelevant. They just shouldn't *be* here.

Officers offered various practical reasons for this. As I shall argue in a moment, however, there may be other non-practical – but perhaps more significant – reasons why men want to keep women out of male prisons – one of which revolves around the issue of identity. The first practical reason offered as to why women are unsuitable for staffing male prisons is that women officers are not allowed to strip-search male prisoners. Some male officers argued that this in itself creates difficulties, particularly if a large proportion of the staff on a particular shift are female. They also believe that women lack the physical strength to deal with difficult prisoners. In short, working in a man's prison is a man's job:

> Despite all the C&R techniques, women are not as capable of dealing with violent and aggressive inmates. Big inmates can throw them around much more easily. And in the C&R training the women can't hold the short shields up for long enough. But anyway we're stuck with them now aren't we? (Male officer, Garth)

Similarly: 'Women staff are the weak link in the chain in riot situations and in hostage situations' (male officer, Lancaster Farms). And again:

> Male staff resent female officers being in the jail – I don't give a stuff what the rest of the staff tell you. Because they're not seen as doing 100% of the job – they can't strip-search male prisoners for one thing. Yes they do have good mothering instincts, and they can defuse situations, but male staff – including me – see the woman as the weaker officer. (Male officer, Wymott)

Male officers (and indeed female officers) hold conflicting views about the qualities that women officers bring to male prisons. As I suggested in Chapter 5, however, that women officers are a 'calming' and/or 'normalising' influence is a perception held by many of their male colleagues: 'Women have been very good for the job … they're a civilizing influence and they can defuse situations (male senior officer, Garth). Similarly: 'They're calming, and respectful [to the inmates]. Inmates don't confront women as much as they do men' (male officer, Garth). And again:

> I think it's been a good move [bringing women officers into male prisons]. They defuse difficult situations, whereas men tend to aggravate – to be confrontational. I think that's why a lot of the violence has gone out of the job. (Male senior officer, Garth)

For some male officers, however, the notion that women officers are a 'calming influence' is: 'A load of rubbish. I can't really see how it's calming at all, if you're in a prison for five years and they only see their wives on visits, and then you get women officers coming in stinking of perfume' (male officer, Garth).

From my observations, I would agree that not all women officers are a calming influence. Nor do they all try to be. On the contrary, at least one of the female officers I observed during one of my visits to the VP unit at Wymott was abrupt, insensitive and deliberately provocative towards certain prisoners. Here is a clip from the fieldnotes I wrote at the time:

> A prisoner came into the office and asked Bernice, a young female officer, about his requested transfer to normal location. She was abrupt with him – offhand and sarcastic. He complained that when he was in the segregation unit he had signed a compact to say that if he gave respect to staff he'd get it back, yet now he found that this was not happening. As he walked out of the office she made faces behind his back – she was trying not to let him see she was laughing but the prisoner accused her of smirking about him. She struck me as an officer who had a (recently acquired?) hard edge, and who would *not* be a calming influence on anybody. On the contrary, she seemed to want to upset the prisoners. Later, when I asked the officer about this episode, she said that the inmate had 'a serious attitude problem' and that he was a 'gob shite'.

The way in which this officer dealt with this prisoner was no different from the way in which some male officers deal with prisoners. Just as male officers are not 'naturally' aggressive and uncivilised, neither are women officers 'naturally' or inherently calm and sympathetic. The vast majority of the female officers I observed and spoke to *did*, however, rely almost entirely on their skills of communication and persuasion when dealing with prisoners, just as many of their male colleagues did. It would therefore be a mistake to dichotomise the behaviour and attitudes of male and female officers, since many male officers also prefer a progressive, non-aggressive, human service approach. Male officers may, however, experience more peer pressure than their female counterparts to adopt a confrontational style.

Other reasons offered for women officers' unsuitability for male prisons revolved around the claim that women are both vulnerable and scheming. In terms of the former, I have already noted the commonly held belief that women officers are vulnerable to being 'sweet-talked' by prisoners. In terms of the latter, some officers believed that women officers were oversensitive to the coarseness of prison life, and that they were prepared to overplay this to make money:

Stuff that is not accepted on the outside is part and parcel of prison life ... [But] Some women are quick to take affront, and they've got harassment in their minds at all times ... They're money-grubbers. [In what sense do you mean? Do you mean that they are after compensation?] Yes.

A small number of male officers said they resented having to stop swearing and telling the kind of jokes and stories they had always told just because women had come into the job. Not only did they find this constraining, they believed that disgruntled women officers might deliberately put their jobs at risk: 'you have to be careful in case a woman wants to get out of the job and claims sexual harassment to do it' (male officer, Garth).

So why are women prison officers treated in this way by some of their male colleagues? It is perhaps reasonable to suggest that the chivalry/sexism debate that continues to rage in relation to female offenders is also pertinent to the treatment of women *working* in the criminal justice system. As the literature on the treatment of offending women in the criminal justice system illustrates (see, for example, Worrall 1990; Heidensohn 1985), the debate revolves around whether or not female offenders are, as a result of their 'doubly deviant'[6] status, treated with chivalry or contempt by the police, the courts and in the prisons. Heidensohn (1985: 32), for example, considers three propositions which are generally asserted about women in the criminal justice system, namely 1) that the system is 'chivalrous', protecting women from its full rigours and passing lesser sentences than on males committing equivalent crimes; 2) that the system is deeply sexist, reinforcing sexually stereotyped notions of role behaviour; and 3) that by attempting to 'protect' women, courts may pass sentences that are unduly harsh. Any one (or a mixture) of these responses may be noted when observing the treatment of female offenders in the criminal justice system. Arguably, the treatment meted out to women officers by some male officers may reflect similar resentments about the 'proper' role of women. Women disrupt the close association between the prison officer role and the performance of masculinity; if women are allowed to do the job, and if they can do it as well as their male counterparts, the job is 'no longer a viable resource for constructing masculinity' (Martin and Jurik 1996: 175).

Not all women officers are prepared to tolerate sexist treatment. Older female officers, particularly those who have been in the job for some time, are more likely to have the confidence to tell sexist men where they stand than their younger, less experienced counterparts. When asked if she had suffered from sexist comments or behaviour during her ten years in the service, this officer, a woman in her mid-thirties replied: 'I do get them sometimes, but not often – they wouldn't dare! I'd chew their heads off!' (acting senior officer, Garth).

I met numerous confident, strong-minded women officers during my fieldwork. They were competent individuals who would have absolutely no truck whatsoever with sexist behaviour from male colleagues. One of these women, an experienced senior officer with nine years in the service, said that she and her female colleagues on the wing simply would not allow old-school male officers to be 'high and mighty' with them. As she rather more graphically put it: 'Boring old farts who have had a long time in the job and try to throw their weight around would be given short shrift on this wing I can tell you.' Officers such as this one have the confidence to mock and tease just like their male colleagues. The following extract from my fieldnotes is illustrative of this:

> During our conversation about the treatment of women officers in men's prisons, Jock, an overweight, middle-aged male officer – a jokey Liverpudlian – came into the room. Sylvia took the mickey out of the way he runs to an alarm bell and called him a 'knock-kneed, knackered old nose-bag!' Turning to me, she said 'It's worth the alarm bell going off to see him running! He runs like this' [she mimicked his knock-kneed run]. Jock [kind of] laughed.

Many female officers believed that some of their male colleagues brought control problems on themselves through their confrontational, antagonistic stance towards prisoners. Commenting on her male colleagues' usual response to unco-operative prisoners, this middle-aged female officer observed:

> Men, they love a fight. They can't wait to get the locks on. The men love a fight. They *love* it. You can see 'em itching … They push each other out of the way to get hold of 'em. [In what circumstances?] If one's getting stroppy mainly … If there's one [inmate] getting stroppy, they're pushing each other out the road to get in the [cell] door. You can *see* the excitement. But it's not for me. [So how often do they get the chance for such action?] Oh, at the most about once a week. (Female officer, Wymott)

When women officers are harassed, ridiculed and ostracised by their male colleagues, it may be because they are seen as representing a threat to their capacity to perform this sort of 'masculinity':

> I think men are frightened of the fact that we don't need to fight. There's no need to fight in prisons. If you respect the cons, and you are respectful, you will get results. They *must* trust you, and believe you will do as you say. And you must be *calm*. If you're gonna come in and do a John Wayne, you'll be treated like a John Wayne. (Female officer, Lancaster Farms)

I would not wish to give the impression that all male officers dislike working with women. On the contrary, many of the officers who took part in my research took a very positive attitude towards their presence. In particular, they said they found women less threatening than men to work with, and liked the way that they were able to 'cut through the macho bullshit' in ways that they themselves felt unable to do. There is actually a good deal of sociological evidence that men sometimes do find it threatening to be in a group of other men because men often take advantage of any weakness that another man might show (on this see Seidler 1992). As Seidler notes, men also often claim that they feel much closer to women and that they talk emotionally with women in a way that they do not with men. In the prison, the only real opportunity that male prison officers have to talk emotionally – and privately – with women is when they are working the night shift.

Front stage, back stage: time, space and emotional expression

At night, prisons have a very different 'feel' about them than they do during the day. During the day there is noise and bustle. At night they are often deathly quiet. On the occasions that I spent whole nights in the prison, I walked round with officers on patrol and, in the process, we visited staff on the wings. We were met by officers walking around in their slippers or trainers, and wearing comfortable old sweaters and fleeces over their uniform shirts. As I mentioned in Chapter 2, officers passed the night doing a variety of activities; some knitting, some doing crosswords, some reading magazines or watching TV (many wings have a portable television in the office). In short, the wing office is, at night, a particularly domestic space.

Spatial metaphors employed by Goffman (1959) describe ways in which space is used to sustain performances, maintain appearances and manage the flow of information about individual actors, groups or institutions. His concept of front- and back-stage areas, for instance, demarcates territories and informational preserves. It struck me that during the night shift, prison officers are in a state of liminality.[7] That is, they are in an ambiguous state of being *between* states of being (Gennep 1960). The night shift provides a space where prison officers are able to move between statuses; in a space where there are no prisoners about and few staff, officers are not required to *perform* prison officer, either for the benefit of prisoners or fellow staff. The status of staff working in prisons at night is thus blurred; postures are relaxed and uniforms dishevelled or partly abandoned. In short, the body speaks a different language at night. I also found that at night, the more usual prison talk was almost entirely replaced by talk of a more personal nature; talk of personal problems such as financial worries, marital difficulties and failed romances were pronounced. When prison work is spoken about at night, the content of the conversation is likely to include officers' difficulties and anxieties about doing it.

Peer pressure to perform the 'hegemonic masculinity' valued so highly during the day shift, then, is much less pronounced at night. The night shift allows the male officer to let his 'guard' fall; on this shift he can have sustained contact with male and female colleagues, in contrast to the day shift when he is much busier, when there is a relatively large number of male officers on the wing and when conversations are necessarily short and carried out within earshot of colleagues and prisoners:

> Male officers will open up to you more at night ... old ones as well as young ones. [Why is that do you think?] 'Cos you're thrown together at night for a long time. Nights is good for getting to know your colleagues better. (Female officer, Lancaster Farms)

A senior officer present at the time of our discussion agreed, elaborating on how there was much less need to engage in emotional labour at night:

> Day time, you've got peer-group pressure. In the day time it's very difficult to discuss serious matters of a sensitive nature ... [At night] you haven't got to keep up a front, so staff tend to let their guard down a lot at night. Although nights are unpleasant to do, it's good because it's a time you can slow down – it's chill-out time for all of us.

Speaking metaphorically: how officers see the prison

As I conducted my fieldwork I noticed how commonly and casually metaphors[8] slipped into everyday conversation. As I have already mentioned, prison officers use a variety of (invariably unflattering) metaphors to describe prisoners, and I was intrigued as to what metaphors officers might use to describe the prison itself. As analytic devices, analogies and metaphors can be useful for understanding how prison officers think about and do their job. For example, the term 'crusaders' describes the sense of mission displayed by officers involved in the 'Prison! Me! No Way!' initiative which aims to prevent school children from getting involved in crime. Officers who worked as tutors on this initiative invariably spoke in terms of 'If we can just save *one*'. As we have seen (and as I shall elaborate below) a crusading or missionary analogy also applies to officers who work as Sex Offender Treatment Programme (SOTP) tutors.

When asked to choose a metaphor to depict what it is like to work in a prison, officers offered a variety of responses, some of which contrasted dramatically. For example, as we saw above, some officers offered the metaphor of the *family*. The selection of this metaphor is clearly intended to emphasise the emotional bonds that tie officers to fellow staff. Interestingly, whilst the family envisaged by most officers consisted entirely of prison officers, the family envisaged by one or two officers included prisoners (perhaps unsurprisingly, the prisoners were seeing as having the role of dependent children and officers the parental roles). In contrast, several officers proposed the metaphor of a *machine*. When prison officers used this metaphor they did so to emphasise imprisonment *as process*; prisoners were merely a commodity to be processed through the organisation that had its own routines, procedures and timetable. I was offered many more metaphors (see the Appendix); most were variations on a theme (comparisons with other institutions such as schools and hospitals cropped up time and time again) but others drew upon television sit-coms such as *Porridge*[9] and *Dad's Army* to illustrate the comical, emotional and human side of prison life. *Dad's Army* was drawn upon by one female officer to describe the variety of characters and the nature of day-to-day interactions within her own work group:

It's like Dad's Army in here! [For example] Greg's 'Pikey' – 'I can't do that, my Mum won't let me!' – and you always get one with a watch under his coat to flog – the spiv. And you've got your Captain Mainwaring … your military type. That line-up of Dad's Army – it's just like us in a morning! (Female officer, Garth)

The metaphors that officers chose depended, in part, on the kind of prison in which they worked.

Negotiation and conflict: three specialist regimes

As we have seen, inter-staff conflict about the 'right' role, attitude and behaviour for prison officers is commonplace. I want to expand on this issue now by drawing upon data collected during my interactions with, and observations of, officer-counsellors working in a TC and with tutor officers working on the SOTP. I want to demonstrate how officers working in these regimes perceive themselves and their work, and how they are perceived and treated by colleagues working in more 'mainstream' regimes by drawing upon fieldwork conducted in HMP Portland's Therapeutic Community for Young Offenders and with officers working as tutors on Wymott's Sex Offender Treatment Programme. I begin with the therapeutic community at Portland.

Regime one: Rodney House Therapeutic Community, Portland

Introduction

In the discussion that follows I want to elaborate on the difficulties and benefits experienced by prison officers who choose to work in a therapeutic community for young offenders. Following a brief discussion of the concept of the therapeutic community and its introduction into the prison setting from the field of mental health, I shall go on to discuss the implications of a therapeutic regime for the prison officer role and for relations with prisoners and colleagues working in other parts of the prison. As we shall see, working with teenagers in this kind of environment presents uniformed staff with a range of opportunities, challenges, problems, disappointments and frustrations. While some would not wish to repeat the experience (a small number of those who volunteered to work in the unit have since left it) others continued to find the work interesting and rewarding.

Background

Following the publication of the government white paper *Tackling Drugs Together* (1995) a reduction in the level of drug misuse in prison became one of the Prison Service's strategic priorities (Clarke 1996: 14). The provision of three (pilot) treatment units which focused on education and counselling in the 'therapeutic community' environment (I shall elaborate on the TC concept in a moment) represented part of a new initiative within this broader strategy. The three establishments involved in this initiative were Channings Wood (a Category C training prison), Holme House (a Category B training prison) and Portland Young Offender Institution.

At the time of my fieldwork, the therapeutic community at Portland YOI – 'Rodney House' – was unique in that it was the first such unit for young offenders in the English prison system. The regime was designed for young prisoners seen as needing help with problems of drug abuse. In that prisoners were able to contribute to decisions regarding the regime, and prison officers attempt to foster positive relationships with prisoners, the ethos of the regime was similar to that of the TC in Grendon Underwood and the now defunct 'Special Unit' at Barlinnie in Scotland. The seventy-two bed unit at Portland, which was tucked away in a corner of the prison, opened on 6 December 1996. The aim was that towards the end of its initial three-year period of funding, the regime would have reached a stage at which uniformed staff could take over the duties of the unit 'therapists' (a small number of (relatively young) individuals who had received training from a Christian organisation called Yeldall Bridges, a partnership between Yeldall Manor and Bridges of America). It was also anticipated that Rodney House would eventually become a national resource. Given that the programme was fifty-two weeks long, prisoners selected for the unit were supposed to have at least twelve months to serve. The programme involved three stages of treatment,[10] a 'peer encounter group'[11] and various meetings such as the morning meetings and the afternoon 'wrap-up' sessions.[12]

The concept of the 'therapeutic community'

The therapeutic community approach was part of a general explosion of interest in what was known during the 1950s as 'social psychiatry', which had a strong interest in the deleterious effects of psychiatric hospitalisation such as stigmatisation and institutionalisation (Trauer 1984). Both these processes caught the attention of the public through the influence of sociological studies such as Goffman's *Asylums* (1968). The therapeutic community movement arose as a reaction against the damaging effects of conventional hospitals for the mentally ill. The therapeutic community was distinctive in the way the resources of the institution – both staff and patients – were self-consciously pooled in furthering treatment. This implied above all a change in the usual status of patients who, in collaboration with the staff, became active participants in the therapy of other patients, in contrast to their relatively more passive recipient role in conventional treatment regimes. In the therapeutic community of the hospital, the patients played an important part in the provision of treatment, guided by their intimate knowledge of one another and their intuitive appreciation of each other's psychological difficulties (Jones 1956). It is easy to say how this type of approach, so popular in the 1960s, could be regarded as highly appropriate both for men who had suffered the deleterious effect of many years in prison (as was the case with the prisoners in the TC at Barlinnie) and indeed for the young offenders whom the Prison Service perceive as being damaged (psychologically and physically) by their involvement with drugs.

The 'Report of the Departmental Working Party on the treatment of certain male long term prisoners and potentially violent prisoners' (Scottish Home and Health Department 1971) was the immediate precursor to the foundation of the Barlinnie Special Unit. As the report makes clear, units run on therapeutic community lines 'demand a change of attitude in the staff who operate them', in order to break down the 'them and us' scenario of traditional prison regimes. At Barlinnie Special Unit (hereafter BSU) it was the ability to make democratic decisions regarding the regime, and the positive relationships that were fostered between inmates and staff, that made BSU such a unique element of the Scottish penal environment. It is important to note, however, that, unlike the inmates in the BSU, none of the young prisoners in the TC at Portland were seen as presenting serious control problems to the establishment.

At the time that I conducted my research in Rodney House, participants could expect a daily routine of morning meeting (to announce the daily schedule and recount 'learning experiences'); seminars (on issues such as forgiveness, resentments and responsibility); individual and group counselling (to enable prisoners to explore their own and each others' problems, feelings and attitudes); and 'encounter groups' aimed at resolving community conflicts and challenging 'inappropriate' behaviour at the level of the individual. All programme participants were also assigned a work detail; jobs were on a hierarchical system and provided varying levels of responsibility and authority. At all times, uniformed officers worked alongside the 'therapists' in the delivery of the therapeutic regime.

I have to say that it was something of a surprise to me to come across (quite accidentally) an experimental TC being run in a young offender prison whose identity has long been centred around its 'robust', 'no nonsense' and 'strict' regime (see Leech 1995; HMCIP 1996). That a former governor was successful in his bid to set up and run the unit was due, I was told, to the availability of a suitable housing block entirely separate from the main prison.

Culture shock (again): starting work in Rodney House

The TC regime places very different demands on prison officers than do more traditional prison regimes. Officers are likely to experience certain difficulties when making the initial transition from one to the other; for 'mainstream' officers starting work in Rodney House the initial problem was that of adjusting to a regime in which some authority is delegated to prisoners. It was extremely difficult for officers to make this adjustment, given that they 'come from a culture where what we say goes' (TC officer pers. comm.). According to one of my interviewees, the central problem for an officer starting work on the unit was that of acquiring the confidence to 'let go' – to be able to 'stand back' and allow young prisoners on the unit to make decisions as to the running of the unit (as I have already suggested, the most distinctive attribute of a TC is that it is run largely by the residents themselves under the supervision of pro-gramme and prison staff). At the time of my fieldwork, the requirement to do so was inducing feelings of anxiety and frustration amongst all the officers working in the unit, partly because the prisoners themselves found it difficult (given their prior experience of conventional prison regimes) to make decisions and to act with the autonomy and responsibility expected of them in the unit. Officers' anxieties and frustrations also arose from the fact that they themselves were simply not used to negotiating with prisoners. As one TC officer noted, commenting on the traditional Portland regime: 'In this prison, its either "Yes" or "No" because officers want to have total control. They're not interested in "Maybe".'

The stigma of 'deviant' officers

It is important not to overlook the influence of such units on their host prisons. Staff choosing to work in 'special' units (and in other specialist units such as those running sex offender treatment programmes) often tend to be viewed negatively by staff working in more conventional prison settings. For example, officers working in special secure units (SSUs) were resented for regarding themselves as 'elite' (Walmsley 1989) while officers working in TCs, on the other hand, are often seen as 'softies' or no longer 'one of the boys' (White 1974). In HMP Barlinnie there was a great deal of resistance to special unit staff; during an earlier piece of research I carried out in the BSU in 1994, I was told by a principal nursing officer (this officer was also a member of the SHHD Working Party which recommended the setting up of the unit) that:

> The staff outside the unit were extremely hostile, particularly to the young staff. They went through hell. Those of us that carried a bit of rank, and all the rest of it, we didn't get that mess. Nobody was gonna take *us* on. But as soon as the young staff came through the gate, they gave 'em a dog's life ... bloody crude name-calling all the

time, oh it was terrible. Most of 'em stuck it, but some of 'em didn't.

In sum, officers working in ways that run contrary to 'the norm' (i.e. interacting with prisoners in ways that appear to run against the traditional ethos of a particular establishment) are likely to be ridiculed or challenged by more conservative staff. As one male officer working in Rodney House observed: 'I've faced resentment ever since I came here. I think [it's because] any staff that does things that's not what a "normal" prison officer does is seen as a threat.' As we shall see, there was a significant degree of antagonism towards Rodney staff, and officers working there were regularly given 'advice' about the 'proper' way to deal with young offenders and the role that they, as prison officers, should be playing instead.

Negotiating order: anxiety and opportunity

As I indicated in Chapter 1, some prisons place particular emphasis on situational measures for maintaining order. Others emphasise more social means of control, in which a greater level of negotiation takes place between staff and inmates, possibly involving the participation of prisoners in the construction of their own regimes. As we know, most prisons tend, in practice, to utilise a mixture of both situational and social measures; Portland, interestingly, utilised both measures but in entirely separate regimes. That is, the control measures used in the 'main' prison were almost entirely situational while in Rodney House, control was almost entirely social. Rodney House attempted to encourage inmate responsibility, co-operation and self-restraint.

The 'dialectic of control' in prison settings is much more visible in the TC than in mainstream regimes. That Rodney inmates were able to negotiate openly (and often successfully) with officers tended to irritate and anger some of the staff working in the main prison. It may have been that these officers simply refused to acknowledge that prisoners are always able to influence the actions of their keepers (albeit to greatly differing degrees) since to acknowledge this may have been to undermine their own sense of authority and identity. It was interesting that Rodney officers (a 'seasoned' group of predominantly male staff) tended to equate the process of negotiating with prisoners with 'giving away their power'. They were at pains to describe how difficult it had been (and to a large extent still was) for them to 'give away' some of their power to these young prisoners, given that 1) the 'do as I say' culture was ingrained in Portland's uniformed staff; and 2) TC officers lacked many of the specialist skills necessary to enable them to play their required role in the unit. Perhaps unsurprisingly, the officers that had, at the time of my research, already requested to leave the unit were also the officers who had not yet received the training received by those who had joined the unit earlier. In consequence, new officers to the unit were obliged to look through the manual to see what was supposed to happen in the next part of the programme and, understandably, found it disconcerting, indeed intimidating, to have to stand in front of a group of inmates as a 'tutor' when they felt woefully under-trained (pers. comm.). As one of the first officers to join the unit put it: 'If I dropped dead in a class, these new lads wouldn't be able to carry on. These lads know that. And I feel sorry for them.'

The problems of a TC officer

The uniformed staff on Rodney house had elected to join the unit for a number of reasons. The reasons given by the majority were that they 'wanted to try something new' and that they 'wanted to do something rewarding'. One officer had simply 'got tired of the hassle on the other wings' and another, who confided that he was pursuing a career change, 'wanted to learn counselling skills'. Once they started work on the unit, however, officers encountered unanticipated problems. One such problem was that compared to the mainstream wings, the regime in Rodney House was very demanding of staff time. This relatively high degree of direct access to officers made working in the TC extremely tiring. A senior officer explained that while on the more traditional wings at Portland, an officer might only see an inmate for brief periods two or three times a day, in Rodney House: 'It's "Sir! Sir! Sir!" – questions all day! So there's no rest from them. It's tiring and stressful ... See, there's another young man here now [an inmate has appeared at the office door].' Similarly, this time from an ordinary-grade officer:

> They're always demanding, always asking. Also, once you're on the unit, you're here all day, unlike on the other wings where staff are detailed out of the wing as well ... [In here] you've virtually got a static population, with no movement.

Like most officers who work in young offender institutions, Rodney House staff were aware that young offenders are often desperately in need of the kind of attention that could be expected of a parent, and as such they often placed officers in a surrogate parent role. Sometimes this is made painfully explicit: 'I've been called Dad. I've been called Mum ... They think of us as their parents these do' (male senior officer).

While several officers claimed that they preferred to work in the unit precisely because there was more contact with prisoners than in the 'main' prison, others found the high degree of contact taxing: 'It's good fun on here. Some of the other officers, though, find it very hard, 'cos they never get chance to get away from 'em (male officer). It is clear from the latter comment that working in Rodney House could be claustro-phobic. Indeed, unit staff had had to get used to working with a relatively small team of officers in a relatively small space. Several officers also found it frustrating that many of these young prisoners had not yet grasped the fact that, unlike in the 'main' prison, there was a delegation of authority in Rodney House and that consequently there continued to be: 'a queue of young men at the office door asking silly questions.' (Senior officer)

Rodney House officers had to deal with five central problems, namely 1) antagonism between TC and non-TC staff; 2) the tendency for prisoners to revert to the norms of traditional prison culture once they were away from the 'teaching' area; 3) the difficulty of getting prisoners (and indeed themselves) out of a 'Them and Us' mindset; and 4) the problem of what officers termed 'role conflict'. Finally, Rodney staff faced the problem of balancing the needs of the unit with the needs of the prison system as a whole.

The tendency for Rodney prisoners to revert to the norms of traditional prison culture once they were on their own landings – a space that they perceived as lying outside the boundaries of the therapeutic regime – was a significant problem for TC officers. For one officer who had requested a transfer out of the unit, the discrepancy between the prisoners' 'upstairs and downstairs' behaviour was what irritated him most of all. From his perspective, it indicated that they were not taking the regime seriously – that they were simply *performing* the role of responsible prisoner. Indeed, several of the officers in the unit suspected that most of the time, they were just 'getting the spiel' from the prisoners; that is, they were simply 'making the right noises' and acting in the ways that they thought staff expected them to act in the 'therapeutic space' of the classroom, meeting room and so on. The fact that, as one officer put it, 'they go upstairs and revert to wheeling and dealing, bullying, borrowing and lending' frustrated staff, and made them feel that these young men were 'just taking the piss' (pers. comm.). As a result, every officer in the unit had felt, at some point, that he wished he had not volunteered to work there. According to one senior officer, every officer felt some degree of frustration and impatience, 'particularly with the inmates that are showing little effort'. He acknowledged, however, that it was unrealistic to think that every prisoner who entered the programme would complete it; what was revealing, however, was the contrast in analogy used by therapist and senior officer to describe the TC process. According to this officer: 'As the therapist says, "When you're panning for gold, you're bound to find a few stones". We [the uniformed staff] say that "Shit floats and when it does we'll scrape you off!"' Those prisoners that *are* 'scraped off' are removed from the unit and returned to 'normal' location.

The 'Them and Us' mindset is difficult to dismantle, even in the TC, since it reflects both prisoners' and officers' past experience of prison life. Many of the young prisoners in Rodney House were finding the regime difficult to cope with, partly because they were unable to see officers as anything other than 'a uniform' – as authority figures. Their prior experience of prison had been largely negative, so when Rodney officers spoke of 'therapy', 'care' and 'respect' it was taken with a (very large) pinch of salt. There was also, as the prisoners put it, the problem of 'the con-screw thing' (TC prisoner pers. comm.). It is extremely difficult to persuade inmates to abandon the codes of the inmate culture, in particular the inmate code of 'no grassing' (e.g. informing officers if a new prisoner has brought drugs into the unit from the 'main' prison) since, if we are to believe Gresham Sykes' analysis, the codes of the inmate culture generate solidarity, and function to make imprisonment less painful. If a unit such as Rodney House was to 'work' however (in the sense that its prisoners remained drug-free and able to provide each other with the support to remain so) staff must somehow manage to generate, amongst the prisoners, a sense of ownership – a belief that the unit is *theirs* as much as it is staff's.

There are practical reasons why TC prisoners might not want to abandon the traditional inmate culture. In the prison setting (as outside it) self-identities are often bound up with notions of 'Us and Them'. Indeed, as numerous writers have pointed out (see, for example, Willis 1977) resistance is a common working-class cultural form (which is presumably also drawn upon by (working class) uniformed prison staff). Many prisoners are thus likely to see 'incorporation' into such a regime as a *loss* – as having been manipulated, won over (as prison officers often do when they submit to the demands of their managers). As Liebling *et al.* (1997) note in their evaluation of the Incentives and Earned Privileges Scheme, how an inmate appears in front of his peers might be more important than getting an extra £2.50 a week or the use of a duvet brought from home. Just as co-operative prisoners in Rodney House were often known as 'screw-boys' by new prisoners into the unit, or by those unhappy with the TC regime (unit prisoners pers. comms.), prison officers in every prison are aware that staff who co-operate openly with management are invariably seen as 'yes men' or, more graphic-ally, 'brown-noses' (various officers pers. comms.). For prisoners, the problem is immediate; they have to decide whose 'side' they are on, not least because staff and other prisoners may demand that they decide.

For TC officers, aspects of the traditional 'screw' culture can be equally hard to shake off. Different working styles could be observed even amongst officers working in Rodney House, where one might expect staff to hold roughly similar values and beliefs about imprison-ment and prisoners. In reality, however, there were one or two officers who were very definitely perceived as 'screws' by the inmates, and who seemed to be clinging to the attitudes and behaviours common to their 'landing screw' counterparts and to more traditional staff cultures. This was illustrated when one of the therapists wished to discuss with a TC officer the fact that an inmate who had been thrown off the unit for drug use had threatened to kill himself now that he was back in the 'main' prison. The officer (who has himself since returned to the main prison) laughed the therapist's concerns off, asking her in a cavalier fashion, 'Does he want any help?' Most other Rodney officers, in contrast, seemed more willing to listen to the prisoners' problems, and seemed generally 'gentler' in their approach. It was interesting, none the less, to note the 'tone' of various notices that had been Sellotaped, by officers, to the wing office door. They read, in ascending order: 'No Inmates', 'Knock and Wait' and 'Local Branch of "Refuse and Resist": Our Motto is No!' Arguably, the presence of such notices indicate that the values and practices of old-style jailing had not been completely abandoned by unit officers. Indeed, several officers confessed that even though they subscribed to the ethos of the TC, when they got frustrated, stressed or tired, they sometimes 'forgot themselves' and briefly reverted to being a 'screw', refusing even to listen to a prisoner's request or 'banging up' a prisoner for a relatively trivial matter. Unfortunately, while this can provide a quick (albeit temporary) source of peace, a reversal, however brief, to this type of behaviour may demonstrate to TC prisoners that the 'community' with which they are encouraged to engage is just a charade.

A more fundamental problem for TC officers was what they described as 'role conflict'. Two of the officers had found this so difficult to cope with that they had requested transfers out of the unit. While they claimed still to 'believe in' the TC philosophy, they found the role they were expected to play in Rodney House much too stressful. They were unconvinced that someone wearing a uniform, and with the power and authority to punish, could at the same time 'counsel' inmates and persuade them to confide their innermost worries and fears. The problem of role conflict is one that is difficult to solve; unsurprisingly it is a problem discussed in an array of literature concerned with the 'care and control' dichotomy inherent in the 'soft policing' role of social workers, health visitors and so on.

Rodney officers had other frustrations and resentments. A significant frustration stemmed from the duality of their role. Because their role encompassed security as well as therapy, they found that once their shift had started they barely had time to draw breath. That the therapists were always in one role had knock-on, practical significance. Officers, who shared the delivery of some sessions with therapists and ran others on their own, resented the fact that after these sessions – which were often stressful and emotionally draining – they had immediately to 'go and feed and listen to a hundred questions' while the therapists were able to go for a coffee and relax (numerous officers pers. comm.). Finally, there was the problem of balancing the needs of the unit with the needs of the prison system as a whole. Although it was a specialist unit, Rodney House had to play its part in coping with the rapidly increasing prison population. In consequence, the unit suffered a dramatic rise in numbers before the programme was fully 'up and running', and this presented significant difficulties for both prisoners and staff.

Staff conflict

As I have already indicated, the idea of giving prisoners autonomy and the opportunity for self-expression is anathema to many of the officers working on the 'main' wings of Portland Young Offender Institution (and, as noted earlier, to many officers in many other prisons). That Rodney officers were perceived as 'too soft' with inmates was made apparent when an officer from the main prison, on making a rare visit to the unit (non-unit staff generally tended to keep away) and overhearing that unit officers were having certain difficulties with a number of inmates, told the officers simply to 'Batter 'em. That's the answer!' This was met with a somewhat hostile response. One TC officer replied angrily, 'No, we're trying to do something different with them, they already know *that*'. A second officer, also clearly irritated, nodded in agreement: 'Yeah, they've known too much of that – violence.' When I asked unit officers if they were a 'different breed' of officer from their colleagues working in mainstream regimes, Rodney officers replied that they simply wanted to try a different way of working, because:

We've seen that the other way doesn't work. [As a result] They hate us over there. They think we molly-coddle them, but really it's harder over here – for us and for them. They [the other officers] try and make fun of us. [They say we] sit them on beanbags and talk to them all day. (Male officer)

Responding to my questions about the (largely hostile) attitudes of staff in the main prison to Rodney unit's (relatively liberal) regime, the unit governor explained that there was 'still a minority – a nucleus – who don't agree with what Rodney unit does'. This was, I think, a serious underestimation of the amount of resentment directed towards the unit at the time of my visits. The issue of control (and who had it) seemed to be at the heart of this resentment of the unit; as one ('hard-line') officer from the main prison put it, 'What I want to know is, who's in control down there?' Antagonism towards Rodney staff was not lessened by the fact that some of the inmates were said to be regularly irritating night staff by shouting out of their windows, playing their radios loudly and relying upon their TC 'specialness' for protection. Unsurprisingly perhaps, officers on night patrol were not amused when prisoners apparently told them 'You can't touch us, we're Rodney inmates!'

At the time of my fieldwork a great deal of resentment was being directed towards the unit, particularly about a perceived discrepancy between the staffing levels on the unit and the other wings. At a joint Prison Officer Association/senior management meeting I attended (at the invitation of the POA) representatives of the POA claimed that the TC was overstaffed on weekend evenings. They were annoyed that although TC inmates were locked up at these times, four officers remained on the unit. Meanwhile other wings were so understaffed that officers were, as the POA secretary put it, 'on their arses'. A somewhat heated discussion ensued between the POA and the governor in charge of the unit.

(Sticking to the) emotion display rules
Despite the taxing nature of the prison officer role in Rodney House, there was surprisingly little emotional and social support for the officers working there. At the time of my fieldwork, the only support available was the (newly invented) monthly 'staff-sensitivity meeting'. During one of my visits, a small group of officers were being told by the unit therapists that these meetings were soon to take place, and that their purpose was to provide peer support, give all unit staff the opportunity to express their concerns and anxieties and provide opportunities for suggestions as to how these could be resolved. On overhearing parts of the conversation, an officer arriving on the unit to start his shift asked what they were all talking about. Looking up and laughing, one of his

colleagues replied '[We're having] Staff sensitivity meetings – don't tell the rest of the jail!' There was clearly some unease about 1) the require-ment for officers to discuss their emotions; and 2) the possibility that staff in the 'main' prison might hear about Rodney staff discussing their emotions at work. Indeed, it later transpired, during a conversation I had with one of the prison psychologists, that these meetings had been less than successful; some officers had refused to attend at all and it had proved 'difficult to get those that did attend to open up'.

Emotional expression in Rodney House

Afternoon 'wrap-up' meetings in Rodney House focused on the day's events, and was the meeting in which special announcements were made about rewards, sanctions and administrative matters concerning prisoners. During one of my visits to the unit I was present at a 'wrap-up' session which focused on an inmate's imminent departure from the unit. This was quite an emotional experience for a number of unit staff, and indeed, for me. Joe, a young man who was to be released the next day, was given a certificate for his efforts on the programme, and he himself gave out thank-you cards 'for Mr Jackson and his crew', expressing his thanks to 'the penguins', especially 'my mate Mr Wood', his personal officer. He had hugs for the therapists and a kiss for the programme manager, which brought about catcalls from the rest of the inmates. He gave his best wishes to his fellow inmates, and encouraged them to stick to the programme; as he did so I noticed that several inmates were sitting with an arm around others' shoulders – something that I have not seen on the wings of any other young offender institution.

During my visits to the unit, I was approached by several of the prisoners and asked why I was there. When I told them that I was interested in, amongst other things, staff–prisoner relationships, all of them remarked upon the difference between mainstream and Rodney staff. Their comments about their interactions with some mainstream officers were disturbing, but they also pointed to the positive nature of relationships within the unit itself. As one young man put it:

> Some of the officers here have really changed over the past few months. You can have a laugh with them ... One or two of them are really great. [So how do they compare to staff on the other wings – in the induction unit, for example?] Well if you don't call the officers there Sir they shout at you 'You fucking call me Sir!' [When asked about the segregation unit, he replied] There's lots of verbal abuse and that ... and they bang your head on the wall and that. I don't want any of that anymore. (Inmate M)

Similarly, according to inmate P: 'On Hardy wing [the induction unit] they treat you like scum … they slap you around.' And again, this time from inmate S: 'It's a nightmare on Hardy. If you don't say Sir, or if you say Boss instead, they smack you round the head.'

Day-to-day negotiation in Rodney House

In Rodney unit, the vast majority of infringements of discipline were dealt with in-house in the form of 'encounters' (within the encounter groups mentioned above). In general, Rodney officers tended to use the adjudication system 'as a tool – to wake them up a bit – rather than as a punishment' (senior TC officer). This officer went on to say that because of the nature of the regime, TC inmates sometimes 'forget where they are' (i.e. in prison) and had a tendency to become 'disrespectful' as a result, particularly to the unit therapists (who were, by and large, all young women barely older than the inmates). On the occasions that this happened, officers felt the need to assert their disciplinary role; consequently, one of the 'nickings' that took place during one of my visits (and which *did* result in a governor's adjudication) was for being disrespectful to a therapist. Significantly, however, I was told that there was a much lower level of other kinds of indiscipline – in particular fighting and assaults – in the TC than there was on the other wings. It could be argued, however, that TC officers were somewhat 'compromised' in their dealings with offences against discipline in the unit. Arguably, they had a vested interest in having a low number of adjudications because they were keen to demonstrate the TC was 'working' in the way that it should. Clearly, inmates also recognised this, and were likely to exploit this knowledge, i.e. 'play the system' for their own (rather than the community's) benefit. That is, a few may have deliberately broken the rules in the knowledge that an admittance of blame (courage to admit fault and express regret are highly valued in this type of regime) would invariably result in an informal warning. In short, Rodney prisoners who had broken a prison rule frequently negotiated with officers not to be 'put on a governor's' – to a degree not found in many other young offender institutions. The following cell-searching scenario (drawn from my fieldnotes) may suffice to illustrate such negotiations:

> A searching team (from the 'Operations Group' located in the main prison) found, in a cell on Rodney House, a Walkman which did not belong to that inmate. One of the operations officers took it to the wing office and asked the SO what he wanted them to do, saying that he would be happy to put in a report to the governor if that was

what the SO wanted. However, the searching team was quickly followed into the office by one of the TC officers who emphasised, as the culprit looked on, that 'the inmate had opened up to the Walkman not being his and that's what we're trying to instil into them isn't it … That they should take responsibility?' In the end, the SO told the searching team that they would deal with the matter 'in-house', whereupon the team left the unit. Arguably, a searching team might resent having to write 'Nothing to report' when in actual fact, they have. A similar scenario ensued in relation to paper and envelopes apparently taken from one inmate by another. Here again the inmate was able to negotiate with the officer through the anticipation of forgiveness and the expression of regret. In this way, TC staff and inmates 'do deals' with each other. It is a reciprocal relationship; the inmate admits his wrong-doings and the officer gives him a warning (rather than a 'governor's') as a 'reward' for being responsible enough to own up. Both know that by avoiding an official adjudication, both win out.

Regime two: the Sex Offender Treatment Programme, Wymott

Introduction

In this section I focus on officers' experience of working as tutors on the Sex Offender Treatment Programme (SOTP) that was running in HMP Wymott's vulnerable prisoner (VP) unit at the time of my research. This programme operated on one wing of the unit and each programme ran for approximately six months. At the time of my fieldwork, just over half the uniformed staff on this wing were SOTP tutors. Each group ran sessions three mornings per week, but tutors told me that there were plans afoot to run the programme five days a week; indeed some of the tutors had actually already started doing this. This fast-track programme would, of course, allow a greater number of offenders to go through the programme within the allocated period of time (and thus make it easier for the prison to reach its performance targets).

To set this discussion in context, I want, first of all, to outline the rationale for the introduction of Sex Offender Treatment Programmes into prisons. I intend then to describe the experiences of a small number of prison officers who have worked as SOTP tutors, using their own words to illustrate particular points. In the process, I also highlight the resistance of some non-SOTP officers to involvement in this kind of work. While a number of other issues could be raised in relation to such programmes (for example about their effectiveness and the quality of staff training) it is not my intention to do so here (or at least only in passing). I do not intend here, then, an evaluation of the SOTP; rather I want to highlight the impact that delivering the programme can have on officers' work and personal lives.

Background

Sex offenders have increasingly been the focus of attention by the criminal justice system (and indeed the media) over the past decade. Moreover, following a guideline judgment from the Court of Appeal in 1986 (*R v. Billam*) and the introduction of the Criminal Justice Act 1991, custodial sentences for sexual offences have increased in length. In the white paper *Protecting the Public* (1996) the trend continued (Worrall 1997). The question that remained, however, was what to *do* with such prisoners in order that they might not re-offend on release. On 7 June 1991, the then Home Secretary announced that a new treatment pro- gramme for sex offenders would be introduced into twenty prisons by the end of the year. These multidisciplinary programmes (the majority of tutors are prison officers, the rest are 'civilians' from departments such as psychology, education and probation) were to be closely monitored for their effectiveness (it was claimed in a Prison Service briefing that a reduction of 50% in the recidivism rate was achievable). It is worth noting that the sex offender initiative came at a time when prisons were already trying to cope with the effects of the progressive reductions in staff hours through Fresh Start. Many regimes were already limited and under extreme pressure. The history of attempts to provide specialist programmes in prison for groups such as sex offenders has shown that such programmes are always 1) exposed to staffing and resource prob- lems; and 2) criticised for the poor quality of the training given to prison officers preparing to take on such work (see Waite 1994).

It is clear that Sex Offender Treatment Programmes crucially depend on prison officers being able to develop a positive and open relationship with the prisoners with whom they are working, in order to encourage honesty and, ultimately, remorse for the offence. Prisoners participating in the programme are expected to reveal the full extent of their offending histories in a group setting. Truth-telling is, however, often difficult, embarrassing and painful; in the context of the SOTP it is also extremely unlikely if participants 1) believe that the information they disclose will be misused by tutor officers (and indeed by other prisoner partici- pants[13]); and 2) are unsure whether the officers (and indeed other par- ticipants) will still treat them as human beings once they have disclosed the particularities of their offences. Offenders' truth-telling has impli- cations for officers too. It demands that tutor officers overcome a significant problem, namely the tension between professionalism and emotionality. It is clear from the literature on psychological trauma that engagement in therapeutic work poses some risks to the psychological health of those who do it. Therapists themselves may become traumatised by the stories they are forced to hear as they attempt to treat their patients, and nightmares and invasive thoughts are common. A number of officers told me that when delivering the SOTP they often felt a mixture of negative emotions, including anger, frustration, revulsion and disgust. Some had also felt distressed, particularly those who had identified with the victims of the crimes. Officers who have young children, for example, can find it particularly distressing to hear a prisoner describe, in graphic detail, his offences against children of a similar age to their own.

Day-to-day interactions with prisoners convicted of offences against children are thus problematic for some tutors, even very experienced ones:

> Their offences are sometimes so heinous it can colour your thinking, especially if it's offences against children, and you've got children yourself ... The professional answer [to your question about whether I suppress my emotions] is that you're supposed to treat everyone with the same level of professionalism. But that's not always easy.

Similarly: 'Sometimes, when you hear what they've done, you want to punch them. I've managed to keep it together but it's not easy.'

Although most officers do manage to keep their emotions under wraps throughout each session, their emotions may be in turmoil. 'Ecstatic', 'gutted' or 'shell-shocked' were the terms one officer used to describe how officers can feel at the end of a session; since none of these emotional states is acceptable on the wings, staff have to 'come down' first. The purpose of debriefing sessions, which are built into the programme, is to do precisely that; they allow staff time to unwind, and to take stock of their emotions, and officers are not supposed to resume their place on the landings until debriefing has taken place. The officer tutors at Wymott *did* have access to a debriefing room – an 'emotional zone' in which they could express (and talk through) their emotions; here, officers could, in short, 'let off steam' out of earshot of both prisoners and non-SOTP staff. After one session, the tutors told me that one young officer had been so angered by a prisoner's disclosures that, once in the debriefing room he had slammed his stave[14] down so hard on the back of one of the chairs that the stave broke in two. I was concerned to find, at a later point, that debriefing sessions could be cut short or

215

abandoned if the landings are short-staffed. Because SOTP resources were not 'ring fenced', senior officers were able to pull tutors out of debriefing sessions if they were needed elsewhere. As this tutor noted: '[Debriefing's] gone downhill recently, 'cos there's no-one to do it. There's no resources, although we were told they would be there. You just have to make the best of it ... to plod on.'

A limited amount of formal counselling was, however, compulsory. The rationale for *compulsory* counselling is to avoid staff declining the offer of support for fear of being seen as 'soft' or unable to cope. Additional counselling was available for both tutors and their partners if they felt they needed it, and a twenty-four-hour help-line was also in place. This independent service (volunteers were ex-healthcare staff) was funded by the prison, and it could refer tutors and their partners on for further counselling if it was felt that this was necessary. Most of the tutors I spoke to felt that some sort of counselling was important; certain sections of the programme are particularly distressing to deliver, and officers may find it difficult to leave behind their distress at the prison gate. Although, as I have said, formal avenues for coping were available, SOTP officers also employed a variety of informal coping strategies to survive the pressures of the task. In fact, these strategies tended to be preferred by tutors. Several officers said that they would prefer to be 'counselled' by fellow tutors than by specially trained counsellors. This was because 'the counsellor is basically a stranger. [In contrast] You get very close to your SOTP colleagues' (female tutor pers. comm.). The support of an understanding partner is seen by some as crucial for maintaining a sense of normality. Indeed, a few of the SOTP tutors I interviewed (the majority of tutors in this unit were men) said that they relied heavily on their wives for support in times of stress and self-doubt. Sometimes, this need for support spills over into explicit requests for guidance in dealing with particularly 'difficult' inmates:

> I go to the gym on a regular basis. I find going for a run or punching a bag gets the frustration out of me ... Also I'm fairly lucky in that I can talk about what's going on with my wife. I don't er, I don't sort of use names, but I'll say I've got problems with this one, and he's saying one thing, and the deposition's saying another, and I'll ask her 'As a woman, how would you tackle it?' because now that we've lost the female probation officer ... it's, well, it can be a bit of a boys' club [there are no female officers in this group]. And what I mean when I say that is, as a man, there's things you might not pick up on ... And you need that. So I use my wife as a springboard for that, and she's happy to do that. Some of them wouldn't want to

expose their wife though. Mind you I tend to scale it down, 'cos obviously, you don't want to talk graphically about what some of these people have done, 'cos they're not nice, some of the offences. (Male officer and SOTP tutor)

For other tutors, the idea of contaminating home life with details of sexual offending was unthinkable. They resorted instead to very different coping strategies:

It doesn't disturb me [listening to their offences], it *astonishes* me. Some of the stuff's outrageous. But you can't talk to the Missus about it. So I go to a night club and I can scream my head off, 'cos the music's that loud they think I'm singing! (Male, middle-aged officer and SOTP tutor)

Arguably, this comment goes some way to illustrate the intensity of SOTP work. As we shall see, however, officers face an additional problem, namely the stigmatising character of the work itself.

Contamination and conflict: the impact of 'dirty' work

Using 'contamination' and 'conflict' as central concepts, I want to discuss now some rather different impacts of SOTP work. I will argue here that prison officers who do it wrestle daily with various types of conflict, some generated by the programme's emphasis on truth-telling (which I have already touched upon) and others generated by the occupational culture of the prison in which the programme is being run. First, officers who do SOTP work often have to cope with a sense of inner conflict, in that while they may have a strong desire to reform sex offenders, as I have already suggested this aspiration may co-exist with a revulsion of such offenders and their crimes. Amongst some SOTP officers there is a strong fear of moral contamination – that they are being 'tainted' by the work itself. By this I mean that they fear that prolonged contact with SOTP participants – which, as I have already discussed, involves them having to listen to graphic details of their sexual crimes – might change their *own* perceptions, attitudes and behaviour. In short, some of my interviewees felt that instead of changing sex offenders, the sex offenders might be changing them. There is evidence that involvement in the SOTP can cause officers to question their own sexuality and affect their sexual behaviour with their partners. SOTP officers also find that they have become much more aware of their behaviour with their own (and others') children, and how others might view it. Tutors also said they had become anxious about physically touching their own children, especially during bathing. As one female tutor put it: 'It makes you question your behaviour with your own kids ... You get nervous about touching your own children in the bath ... the way that you're holding them; where you're putting your hands.'

Without exception, all the tutors I spoke to had placed new limits on physical interaction with their children, either because they were 'unsure how offenders had started' or because they worried how their behaviour would be construed by others. Recent media reports of suspected child abuse cases had exacerbated their fears. A few years ago, Colin Turner, a higher psychologist from HMP Dartmoor, issued a survey questionnaire to staff conducting the core SOTP in the prison. Focusing on the emotional impact of the work, he reported very similar findings to those reported here (and in Crawley 2000b). Turner noted that nearly half of those with children felt that being involved in the programme had affected their relationship or behaviour with their own children in some way. They had certainly become more protective of their children, often to the extent of radically restricting their movements outside the house.

Secondly, tutoring can result in marital difficulties. Some officers found that their partners were less than happy that they worked on the programme, not least because of the sexual difficulties that tutoring had introduced into their lives. Indeed, several tutors reported sexual problems directly attributable to the 'contaminating' nature of SOTP work. One reported having become 'completely disinterested in sex'. Commenting on his (hopefully temporary) loss of libido, he explained that 'things they've told us in the sessions keep popping into my head, and it puts me off'.

Thirdly, officers who work as SOTP tutors may experience conflicts with colleagues. Some non-SOTP officers may resent tutors' willingness to work closely with sex offenders and treat tutors almost as 'nonces by association'. As Woolf (1991) commented, there are many staff within the prison system who share the prisoners' hatred of sex offenders; this hostility can attach itself to SOTP staff. Several of the tutors said that they had been criticised by some of their non-SOTP colleagues, even those who worked on the Vulnerable Prisoner Unit in which the programme took place. They had been told that this was not 'proper' prison work and that there was 'something wrong' with people who wanted to do it:

[Do any of your colleagues think that you should not be doing this kind of work?] Oh yes. They ask us 'What you working with them nonces for? Are you a nonce? Do you get off on it?' I think it's 'cos they've no idea of what we do. (Male officer and SOTP tutor)

Similarly:

> [Do you ever get any antagonism from any of your colleagues about you doing this kind of work?] Oh yeah. Quite regularly you get 'It doesn't work' or 'How can you listen to them?' or 'You just want to lock the buggers up!' (Male officer and SOTP tutor)

With regard to whether the rehabilitation of sex offenders is actually possible, many of those who had chosen *not* to work as tutors believed sex offenders to be irredeemable. As one senior officer concluded:

> Sex offenders are genetically abnormal ... no amount of therapy will make a blind bit of difference. [What do *you* think should be done with sex offenders?] I think they should be drowned! Actually they would have been taken round the back, beaten, and burnt at the stake 200 years ago.

Regime three: I wing, Wymott

Introduction

At the time of my research, Wymott's I wing[15] was not, strictly speaking, a 'specialist' unit. Little rehabilitative work was carried out there since the vulnerable prisoners living there were largely regarded as 'deniers' – prisoners who, although charged with sex offences, denied their guilt and their blameworthiness. As such they were deemed unsuitable for the SOTP. None the less I want to include the I wing regime in my discussion of staff conflict because the prisoners held on this wing were, like their counterparts in the SOTP and elsewhere, a despised group. Not only were they seen as 'nonces', many of them were also old. In consequence, I wing staff also found that their role (and ultimately their prison officer identity) was challenged by mainstream staff. In short, the work of I wing staff, like the therapeutic work of TC and SOTP officers, was not regarded as 'proper' prison work. Rather, I wing officers had been described by some staff on other wings as 'nonce nannies' (pers. comm.).

Sex offenders' crimes often remain hidden for years. This is particularly the case where their crimes have involved their own children. When these offences come to light (which is often not until these children are grown up) the perpetrators may already be well past middle age. Sometimes they are old (Crawley and Sparks 2003). Working with elderly prisoners has certain important implications in terms of 1) the nature of the work itself; 2) it's impact on the officer's self-identity; 3) officers' relationships with 'mainstream' colleagues; and 4) the nature and quality of staff–prisoner interactions.

Not proper prisoners? Not proper officers? Working in the 'old folks' home'

I wing had an 'enhanced' regime where ageing prisoners wandered about, sat in the TV room (there was a resident 'couch-potato'), read the papers (there was a communal reading room), chatted to one other, made cups of tea and hung around the wing office. At the time of my fieldwork, a significant proportion of I wing's population were over the age of sixty-five (the oldest prisoner was seventy-nine); there were, however, a small number of younger prisoners living there and employed as wing orderlies. The majority of the older men were first custodials (i.e. they had not served a previous prison sentence) so they were not 'prison-wise'.

Older, more experienced officers are often more suited to working with this kind of prisoner than their younger, less experienced counterparts. Of those who worked on I wing at the time of my research, a few were there simply because they were 'tired of fighting' (pers. comm.) and wanted a more predictable working environment which generated less anxiety and stress.

Working on such a wing can generate a strong sense of job satisfaction in those who enjoy interacting with prisoners. Not all older, experienced officers want this level of interaction however, and not all find satisfaction in the work. On the contrary, while they liked the pre-dictability of the environment (there was very little confrontation on I wing, certainly not towards staff at any rate) some of the staff working on the wing were not at all interested in talking to prisoners. Most of the younger staff detailed to work on I wing did not like working there either, because the work did not present a challenge – or at least not the right sort of challenge: 'The main thing we have to put up with in this co-operation is the mithering ... There's a hard core of mithering old bastards – "scuse the language" – who outstay their welcome in this office. They talk drivel' (male officer). One officer, a young man in his thirties, described I wing as being 'more like an old folks' home than a prison', largely because of the extreme age of some of those living there. George, the self-styled 'overseer' of the wing (there was no senior officer in charge at that time) accepted this analogy:

> This wing's not a challenge for the younger element, 'cos they're not gonna find anything on searching, etc. It *is* like an old people's home – just look at them sitting there [gesturing to a group of elderly inmates sitting in the newspaper corner]; it's like an old folks' parlour. This *is* an old lag's wing – for officers too.

While George was very content to do this type of work himself, he was none the less aware that it might not be the most suitable regime for newly recruited staff: 'The younger element can get a false sense of security [working on a wing like this] 'cos it's not traditional prison work.'

Working on I wing certainly failed to present its young officers with the challenges that they felt the prison officer's job should be about. I wing prisoners largely did as they were told and there was none of the rough and tumble found on other (non-VP) wings. Since the completion of my research, the regime and purpose of I wing have changed considerably. The staff group now includes a number of younger officers (male and female) who work positively and with enthusiasm with this prisoner group.

Discussion

Various aspersions are cast on prison officers who work in therapeutic regimes. As we have seen, officers in the therapeutic community are often accused by colleagues of being 'too soft' with prisoners, and consequently, not in control of them. As we have also seen, officers working as SOTP tutors are often stigmatised through association; the dominant cultural norms of uniformed prison staff encourage officers to rail against 'deviant' colleagues who are willing to work closely with prisoners seen as 'nonces' and 'beasts'. Similarly, officers who choose to work with elderly prisoners are seen as not doing 'proper' prison work because it is seen as too quiet, too predictable and too safe.

Spoiled identities: the 'deviant' prison officer

Officers working in specialist regimes such as these run the risk of acquiring a spoiled identity. That is, their willingness to work either with despised groups of prisoners or in regimes which espouse values contrary to traditional occupational norms may expose them to hostility and ridicule from other, 'mainstream' staff. As we have seen, SOTP tutors, like the sex offenders themselves, are often at the receiving end of derogatory remarks (for example about their sexual predilections) as a result of their willingness to work with this prisoner group. Arguably, the most obdurate aspects of occupational cultures in prisons – particularly the high value placed on machismo – become more visible in such settings. That they are making efforts to prevent future victims is the weapon SOTP tutors most use to counter 'mainstream' attacks:

My stock answer to their insults is 'Well have you got kids? Yeah, well right, I'm trying to do something so that when that person comes out, it's not your kid that's the next victim'. And I say it like that, and I say 'What are *you* doing?'

Renegotiating spoiled identity

The management of spoiled identity is an important component of the interactional skills of stigmatised individuals. Those whose actions or identities are challenged draw on a variety of strategies and techniques in an attempt to 'restore disrupted meaning, repair fractured social interaction, and re-negotiate damaged identities' (Hewitt and Stokes 1975). These strategies include the resort to socially acceptable 'vocabularies of motive' (Gerth and Mills 1954) – strategies often employed by those tainted by the stigma of 'dirty work' (Hughes 1971) and other forms of devalued behaviour.

Officers working in TCs and on SOTP s attempt to renegotiate their spoiled identities by asserting the positive value of their role in the face of claims to the contrary. The justification most often used is an appeal to higher loyalities (for a discussion of this in the context of policing, see Mulcahy 1995). As I indicated above, in the context of SOTP work officers justify their 'dirty work' by asserting that it may prevent further child victims. In the context of the TC, officers stress the value of their work in terms of helping young prisoners to become drug-free, responsible adults. To varying degrees, these strategies 'work' in the sense that they provide alternative credible identities to otherwise 'deviant' prison staff. It struck me that officers working on I wing, in contrast, where no 'treatment' was carried out, might find it more difficult to renegotiate their (spoiled) identities since their role *was* largely limited to 'looking after old folk'.

In recent years there has been increasing recognition of both the plurality of masculinities and the domination and subordination of particular masculinities – hence the notion of 'hegemonic' masculinity; that is, taken-for-granted dominant forms of masculinity that are powerful partly by virtue of overt dominance and partly through their taken-for-grantedness (Fineman 1993: 151 but see Connell 1987). 'Subordinated' masculinities, by contrast, are often discredited; men face pressure to conform to the status quo (Smith 1989). Yet men do think about, and perform, masculinity in quite different ways. As we have seen in earlier chapters of this book, controlling prisoners often involves everything *but* a physical response. For many officers, being 'manly' in the face of threat is not about being physically aggressive; rather it is

about staying calm and maintaining a sense of dignity and professionalism. Here the ability to risk the body in performance is directed
towards achieving a non-confrontational outcome, without losing face
(for a discussion of this in other contexts, see Jefferson 1998).

Although individual acts in prison are often sustained by a powerful
culture of masculinity, this culture is not homogeneous; on the contrary it
'contains internal contradictions and fissures out of which other,
empowering and positive patterns of behaviour have developed as a
challenge to traditional networks of domination and subordination' (Sim
1994: 101). According to Sim, the BSU in Scotland was 'the clearest
example yet of the challenge to [hegemonic] masculinity in prison'. I
have tried to show that masculinity *is* performed differently across
prisons and even within the same prisons and prison wings; in the
context of young offender institutions, Portland's TC is a striking
example of this. In Rodney House, male officers attempted to adopt and
develop versions of masculinity that were qualitatively different from
those employed by staff on the mainstream wings of the prison, in that
they elevated communication and negotiation rather than physical force
and confrontation.

Notes

1   These jobs have 'gone' in the sense of either having been contracted out to
    private services or performed by the new operational support grade (OSG).
2   The Prison Service Statement of Purpose is as follows: 'Her Majesty's Prison
    Service serves the public by keeping in custody those committed by the
    courts. Our duty is to look after them with humanity and help them lead
    law-abiding and useful lives in custody and after release.'
3   The work that prison officers describe as 'teaching' encompasses all those
    classes, sessions and courses designed to improve prisoners' thinking,
    communication, interaction, educational and practical skills.
4   There is widespread agreement that there are many mentally disturbed
    people in prison who would be better off in hospital. In 1994, 5.6% of all
    prisoners were considered by prison doctors to be in need of mental health
    care (NACRO 1993: 3).
5   Workplace bullying is a significant problem within the Prison Service,
    evidenced by comments from numerous officers (see especially Chapter 5),
    from various articles in the *Gatelodge* magazine and in literature provided by
    the Prison Service Staff Care and Welfare Service (PSSCWS). Several
    experienced officers reflected on the fact that despite a plethora of anti-
    bullying programmes for prisoners, management bullying of lower-ranking
    staff had increased over recent years. Bullying takes place at all levels of the

service; probationers may be bullied by longer-serving officers, experienced basic-grade officers by both their peers and by senior officers, senior officers may be bullied by principal officers and principal officers by the governor grades. Officers in their probationery year are particularly vulnerable to bullying; higher-ranking uniformed grades know that they are afraid to refuse because they need favourable progress reports to achieve a permanent contract.

6   In that they have broken both the criminal law and the social rules about the 'proper' behaviour of women.

7   The concept of liminality first came to anthropologists' attention through the work of the Dutch ethnographer Arnold van Gennep, a contemporary of Durkheim.

8   Metaphors are potent devices for embellishing our thinking and seeing; for conveying special meaning in a powerful yet succinct manner. Metaphors offer tidy and evocative analogies for complex social processes (for an interesting discussion of the use of metaphor in a range of organisations, see for example Fineman and Gabriel 1996).

9   It was interesting to note that the prison sit-com *Porridge* was regarded by many prison officers (particularly long-serving officers) as accurately reflecting the dynamics of staff–prisoner interactions. Most other prison dramas (in particular Linda la Plante's *The Governor*) were rejected as 'unrealistic rubbish'.

10   Stage 1 (orientation) is designed to impact a basic understanding of the therapeutic community concepts and principles. Stage 2 (primary treatment) emphasises the values of 'right' living and strengthens skills for independent decision-making. Stage 2 (re-entry) prepares prisoners for 'graduation' from the unit and where applicable his release into the outside community.

11   This is the therapeutic community's most important therapeutic mechanism. The purpose of such groups is to heighten self-awareness of negative behaviour by means of peer confrontation.

12   The morning meeting, held after breakfast, attempted to motivate prisoners to face another day with positive attitudes. The afternoon 'wrap-up' meeting focused on the day's events, and was the time when announcements were made about rewards, sanctions and administrative matters concerning prisoners.

13   In part, prisoners judge each other by the nature of their crimes. Even amongst sex offenders there is a 'hierarchy', with particular prisoners (usually those who have committed serious sexual crimes against young children) relegated to the bottom of it. Although SOTP participants must agree to keep group discussions confidential (i.e. not discuss them outside the group) prisoner participants do sometimes renege on that agreement and divulge information to other prisoners.

14   All prison officers in England and Wales are equipped with what officers call a stave – a short wooden weapon rather like a truncheon.

15 Since the completion of my research the regime and ethos of I wing have changed significantly. The wing is now, as a result of the hard work of a number of motivated individuals, a designated 'elderly and disabled community' (EDC) offering facilities, resources, activities (and even work) that are appropriate to its relatively large elderly and disabled prisoner group.

Chapter 8

Bringing it all back home?
Stories of husbands and wives

I want, now, to consider the impact of prison work on officers' home lives and their families. Although this is also a topic seldom discussed in the sociology of the prison, I intend to demonstrate here that the impact of prison work on husbands, wives and children can be profound.

In the American prison context, Kauffman (1988) provides persuasive evidence that the nature of prison work can alter home life significantly. In the British prison context, research into the topic is much more limited and largely quantitative; the Home Office (1985) survey of prison staff attitudes provides one of the few British studies of the social costs of prison work. While this survey does not provide data that are particularly 'rich' – respondents simply answered preset questions – it did, none the less, suggest to me some useful starting points from which to undertake my own research on the issue. I found certain aspects of the survey particularly interesting, for example the authors claims that 1) 46% of discipline officers felt 'under a strain' in their work; 2) 55% of discipline staff sometimes preferred not to disclose their occupation to others; and 3) most officers perceived that their attitudes and general outlook on life had been changed by the job. I wanted to know more about the ways that prison officers' interactions outside the prison setting might be influenced by the work that they do, and the implications of this for the lives of their partners and children. I was also interested to know the extent to which prison officers discuss their work problems at home, and the extent to which their partners are able to provide support given that they often do not know what the work actually involves.

Prison 'spill-over'

My interest in these questions was initially sparked by various off-the-cuff comments made to me by prison officers. As they talked to me about their work I became aware of the prison's capacity to 'spill over' into the home. This process of spill-over was one that I was keen to understand, but it was clear that to do so in any depth I would need to speak to the families of prison officers themselves. I was not sure how possible this would be, not least because some officers were initially wary about me even interviewing *them*, but my frequent presence on the prison wings, and the consequent relationships that developed between myself and the officers working there, made this process easier than I had anticipated. I was extremely fortunate that a small number of officers agreed to ask their wives if they would participate in the research. With their help I was able to conduct a series of in-depth, informal interviews with the wives of seven prison officers and with the children of two of them (a boy of ten and a young man of seventeen). Three of my interviews with these women were carried out on a one-to-one basis in their own homes, as was my interview with the seventeen-year-old. My interview with the boy aged ten was carried out in the company of his mother. The wives of the remaining four officers were interviewed altogether, and this group interview took place during the evening in the home of one of them. During this interview (which lasted nearly four hours) their husbands went out together to a nearby pub and did not come back until the interview was over (and the pub was closed). Initial interviews with all seven wives took place out of earshot of their husbands. During the three one-to-one interviews (each of which lasted for approximately two hours) each officer volunteered to stay out of the room while his wife was being interviewed but joined us later where we continued our conversation over a cup of tea or a glass of wine. Subsequent to these interviews, I was able to return to re-interview each of the seven officers in their own homes and in far more depth than had been possible in the prison setting, where they had admitted they had been a little cautious of speaking too frankly. This was because, as one of the officers put it, 'walls have ears'. My interviews with these seven women and their husbands form the basis of this chapter. For obvious reasons, names of all interviewees have, of course, been changed.

Methodologically, it is important to note that all the wives were in their forties and fifties, and married to men who had worked in the Prison Service for many years, one for as long as thirty years. As such, their views on (and knowledge about) the service, and on the impact of the job on home life and health may differ markedly from those of younger women whose husbands or partners are new to the service. Unfortunately I was not able to interview the husbands of any female officers during the period of the research; the prisons in this study were staffed predominantly by men, and so the number of interviews I was able to carry out with female officers was comparatively small. One female officer's husband did agree to be interviewed, but the interview did not take place because he was subsequently too ill to participate. The impact of prison work on the partners of female officers is clearly, of course, an important part of the story. From my conversations with female officers themselves, it is clear that men whose wives work in prisons, while they themselves work in other occupations, can (perhaps unsurprisingly) also find it difficult to adjust to the changes in their wives' attitudes and behaviour as they become prison officers. As we shall see below, female officers, like their male counterparts, may also recognise that they have been 'changed' by the job.

This chapter is structured around a number of key themes. First I examine wives' concerns about the impacts of the job on their husbands' health and well-being. I then discuss their assertions that their husbands have been 'changed' by the job, and that the prison has shaped (and reshaped) home-based relationships and interactions. Revisiting the concepts of 'stigma' and 'contamination' I then explore the ways in which wives feel that the (largely negative) public image of the prison officer rubs off on to them, and the ways in which their (indirect) contact with the prison impacts on their relations with others in the community. Finally I discuss the impact of prison officers' work on their children.

Danger, safety and health

All the wives I interviewed had concerns about the impact of prison work on their husbands' physical and emotional well-being. While four of these women were primarily concerned with the possibility of injury from prisoners, the rest were more concerned about the long-term effects of the emotional nature of the job: 'You don't know what effect it's having over their bodies. The range of emotions, like your adrenalin going up and down like a yo-yo all the time and having no set pattern of release' (Anna, wife of officer working at Portland).

These women were aware of the stressful nature of prison work, and they were also aware of the circumstances and events that tended to put their husbands under stress. Anna, for example, believed that inconsistencies in prison work practices and unexpected changes in staffing arrangements were a significant and routine stressor:

I think Pete finds it very stressful if he goes in and he hasn't got Dan with him, or Terry, or any of his regulars. One might be on leave, one might be on sick, and he comes home and I notice the difference then. He's very tense … he's had chaps in that's never worked on his wing, or they're new boys to the job anyway.

Jenny, whose husband also worked at Portland, agreed:

The same goes for Dan. If Pete's away, and he's doing Pete's job, and he's got a young team around him who are strangers – what he calls 'strangers to the house' – he says then his job is twice as bad, because he's got to control the inmates *and* he's gotta tell the officers what to do.

Two of the wives also identified management bullying as having damaged the psychological health of their husbands. Mary, whose husband worked with young offenders, cited bullying as the most significant contributor to her husband's nervous breakdown (and subsequent loss of confidence) after almost thirty years in the service:

erm, there was one point, erm, which was two, probably three years ago now, that it [the job] wore him down to the extent that he did take time off … about three months it was. And, erm, and he … there were some elements of depression, but most definitely it was, I would suggest that it was stress and anxiety that was the problem. [Well what was the stress about?] About people! About management! [Oh, *management*, rather than the prisoners?] Yeah. Yeah, yeah. I don't … do you know I don't think that … I don't think the prisoners cause him any stress, any undue stress. He manages. He manages well. I mean from my understanding, it was a case of bullying. Although Frank actually didn't … he didn't call it bullying, but what he said … you know, odd bits that he's said to me, I've thought, you know, this really is. It really *is* bullying. [So what did you think it was about it that constituted bullying?] Erm, right. It was more, I would suggest, verbal abuse.

Mary knew, however, that most prison officers – perhaps particularly long-serving officers – are reluctant to talk about stress at work. Drawing upon her own experiences as a psychiatric nurse, she noted that even in the wider community, stress is simply not seen as a man's problem:

If I get a woman referred [to me] its for stress and depression, and a woman will talk about stress and depression. If I get a man referred, it's for chest pains. It's only because the GP has recognised that these chest pains may be stress that he's come to see me, but so far as the person who's being referred is concerned, it's a physical problem. 'Cos men get physical problems, men don't get stressed!

All seven wives wanted to emphasise, none the less, that there were some *positive* impacts of the job, in particular the (inter-staff) friendships that had developed over the years and the capacity of the job to generate self-esteem and a sense of identity and purpose. All were aware that the job was all consuming, and they were unsure how their husbands would cope when they had to retire. As Sheila noted, from seeing others retire, it was as if once officers left the job they simply gave up:

> A lot of it, I think, is because they've had nothing after the Prison Service. Nothing to do, nothing to go to ... Because I mean once you put on your prison officer's hat you're on a high. You're in there, you're in the job, you're doin' it. Action. Yeah, action. Alright, they might have a quiet shift, they might play snooker, they might watch a film, but it's not always like that. But once they finish, once they retire, once they come home, and finish, that's it ... Certainly there's not many have a long retirement ...

Indeed all seven women had known, or had heard, stories about long-serving officers who had died very soon after retiring from the service, usually as a result of a heart attack (what officers often describe as a 'bluey') or a stroke, and they found this very worrying. It was interesting that on the prison wings, numerous officers had voiced the same concerns, but *they* tended to blame early deaths on years of shift-working, long working days (especially prior to Fresh Start), the unpredictability of the landings and the constant requirement 'to accept and soak up aggression' (pers. comm.).

Interestingly, several of these women had never even *heard* of the care teams that were operating in their husbands' establishments. Discussing the problems that had recently beset her own family, including her own serious ill-health and the subsequent near-nervous breakdown of her husband (who was trying to hold down his job in order to support his wife and two young children), Judith, whose husband worked at Lancaster Farms, had remarked:

> To me, there should be a team of workers up there, care workers – I don't know what *you'd* call 'em, so that when a prison officer gets

stressed up with *anything*, they can go to somebody and talk to ...
They need somebody there ... [Well from what I can gather, they
have this sort of care team that ...] Well I'll be honest with you, if
there's a care team up, up in ... I would like to know who they are,
because to be honest, to me, they don't give two hoots about prison
officers.

Those wives that had heard of the care teams tended to view them in
largely negative terms:

[How much, and what kind of support do officers suffering stress
receive from the Prison Service?] None at all. None at all. [What
about the care teams? Did they come to see Frank when he had his
nervous breakdown? Have you *heard* of the care teams?] Yeah.
[Were they any good?] I don't think anyone ever approached Frank.
Certainly, the governor came round out one day, and .. and I believe
that he came out to say, virtually, come on, pull yourself together,
let's have you back to work, and he caused, he caused us a great
deal of distress ...[Do you think he meant well?] I don't think he
understood what he was doing. (Mary)

The wives who had not heard of the care teams could recall situations in
which they themselves would have appreciated emotional support –
particularly when their husbands had been required to attend a prison
riot. For wives and partners sitting at home waiting for news, riots
generate fear, worry and anxiety, not least because they may find it
difficult to obtain even basic information from the prison. As this officer
working at Strangeways at the time of the riot commented:

A lot of wives were really worried because *they* weren't there facing
it. They were just seein' what was happenin' on TV and hearin' all
these horror stories ... One of the worst things that ever happened,
it shouldn't happen again, is that *some* officers – especially the ones
that came from other prisons – it was two or three days before they
could actually get out of the prison, get to a phone, and contact their
family to say where they were. And it was a disgrace. (Senior
officer, Lancaster Farms)

Or as Judith recalled:

They had riots up there and I didn't hear a word for three days. I
didn't know if he was ruddy knocked out or whether he'd ... I

mean a cell had caught on fire and a prisoner had got killed. I didn't know what the heck had happened.

Similarly, from Anna:

I know when I first came to Portland, they had a couple of blow-ups in succession and I know, like, five past nine you haven't heard a thing, and then you've got somebody else's wife ringing 'Has so-and-so rung up?' And you can't do nothing. You've just got to sit there and wait until they come home. [When they come home] *They're* laughing, because they *know* what's happened. But there's no liaison with wives. To me, that was very reminiscent of when Pete was in the army [in Northern Ireland], when all you've got is that television, and you're lookin' and you're thinking well I hope that isn't him, you know, three soldiers die in a land bomb or whatever it is, and erm that is how I felt then, because nobody will let you know, you know.

All the wives agreed that the 'not knowing' was the worst aspect of their husbands being involved in attending riot situations. Moreover, they felt that the service's procedures for providing informing for wives at these times was totally inadequate and hence unacceptable. They also noted that when 'trouble' arose, the prison (and what was going on within it) became all-important to their husbands; other prison officers became 'family' and 'outside' (i.e. home) life temporarily forgotten:

in the prison, there's nobody at all. I mean the men have got their union and everything else, but when there is a problem there is no body that forms that *you* can ring in and say what's this that happening. If you *do* ring in, and somebody bothers to answer the phone, and you can actually get through to somebody, nobody knows anything anyway. It's like the family, and all outside life is unimportant. (Anna)

Rose, the wife of a senior officer working at Lancaster Farms, spoke in graphic terms about her efforts to get information about her husband during the Strangeways riot:

We didn't know what, er, I think Sunday lunch-time it started, and er I think it was Monday night I think [when I found if he was okay] ... but we were all in the same boat, and me and my neighbour went down, it was really late at night ... cos we hadn't heard from 'em and we just happened to see Arthur, on the … taking a load of prisoners out of jail on a coach. We just happened, through a pure fluke, we just caught a glimpse of 'im, so we knew that he was alright, but my mate didn't know about her husband till a few hours later. [Was there a procedure in place where you could find out, or ring in, about what was happening?] No. It was total chaos. It was total chaos. The jail was burning … we'd got … my neighbour had got Sky – in them days it was something to have Sky – every hour reports, er, prisoners dead, officers dead, bodies lying all over and we just couldn't find anything out. Even the police down there, when we got down there, we said 'Look, can you *tell* us, 'cos we've heard on the news there's … [unclear] officers been found dead, on Sky News'. He says 'I can't love', he says 'No, you'll just have to go back. You can't come through … You'll just have to go back home and wait'. I mean I'm not the only one. There was loads of us; we just didn't know what it was all about.

Interestingly, all the wives bar one presumed that in such circumstances (and indeed in most other circumstances) *prisoners'* families would receive better treatment than the families of prison officers: 'See you've got inmates' families ringing in as well and *they've* got access to what's going on haven't they?' (Sheila). And from Anna:

I would think the way the Prison Service is going it is quite … it appears pro-prisoners, where *they* get all the counselling, and their families get all the counselling, because I mean, not, you know I'm not, not to their detriment or anything, but the prison officers who have to cope with *all* of this – all the emergencies, all the going in at the drop of a hat, regardless of what plans you've made, or anything, you can't plan far into the future or, all the disruption to family life, they don't get nothing at all. I mean at a push you can go to the doctor and get, you know, off on sick with stress or something, if you particularly want to protest about it, or your wife insists or whatever, but generally speaking … there's no actual person to actually say, you know, 'Right, off the landing, *now!*'

These comments correspond closely to an observation regularly made by prison officers – that prisoners and their families are 'better thought of' than them. According to Arthur:

[So is anything in place for wives to be given information?] No. They [management] don't give a monkey's toss about wives! Never have. [Really?] Never have. No. They're not interested. *Prisoners'* wives? Ah, now you're talking! Prisoners' wives? Ooh, must let the prisoners' relatives know. They don't *care* about staff.' (Senior officer, Lancaster Farms)

It was a common observation that the families of prisoners have more 'rights' than do the families of prison staff. While, of course, the accuracy of this perception can be questioned, it is important to note that prison officers and their wives *do* believe this to be the case (for a discussion of this in the American prison context, see Hawkins and Alpert 1989; Martin and Jurik 1996). When asked whether their husband's jobs had had an effect on their own health, two of the wives (Rose and Mary) said that it had, but for very different reasons. For Rose, fears about the dangers of the job caused her concern:

> if he's late, I get myself wound up, yeah I do, but not so much – perhaps I'm mellowing a bit – but not, not so much now, but I used to. I'd get myself really wound up. I mean he's had a few ... a couple of good hidings off convicts ... when he was at Strangeways... And the shortage of staff bothers me tremendously. I've thought about putting pen to paper about that many a time.

For Mary, it was her husband's distress that had led to her own. When I asked her whether her husband's job had impacted upon her *own* health, she replied:

> Er ...only that time that it affected Frank's health, and that was afterwards; that was when Frank was getting back to work. Erm, and I think that ... I had, I spent a few weeks feeling quite low, and quite stressed, very very irritable, mainly with, er, with Frank, and er, and I sorted it out in my own head, what it was all about, and it was all about anger, you know. It was how dare you bring all of this trouble here, you know, and erm, it was here you are, going back to work, everything is absolutely fine for you, and here you were left this shrivelling mess, you know! ... And yes I did, I got quite low, about it ... But yes, I can remember that really affecting my life; my own life and my work and health.

Officers differ markedly in terms of the extent to which they talk to their wives about their jobs. Some refuse to discuss work with their wives at all (even though their wives might ask to know more) while a few officers, particularly Sex Offender Treatment Programme tutors, confide in and seek advice from their wives a great deal. The wives of these officers provide an important supplement to, and in some cases a preferred alternative to, more formal sources of staff support.

Officers who prefer not to discuss work with their wives refrain from doing so for a number of reasons. For example they may fear that their wives will be indiscreet or they may simply believe that their wives are not interested. Other officers make every effort to keep their home lives and work lives totally separate because they have no wish to 'contaminate' the relative purity of the home with talk about prison (I shall elaborate on the issue of 'contamination' in a moment). They are also cautious of worrying their wives, invariably concluding that 'it's my job and I have to deal with it'. Others would like to talk to their wives more about the job but know that their wives would rather *not* know. As Rose put it when her husband joined in our conversation:

[When Arthur gets home, do you ask him about the kinds of things he's been doing that day, or do you tend to not want to know?] No. No. [You don't ask him?] No. I don't want to know. [Why don't you want to know, though?] [Arthur interjects at this point] She'd worry about it if she did. [And back to Rose] Yeah, yeah I think I would, yeah. I'd worry more knowing. Yeah, definitely. Funnily enough the girls at work asked me that, 'Ooh don't you worry?' I said 'No'. I said 'Cos I don't know. And I don't wanna know. And he's never offered ... offered it anyway, so no'.

Unable to 'offload' their worries at home, these officers must either share their worries with their colleagues (which, as we have already seen, they are usually loathe to do) or keep their worries to themselves. Of those officers who do discuss their work with their wives, what aspects of the job do they talk *about*? Most officers will happily tell their wives about a humorous event that has occurred during the shift; some will talk about a particular problem that arose at work that day while others will disclose to their wives their frustrations and anxieties about working with prisoners more generally (see above). One principal officer said that he talked regularly to his wife about his work difficulties, some of which she identified as the primary source of his ill-health. The first of these was the resistance to regime changes demonstrated by some of his staff. As Mary reflected:

you know, the group that, erm, [says] 'We've done it this way for so many years we're not gonna change it' *that* frustrates Frank awfully ... When he's trying to help them to move forward ... and I know that he's coming up against brick walls in places [Really?], yeah, a lot of objection to change. A lot of fear in the Prison Service, to change – nearly as much as there is in the Health Service! ... Wherever you go, there seems to be this little group, who, have got it sewn up; the job works for them, and if they look ... they're frightened to death of looking forward, because it changes their routine. It stops them playing pool, it stops them sitting with their feet up on the desk reading the newspaper, 'cos they're expected to do something else ...

A significant source of worry amongst several of the wives was the increasing recruitment of women officers into male prisons. Although it is now widely accepted that women officers can bring valuable communication and conflict-diffusion skills into prisons (see Chapter 7 but also Zimmer 1987; Martin and Jurik 1996) and as a result make them safer environments in which to live and work, unfortunately, the wives of prison officers often have little understanding of the prison environment – perhaps largely because their husbands choose not to talk to them about it. Perhaps unsurprisingly, Rose (and most of the other wives) held stereotypical views about the role of women officers in male prisons, and was convinced that the presence of women officers put her husband's safety in jeopardy:

I don't agree with women prison officers working in men's jails ... I've got nothing against the women involved, 'cos I know them and I go out with them. But I don't approve of them men's jails. [Why, though?] Well I think now, when the staff are so cut back ... if there's gonna be some sort of riot, or some sort of fight, what point's a woman? ... He [Arthur] says ah, but some of them we've got up there can get in with the rest of 'em. I said I don't care, at the end of the day a man will always be stronger than a woman ... I wouldn't like to think my husband's safety depended on a woman officer.

'Changed' by the job

The most commonly expressed remark made by all seven wives was that their husbands had 'changed' since becoming a prison officer (this perception was also shared by virtually every officer who took part in this study). They reflected that their husbands had become 'harder' (in the sense of having become less sensitive) and that they had become increasingly intolerant, cynical and suspicious as the years had passed by. As I noted above, all the officers I spoke to were in agreement that such changes had taken place, commenting also on the *daily* adjustments to persona that were required to bridge the space between home and work. Officers spoke of 'psyching themselves up' for the shift whilst driving to work, and of trying to 'come down' or 'wind down' on the drive back home; many of those officers living long distances from the prison in which they worked were glad of the long drive home precisely because it gave them time to unwind after the pressures of the day. They recognised that their work persona – the 'mask' they had developed for interacting with prisoners (and indeed with colleagues) – was often vastly different from the persona worn at home. The recognition that home/work personas were so vastly different was, for some officers, disconcerting, and to some extent resented:

> … the minute you go through that gate, you change. I mean, none of our respective partners would recognise us how we are in here. [For example?] I don't swear at home. Here, my language is atrocious … It's the same with Angela who's just started in the job – the change in her is tremendous. She's gone from a little quiet housewife to … It's not right that newcomers should be made to go with the flow, but the current just takes you up … (Senior officer, Garth)

Officers claimed that the job had 'changed' them in both positive and negative ways. On the one hand, most felt that being a prison officer had made them more self-assured: 'Door-to-door salesmen are no problem now, 'cos you're used to saying No to murderers and armed robbers. So it's made me more confident.' (male officer, Garth). Similarly:

> You become more assertive … in many things. You know, like at the checkout when you get there and the girl gets funny, says she's closed, I just stay there now. I refuse to budge. Or if the repairman's coming out and he doesn't turn up I'll ring and get stroppy. Before, you might be more submissive, and be prepared to put up with things. Not now! (Male officer, VP unit, Wymott)

And again:

> I'm definitely more confident … Once you've been in this job, you don't suffer fools gladly. If I ask the milkman to leave me a pint of milk and he doesn't, I want to know why. (Male officer, Garth)

Unsurprisingly, women also change when they join the service, and non-service husbands can find it bewildering: 'He says I've changed … He says I go home with an attitude' (female officer, Garth). This officer went on to say that she had become much more assertive and quick-witted since she had joined the Prison Service, and that she took home with her the verbal jousting she engaged in at work. Unfortunately her partner found this very difficult to get used to and this had led to arguments. Similarly, from an officer who had recently split up with her husband: 'He couldn't cope with the new me. He ruled the roost before.'

Interestingly, the increased confidence of officers can also rub off onto their wives:

> I used to be a very weak person ... Since I've married Ted I've got harder. And to me it's a good thing ... I stand up for myself a lot better. I'll not let nobody sit on me, or tell me off. If I see anything wrong, I just go and tell 'em off. [Do you think that's to do with him working in the job?] Yeah. Yeah ... It's hardened him *and* hardened me. (Judith)

As I have already suggested, however, change was not always seen positively. For some officers, the cynicism and suspicion engendered by the job had spilt over into home life to the extent that they were unable even to trust their wives. As this Garth officer put it: 'Sometimes I've dismissed what my wife's said, 'cos I'm so used to being conned here. [How do you mean?] I just think she's trying to get one over on me.' Similarly, from an officer working at Wymott: '*She* says I've changed for the worse – that the job's made me more suspicious. The thing is you get good at weighing people up – and you're usually right.'

This officer's metamorphosis into a more disciplined, wary and analytical individual had cost him his marriage:

> I thought I'd seen everything when I joined, but I knew nothing. My family thought I'd changed; I'd got a lot more confidence. But the change resulted in my divorce. My wife said I'd become more methodical ... I can't stand loose ends. And I try to analyse what everybody says ... [I'm] much more suspicious. And I think that's what made us split up. (Officer, Garth)

The following comment from Rose indicates the ways in which the practices and routines of prison life become the norm:

> Sometimes, he tries to, erm, bring the regime in 'ere really! [Can you give me an example?] Right, say he's cookin' tea. Now, I can be potterin' about upstairs, or hooverin', or whatever, [and he shouts

up] 'Im gettin' tea out now!' and he likes us down here, waitin', while he puts the tea out. Now I'm one of these that [says] 'Put the tea out, I'll be down in a minute', and yeah, you know, he tries to run it like he's in the prison, or, and he tries to boss our Andrew about as well ... Andrew 'll say 'You're not at work now Father!' [Do you think he tries to boss him around like any Dad does, or do you think he treats him like an inmate?] No, I would say he tries to boss him round like an inmate! 'Do this, do that, do the other!' [We both laugh] ... He just gets a bit 'do this, do that, move this, what's this doin' here it shouldn't be there ... 'And you have to say 'Hey, hey, hey, you're not at work now!' ... [In fact] I've noticed it more now, as Andrew has got like fifteen upwards ... I generally co-operate to avoid an argument, but really I don't want to be regulated like that ...

The tendency to control was more marked for officers working in those parts of the prison where rules were applied particularly strictly: 'When he was working in the segregation unit, he couldn't switch off. He demanded our instant attention' (Sue). Officer husbands were described by their wives as either 'institutionalised', 'routinised' or 'routined'. Although the terms 'institutionalise' and 'routinised' have slightly different meanings, these wives used them in the say way, i.e. to indicate that their husbands liked things to run smoothly; they *needed* to have things done at particular times and in particular ways. Arguably, one of the unintended effects of the prison is that prison officers as well as prisoners come to rely on routines, procedures and timetables to reinforce their sense of ontological security. Note the comments of an officer from Wymott who had transferred, twelve months earlier, from administration to the discipline grades: '[You] become pre-occupied with routines ... Routines are drilled into you at training. I never used to be always on at the kids before I came on this side ... [e.g. eating at a certain time, bed at a certain time].'

Some longer-serving officers have adjusted to this pressure and have found ways of reducing the impact of the job on home life:

Me and my wife have got an agreement that the day I start acting like a prison officer at home is the time I leave the job. The Billy Barrett you see at work is not the Billy Barratt you'd see at home ... It has an impact on home life if you let it ... [so have you tried to resist acting like a prison officer at home?] I've totally resisted it. Although my wife has pulled me up a couple of times ... 'Hey, you're not in the prison now!' she says. (Officer, VPU, Wymott)

Some prison officers expected their wives to be suspicious too. Describing his wife as 'the kind of person who within half an hour of having met somebody will have told them all about us' a long-serving officer from Wymott said that whenever he was out with her he felt the need 'to rein her in a bit'. Prompted by his wife, he also admitted his tendency to stare at 'suspicious' strangers whenever they have a night out. While staring suspiciously was, for him, the norm at work, he recognised that 'When I do this when we're out its embarrassing for the wife'. Interestingly, this officer also recognised, as many others did (see above) that he had become much more impatient, particularly when waiting to be served in shops. According to this officer, this is 'because officers get used to people doing as they say straightaway'. As I suggested in Chapter 7, those officers *least* likely to feel that working as a prison officer had changed them were officers who had served in the armed forces. In addition to having prior knowledge of danger, they had already been socialised into a suspicious and wary worldview: 'Me, myself, I don't think I've changed. But I've been in Northern Ireland, and so I'm used to being aware of dangers and suspicious people' (male officer, Portland). Rose acknowledged, however, that it was, of course, impossible to say whether the job alone had changed her husband or whether he would have acquired his particular outlook anyway, just by getting older. Her husband made a similar point:

> [Do you feel that being a prison officer has changed your outlook on life?] The simple answer to that is I don't know. I really don't ... I don't know ... Had I taken different employment, I *may* have been more laid back. But I dunno ... There's nothing to say that I wouldn't have been just as uptight if I'd been ... [in an office] It might have driven me daft, actually, stuck in an office.

Contamination, stigma and revenge

A Home Office survey (1985) found that slightly more than half (52%) of uniformed respondents felt 'quite happy' to tell people they worked for the Prison Service. The remaining 48% of uniformed staff, however, 'sometimes preferred to keep it to themselves'. The survey also found that well over half (61%) of uniformed staff said they felt that they were regarded differently when their occupation was known to others. Some 51% felt that they were *treated* differently. According to this survey, the most common response was that 'outsiders' either regarded them with suspicion and wariness or ignored them altogether. Put simply, 'It was as though others saw upon them the miasma of prison and were keen to avoid it' (*ibid*.: 64). Virtually all the officers I interviewed indicated that they felt, or were treated as if, they had been 'contaminated' by their contact with the prison. As we shall see in a moment, the issue of 'contamination' arises both in the context of officers' interactions with the general public and in the private sphere of the home. With regard to the former, I suggest that while the type of establishment may have little bearing on the likelihood of disclosure, the nature of staff–prisoner relations within that establishment do. Officers who worked in prisons which had positive reputations within the wider community (i.e. prisons where staff were believed, by prisoners and their families, to be helpful and fair) tended to be less reluctant to reveal their occupations than officers working in prisons where staff had the reputation for being abusive and unfair: 'If you work at Lancaster farms, no problem, 'cos it's got a good name. If you work in a jail with a bad reputation, staff's wives might not like to tell people what their husbands' work is' (senior officer, Lancaster Farms). Similarly: 'When I'm out, I don't tell *anybody* my job, 'cos lots of people have been inside. Also, other jails give us a bad name, 'cos they're lock-up jails. [There] It's just ordering inmates about, and they don't forget it' (male officer, Garth).

Context also has a bearing on whether disclosure will (or will not) take place. Certain settings make disclosure unlikely; officer are less likely, for example, to disclose their occupation to strangers in a local pub than to strangers sharing the same hotel on holiday. One strategy that officers regularly use to avoid occupational disclosure is simply to tell strangers that they are 'civil servants'. This is usually sufficient to ward off the three types of response commonly encountered by officers when they reveal their true occupation, namely:

1 The response from fascinated individuals who either want to bombard the officer with questions and offer various banal philosophies about prisons or indulge their fantasies (which murderers do you have? Do you give them a good kicking?) – none of which is particularly welcome during a night out with friends:

> I don't mind telling people what I do, but if I do tell them, a lot of people just want to talk about it all night. And I don't want to do that. They say to you 'I'd beat 'em up, me!', and 'Give 'em bread and water!' (Basic-grade officer, Garth)

2 The response from individuals who would rather not know anything about prisons. When prisons are mentioned in the company of these individuals, the conversation often comes to a grinding halt.

3   The hostile response of anti-authority individuals, especially ex-prisoners who may want to do the officer harm.

With regard to the latter, several of the wives had deep concerns that they themselves (or worse still, their children) might become the victims of assault by disgruntled ex-prisoners. They understood that their husbands, like all prison officers, had been 'contaminated' by the prison and, in consequence, they themselves had experienced 'vicarious contamination'. In other words, they had experienced some of the consequences of being a prison officer without having ever worked in a prison. The public image of the prison officer can impact significantly on the day-to-day interactions of the prison officer's wife. Each wife differed, however, in terms of her willingness to disclose her husband's occupation, and in her perception of the threat her husband's job might pose. Mary, for example, claimed that she was very proud to tell people what her husband did for a living; indeed she welcomed any opportunity to present the prison officer in a more positive light, particularly since his recent promotion to the governor grades:

> [Are you happy to tell outsiders what your husband's job is?] Oh yeah. Yeah, no problem. I don't have any problem at all telling people that he works for the Prison Service. Never have had. Whether he's been an officer, a senior officer, a principal officer, and I mean it's lovely now, saying my husband's a prison governor! Yeah, I'm proud. I'm very proud of what he's done. I don't have any problem at all with it. And I think it's always a chance, you know, there's always an opportunity to make people see it a little bit differently, you know. It isn't the bread and water, they're not slopping out, you know, they're not banged-up for ever more, and I know that cos I've actually seen it.

In contrast, and despite her husband's insistence that the threat to prison officers' families be kept in proportion, Rose said that she would never disclose her husband's occupation:

> [So are you quite happy to tell people what Arthur does for a living?] No. No. No. No. No, I mean obviously, the girls I work with, they know what he does, but … if anybody asks me, you know, or if I have to fill out a form or something, I just put civil servant. [Oh do you?] Yeah. Yeah. [Why? Is that because you worry about repercussions?] Yeah. Yeah. Yeah. I don't publicise what he does … [Does it bother you in case, like … ?] In case I get a brick

through my window! [Does it?] Yeah it does, I have to say. [What, ex-inmates, or … ?) Yeah, it doesn't bother me so much … *here* … [but] it bothered me a lot when we lived in Manchester, you know, when the area we lived in wasn't too salubrious, you know. You were lockin' up the people that you living' with. Erm, but no, I wouldn't … it's something that I don't like. But I'm a bit … I'm funny like that. Even with market research – I don't offer anything voluntary.

Similarly: '[Are you quite happy to tell strangers what John does for a living, or do you tend to be a bit wary?] A bit wary. A bit wary. No, I don't think I would tell anybody about his job' (Jenny). None the less, Jenny did *not* believe that she or her husband were likely targets for victimisation:

[Relating to whether you would tell outsiders what Dan does for a living, have you ever felt that you might be victimised by ex-prisoners, for example?] No. No. No. No way. I mean there's many a time me and John could be walking along the sea front, and these fellas' say 'Good afternoon Sir!' [Oh really?] And I'll say to John, 'Who were they?' And he'll say 'They were my ex-cons' … [from when] he used to work at the Castle or, you know, up at the Farms. They'll say 'Hello Sir' and that's it. [Really?] … I can't see that prison officers wives … that getting victimised is very likely.

While some wives were unperturbed if their husbands stop to talk to ex-prisoners while they are out shopping or having a day out, others disliked it intensely. As Rose remarked to her husband when I interviewed them both at home:

If, like that time we met that fella in Asda, that – we'll see a few of 'em don't we, your inmates? – and he'll stop and talk to 'em. I will walk away. I don't want them knowin' that … I don't want them to know my face, that I'm a part of that. I feel really threatened.

As I have already noted, most officers are aware that, as an occupational group, they are perceived in a negative light by the general public. These seven wives were aware of this too, and they deeply resented it:

I think they think prison officers are big, burly, thick, unemotional bullies … and they *don't* think that they've got children the same age or they've got problems, or that, you know, they cope the best way they can. (Anna)

243

Moreover, both officers and wives felt that negative media reporting and dramatic (often fictional) representations have done little to dismantle this stereotype. Several officers commented that the public view them in the same light as the police; as 'spies' whose primary orientation, even off duty, was that of surveillance. It was because of such stereotypes that wives are often wary of revealing their husbands' occupation. The picture is not an entirely negative one, however. A female officer from Garth claimed that working for the Prison Service had in certain respects *improved* her status in the community (her husband is also an officer). They were perceived by their neighbours as improving the safety of the neighbourhood precisely because of their confident, suspicious and observant disposition:

> If you, for example, see kids mucking about in the street, you don't think; you just dive in ... You feel, in a sense, that you're protected when you're in your uniform, and that carries over to when you're outside the prison – in your civvies. You get used to getting stuck in – it's almost second nature. Also, you're more observant, and more suspicious ... If things don't seem quite right [you'll follow it up]. It's as though your antennae become more finely tuned somehow.

Most prison officers resent the negative picture that the general public tends to hold of them *as people*, and regret that they do not have a more positive picture of what prison officers actually do. As we saw in the previous chapter, some officers noted the public's perception that there must be 'something wrong with' people who want to be prison officers; none the less it can still come as a shock, even to the most experienced and mature officer, when he is asked if he is sexually aroused by locking people up (senior officer, Lancaster Farms pers. comm.). Prison officers, in short, often find that their social lives are to some degree contaminated by the work that they do. One female officer gave, as an example of this, the attitude of other patients to her whilst she was waiting in her doctor's surgery:

> If I have to go to the doctors in my uniform, when I sit in the waiting room, people just move. [How do you mean?] They physically move away from you ... It's as if you smell. You get people who are hostile towards you, say if you go to Tesco in your dinner-hour. You try and bring a civvy coat, but they titter or they follow you around the shop or they'll be openly hostile. [How do you cope with this?] You have to make light of it. (Female officer, Moorlands)

For one female officer the prison's potential to 'contaminate' had both a material and symbolic reality. It was extremely important to this officer that she maintain the boundaries between the purity of the home (clean, secure, safe and 'sacred') and the impurity of the work environment (dirty, dangerous, germ-laden and 'profane'). This was not simply to avoid the pollution of the home by prison dirt but also to avoid the polluting effects of symbolic contact with 'profane' individuals. To do so she engaged in various rituals of purification. One of these, performed without fail on arriving home at the end of each shift, was the immediate removal of her prison uniform – a ritual she described as 'a cleansing process'. She made particular efforts to ensure that her uniform (and all other clothes associated with the prison, including work underclothes) were kept separate from non-work clothes – clothes that were uncontaminated by the prison. Her increased use of disinfectants and bleaches in the home since joining the service, her refusal to drink from a 'work mug' at home and her refusal to discuss prison work or individual prisoners in the bedroom demonstrated her stated desire to keep work life and home life entirely separate. All these rituals constitute what Douglas (1970: 44) terms 'ritual purification'; they serve to remove or avoid what Douglas refers to (*ibid.*: 48) as 'matter out of place'. To understand this we must be willing to abstract pathogenicity and hygiene from our notion of dirt. Dirt as matter out of place:

> is the by-product of a systematic ordering and classification of matter, in so far as ordering involves rejecting inappropriate elements. This idea of dirt takes us straight into the field of symbolism and promises a link-up with more obviously symbolic systems of purity. (*Ibid.*)

Dirt, on this view, is a relative idea. Things are not dirty in themselves: rather they are dirty when they are not where they should be (for example when shoes are placed on the dining-table, or underclothes are lying about in the kitchen). In short, 'our pollution behaviour is the reaction which condemns any object or idea likely to confuse or contradict cherished classifications' (*ibid.*). The actions of this officer may, of course, be exceptional (none of my other interviewees discussed the issue of 'contamination' in quite the same way) but they do, none the less, alert us to the fact that, even for some of those working in it, the prison represents an 'Other', 'profane' place.

The impact of the job on children

The prison officer's job can be hard on children too. Officers acknowledged (as did their wives) that the nature of the work affected the way they behaved with their own children. The fear that one's children might 'get into trouble' – arguably a fear that most parents have – may be heightened by the experience of working in a prison: 'I frighten him [my son] sometimes … I tell him what can happen when you go out … getting into trouble … and about drugs' (male officer, Garth). Officers are aware that they are often too severe with their children, particularly when they themselves have had a bad day at work:

> My missus says I'm too strict with my little girl. [Do *you* think you are?] Yes. [How old is she?] Five years old. Sometimes, if she, say, drops a cup, I shout at her – you know, *really* shout. I can tell I scare her … It's worse if I've had a bad day. [What counts as a bad day?] SO's [senior officers] getting on your case, finding you've been extended for the next day, cons hassling you. (Officer, Wymott)

Those working with young offenders were perhaps particularly likely to treat their children like prisoners when they got home: as Rose put it 'I found Arthur's bossiness got worse as our Andrew got to the same age as the inmates'.

Mary reported that her husband's interactions with their son were limited to requests to perform tasks and household duties. This troubled her; she wanted him just to *talk* to the boy:

> I quite often say to Frank, you know, you tend to treat Mark … he's not one of your prisoners! … There's this air of discipline [to illustrate the point, Mary sat bolt upright] all of the time, and I think that probably the children do miss out, and again, probably a lot of it is personality. But I really do think that a lot is the job, and, and I think Frank has learned to er, ask questions all of the time, erm, he wants an answer – 'What have you been doing?' You know, or 'Pick your clothes up!' or 'I want you to do more of this!' and I very often say to him, 'When did you last hold just an ordinary conversation with Mark?' That's the way that I see it. [So when you say that he talks to him like a prisoner, could you give me an example?] Like he … the only time that he tends to talk to Mark is if he's wanting him go tidy his room, if he's wanting him pick stuff up … er … the only time that he will perhaps have a conversation, say about football, is if I've said to him 'For goodness sake, you never hold just an

ordinary conversation with Mark'. It's almost as though it jolts his memory then. Erm, and he will actually change his tone then, towards him, and he'll actually say 'You alright mate?' you know, that sort of thing, almost as though he's aware that he needs to soften. But it doesn't last! He's back into the disciplinarian image. [Was he like that with your other two?] Oh very much, yes. Oh yeah. Yeah. [But] how different he would have been had it been another job I don't know ...

Terry, the husband of Sue, observed that there is a tendency for those who work with prisoners to be 'over-protective with daughters'. He admitted that whenever his daughter brought boyfriends home, he immediately 'sussed them out', on the grounds that 'in this job, you get good at judging people', claiming that his years of working with prisoners had given him the ability to recognise falseness as opposed to openness and honesty: 'I used to think "What reprobate is she gonna bring in now?" '

Andrew, whose father had worked in the service for a quarter of a century, remarked that on occasion, his father adopted the same tone of voice and demeanour in the home setting that he used at work. He had suddenly been struck by the fact that whenever a friend came to call, his father responded like a prison officer during visits; that is, he stood at the bottom of the stairs and shouted loudly, as he would to a prisoner, 'visitor!' This struck his son as a peculiar way to treat guests, and he had asked his friends if it had struck them as peculiar too. They agreed that yes, it had.

During the course of my research, a number of officers had reflected – sometimes with dismay – on the way that they brought routines home from the prison. One officer, a man in his late thirties, reported giving his young son a rub-down search after noting that chocolate had gone missing from the fridge. Another, convinced that his teenage daughter had taken up smoking, had searched her room from top to bottom for cigarettes. It occurred to him only later that he had carried out the equivalent of a cell 'spin' in his own daughter's bedroom. Both these officers work with young offenders.

Neither are the children of prison officers immune to the feeling that they too have been contaminated by the prison. On the contrary, they are often reluctant to let their school-friends know that their father or mother is a prison officer, because they fear they will be treated with hostility or shunned. One female officer, herself the mother of a teenage daughter, put it this way:

My daughter said 'I'm bringing some friends round. You won't be in your uniform will you?' [Why does she not like you to wear it when her friends are there?] Because of peer pressure I suppose ... What her friends will think. The kids class us very much with the police, who teenagers don't like.

Similarly:

Andrew, my son, he's had a few good hidings 'cos of his Dad's job ... You know [kids saying] 'We know what your dad does' and what have you, and he's had a couple of thumpings, and nastiness, and that, 'cos of it while his Dad was working at Strangeways. (Rose)

Andrew, now in his late teens, is still reluctant to disclose, to outsiders, his father's occupation, because of both a lack of public sympathy for prison officers and because of fears of reprisals. According to Rose:

Last year, he was at college doing sociology, and, erm, his sociology teacher, she was a nice enough woman but, how can we say it, a bit naive. Sometimes, like, sociology – she was away with the fairies! Away with the fairies I think Linda was. And there was another prison officer's lad in the same class, now Linda doesn't know what Arthur does, and she had them for two hours, slaggin' off prison officers, in the lesson ... Erm, and I've been mugged, as well, so our Andrew knew what that did to me, and she's goin' on about, you know, all these nasty prison officers, and all these nice convicts ... Anyway – I'm goin' off the story now – I said [to Andrew] didn't you say anything? He said 'No', he said, 'I don't want people round here to know what my Dad does'. He says if they find out they find out, but I'm not standing up in a class full o' yobs and saying what my dad does.

Concluding comments: moving between two worlds

The extent to which prison officers bring the prison back home can be disturbing, frustrating and vexing for their partners and families. It can also come as shock to the partner of a new recruit. I asked Mary, whose husband had served as an officer for thirty years, what advice she could offer to make the transition from being a wife, to the wife of a prison officer, less painful. After some thought, she replied that if prison officers and their families were at least aware, at the outset, of the problem of prison spill-over, they might be in a better position to recognise it and deal with it in a more effective way:

> I think that I would probably, I would probably advise someone to be very aware of how the job can affect your family life. And, you know, they would need, she would need to work towards some sort of agreement that they would retain what they'd got, because there is so much of – like where the children are concerned – there is so much of habitual behaviour, that eventually creeps in.

The wives who agreed to share with me some of their stories and experiences were all too aware of the emotional demands made on their husbands in their performance of the prison officer role. They were also acutely aware of the difficulties their husbands face in *ceasing* to perform the role of prison officer when they get home. As I have already suggested, some of the resources which prison officers draw upon to perform their role are drawn upon by others working in emotionally charged occupations, for example nursing. Each of these occupations has, of course, its own distinct combination of spill-over. As I have attempted to show in this chapter, the spill-over of prison work derives from four key issues, namely, danger, routinisation, desensitisation and contamination. This combination ensures that the potential for role engulfment is high, and officers' ability to come 'out of role' low. Indeed, as the comments of these wives and officers demonstrate, a striking aspect of prison work is the strain of living in, and moving between, two worlds – only one of which is contained within high walls.

Chapter 9

Conclusions: doing prison work

Throughout this book I have attempted to explore issues that, although largely neglected in the sociology of the prison, are fundamentally important to understanding how prison work is 'done' and the impacts of prison work on those who do it. In developing this book, the concept of 'emotional labour' has proved to be a powerful analytic lens through which to view the prison officers at work. Throughout the book I have used this lens to demonstrate that in addition to being places for the confinement of law-breakers, prisons are emotional and highly domestic spaces in which prison officers must perform and manage emotion in their day-to-day work. As I have tried to show, working in prisons is emotionally demanding and the emotions generated by prison work are many and varied. These emotions are rarely, however, freely expressed.

Clearly, how prison officers feel about the work they do, how they feel about prisoners and fellow officers, and the extent to which (in their efforts to convey the 'right impression' of themselves) they are able to manage and perform emotion have implications both for the nature and quality of imprisonment, for their relationships with prisoners and, equally important, for their relationships with fellow staff. With regard to relationships with colleagues in particular, there is no doubt that the occupational norms of individual prisons can bring to bear profound emotional and psychological pressures on prison officers. Failure to display the 'right' emotions in the 'right' place and at the 'right' time is to risk being constructed as an occupational 'deviant' by fellow officers and excluded from the occupational group. Male officers must also be able to muster some version of the 'masculine' prison officer image; for women officers, however (perceived by many male officers as exerting a

250

'calming' or 'civilising' influence on prisoners) a macho image is unnecessary (though as we have seen, some women officers choose to present one). Prison officers pride themselves on being able convincingly to mask their feelings and, as I have demonstrated throughout this book, they draw upon an array of well rehearsed coping strategies to keep unwelcome emotions in check. The use of humour is a particularly important strategy for coping; from their first days on the prison landings new recruits recognise that humour is an essential part of the socialisation process – that learning to 'banter' is crucial to *becoming* and *being* an effective prison officer. Private feelings can, over time and under pressure, however, 'leak' through the mask, either in frustration, distress or anger.

As I have already suggested, it is within a context of domesticity and familiarity that the emotional performances of prison officers acquire their relational meaning. We know that emotional interchanges are more likely, more meaningful and more fluent in contexts in which there are high levels of intimacy, shared knowledge of context and a never-ending but intermittent 'dialogue' between the social actors involved. The emotional interchanges of family life are the most obvious and best example of this, and as I hope I have managed to show in this book, there are some striking similarities between the nature and structure of relationships in prisons and those in the familial setting of the home. A key aim of this book, of course, is to demonstrate that emotion and emotion work are part and parcel of the predicament of imprisonment, for prison officers as well as for prisoners. Far from being an 'add on' to prison life, emotions – and their management and mobilisation – are actually pivotal to the way in which organisational order in prisons is achieved and undone.

The various staff conflicts I have discussed in this book arise, in part, because the prison has to function as an institution concerned not only with security and control but also, increasingly, with 'treatment' and 'rehabilitation'. These activities must take place in prisons obliged to receive and care for rising numbers of prisoners, despite many (probably most) prisons having insufficient and inadequate resources and the lack of space to do so. When we ask prison officers to take on 'treatment' roles, and to do so under such conditions, we need to be aware that we are making particular demands on them – demands that can bring opportunities, challenges and rewards but which can also create staff conflict, stigmatisation and high levels of occupational stress. In all organisations there are, of course, staff conflicts – many trivial, some less so – and they arise for a variety of reasons. As I suggested in Chapter 1, *all* organisations are emotional arenas; for each one of us the workplace represents an important part of our social existence, so it is perhaps unsurprising that the workplace – in this case the prison – is replete with the same human feelings experienced outside work.

Skolnick's concept of 'working personality' has – to some extent – proved a useful analytic device for analysing the working cultures of prison officers. As we have seen, there *are* certain cognitive and behavioural responses to prison work that are strikingly similar to those found in police work (i.e. the tendency towards cynicism, suspicion, machismo and a strong sense of group solidarity). Although, as in police work, the *strength* of these tendencies depends to a great extent on working conditions and contexts (not least the type of prison that officers work in and the kind of work that officers choose to do), I did find them in all the prisons in this study. None the less, I have come to think that compressing the myriad ways in which prison officers think about, feel about and perform their work into a descriptive 'working personality' is perhaps merely to construct yet another stereotype or at the very least another 'ideal type'. As we have seen, prison officers are a very heterogeneous group, and they respond to the demands and pressures of their work in very different ways. In that the occupational culture of prison officers is shot through with splits and fissures, conflicts and instabilities it makes more sense to speak of prison officer cultures. Throughout this book I have argued that prison officers defend distinctly different visions and versions of the prison officer role. Their attitudes towards prisoners differ markedly, depending largely on officers' views on the causes of crime and the purpose of imprisonment itself. As we have seen, inter-staff resentments, tensions and conflicts as to what counts as 'proper' prison work and who should be doing it are widespread and often intense. Although many prison officers have a strong desire to 'make a difference' in prisons, this is difficult in prisons as they are currently organised. High prison populations stretch resources to the limit and impact on the availability of staff training, often making officers' attempts to rehabilitate prisons a *practical* impossibility. The other key (and long-standing) concern of prison officers – that they are unsupported and undervalued by their managers – has practical and far-reaching effects in the prison. As I have already suggested, it can result in officers being less ready to respond to the needs of prisoners and in officers themselves suffering increasing levels of demoralisation. The need to get staff–prisoner relationships 'right' has already been recognised (Home Office 1984); it is perhaps time for prison managers to get the staff–management relationship 'right' too.

It has been interesting to note, given the solidity of the prison wall, the ease with which the emotions, values, routines and attitudes generated by prison work leak into officers' personal and home lives. Neither the 'people worker' nor the 'bureaucrat' is immune from this; the latter takes home his liking for discipline and order while the former, perhaps especially the SOTP tutor, takes home his anxieties and feelings of moral contamination. As a *way of seeing* the social world of the English prison officer, the sociology of emotions has proved invaluable. It has enabled me to explore the relations between prison bureaucracy, rationality and emotion and the ways in which control (and hence order) in prisons is sustained by various forms of emotional performance and emotion work. I hope that it has also allowed me to convey to the reader some sense of the working lives of prison officers, and of the complexity of their task.

Appendix

Speaking metaphorically: how prison officers see the prison

It's like in an airport waiting lounge when everybody's plane's three hours late, and nobody knows where they're going or when, and everybody's tired and stressed out. A mass of confusion! (Male officer, Lancaster Farms)

It's like *Porridge!* ... Its really comical working in a prison. Not so much *here*, 'cos they're boys, but at Belmarsh we used to have a right laugh. (Female officer, Lancaster Farms)

It's like a kindergarten [So does that mean that you have a teacher's role?] No, it's more like being a Mum for me. You get it from the staff *and* the inmates ... I'm like an agony aunt to everybody! (Female officer, Lancaster Farms)

It's like a boarding school. 'Cos you're always telling 'em off and they can't go home. (Male officer, Lancaster Farms)

It's like a youth club with screws! (Officer, Lancaster Farms)

Once they come through the gate its like a factory; you're just pushing them through. (Male officer, Lancaster Farms)

This place is like a sausage machine; we're forcing them in one end and out the other. (Male officer, Lancaster Farms)

It's like a school. Depending on where you work and that, but you watch them some days, running around like little kids, seeing what they can get away with … It's a bit like being a teacher I suppose. But again, that's only one part of it. (Male officer, Garth)

I see prison officers as a social worker or a waiter – something like that … Or a nurse. 'Cos we're basically looking after people. (Male officer, Garth)

It's along the lines of a YMCA or a school, cos you're doing basically everything for them. (Male officer, Garth)

It's like its own little community really … [with] all different characters, and you're all pushed in there together and you've got to get on. (Male officer, Garth)

It's just like a stricter YMCA. (Male officer, Lancaster Farms)

It's like a senior school. With lots of teenagers and you're the baddy. A schoolteacher, out to spoil their fun. (Female officer, Garth)

I think it's like a creche, 'cos its like having a load of little kids and you've got to put them right now and again. (Female officer, Garth)

I'd say its like a hospital, 'cos of the nature of the people we're getting in here at the moment. (Male officer, Garth)

Aylesbury was like a madhouse. Here it's more like a school … [in what way?] In the way that we try to educate them to do things. I mean you have these sentence planning boards, and you try to sway them over to your way of thinking. And if they can't read or write you try and push them towards education, and if they're weak, you might push them towards the gym. Or you might try and get them to achieve an NVQ – something that will be recognised [outside]. (Male officer, Garth)

It's like a holiday camp – for both inmates and staff. 'Cos its not a hard place to work in, and the place ticks over, and there's a lot of humour in the place … I don't mean like Butlins really – more of a holiday camp-cum-school. The lip they give us … schoolkids get suspended and *they* [the cons] get the block! And they get a two pound fine and they come back laughing at you. No, I can't really call it a holiday camp – more a school. (Male officer, Garth)

There's *nothing* outside that you can compare prison to. Because you're in a small place with a lot of people in it ... Perhaps the closest comparison is to say it's like a ship. (Male senior officer, Garth)

It's like a hospital really. A mental hospital. [Why?] A lot of inmates are all right, but some of 'em shouldn't be here. [Why not?] They're unpredictable. With most of 'em, they come back from the gym and they're wanting a shower and you've got to say no. And you don't know how they're gonna react ... Some of 'em are madmen! (Male officer, Garth)

It is a big family, and yes it is a madhouse ... It all depends on the prison you're in. If it's a big local, then it's a meat factory, you know, it *is* a conveyor belt. I mean it is *here* to a certain extent, a conveyor belt, because a lot of 'em are remands. (Male senior officer, Lancaster Farms)

I'd say it's like a school, 'cos there's common ground between us and school teachers about the kind of things we have to deal with. (Male senior officer, Garth)

To me, sometimes, it's like being a glorified baby-sitter. Because that's, that's what you're doin', yeah. I mean you're just ... you're just lookin' after everything for them like they're kids. (Male officer, Portland)

they're kids and they've got lots of energy and they need entertaining. At night, it's more like a youth club, and they treat you like a Dad. I spend more time with these than I do my own wife. (Male senior officer, Lancaster Farms)

References

Alasuutari, P. (1995) *Researching Culture*. London: Sage.

Asch, S.E. (1951) 'Effect of group pressure upon the modification and distortion of judgements', in H. Guetzkow (ed.) *Groups, Leadership and Men*. Pittsburg, PA: Carnegie Press.

Banton, M. (1964) *The Policeman in the Community*. London: Tavistock.

Barclay, A., Skerry, K., Sneath, E. and Webster, R. (1994) 'Management of dissent in prison', in E. Stanko (ed.) *Perspectives on Violence*. London: Quartet Books.

Barnes, H.E. and Teeter, N.K. (1959) *New Horizons in Criminology*. Englewood Cliffs, NJ: Prentice-Hall.

Bauman, Z. (1989) *Modernity and the Holocaust*. Cambridge: Polity Press.

Becker, H.S., Geer, B., Hughes, E.C. and Strauss, A.L. (1961) *Boys in White: Student Culture in a Medical School*. Chicago, IL: University of Chicago Press.

Becker, H.S. and Strauss, A.L. (1956) 'Careers, personality, and adult socialization', *American Journal of Sociology*, 62: 253–363.

Beehr, T. and O'Hara, T. (1987) 'Methodological designs for the evaluation of occupational stress interventions', in S.V. Kasl and C.L. Cooper (eds) *Distress and Health: Issues in Research Methodology*. Chichester: Wiley.

Beetham, D. (1991) *The Legitimation of Power*. London: Macmillan.

Bendelow, G. and Williams, S.J. (eds) (1998) *Emotions in Social Life*. London: Routledge.

Bensman, J. and Vidich, A. (1960) 'Social theory in field research', *American Journal of Sociology*, 65.

Bittner, E. (1967) 'The police on Skid Row', *American Sociological Review*, 32: 699–715.

Bittner, E. (1970) *The Functions of the Police in Modern Society*. Rockville, MD: National Institute of Mental Health, Center for Studies of Crime and Delinquency.

Bogardus, E.S. (1933) 'A social distance scale', *Sociology and social Research*, 17.

Borman, K.M., LeCompt, M.D. and Goetz, J.P. (1986) 'Ethnographic and qualitative research design and why it doesn't work', *American Behavioural Scientist*, 30(1): 42–57.

Bosworth, M. (1999) *Engendering Resistance: Agency and Power in Women's Prisons*. Aldershot: Ashgate.

Bosworth, M. and Carrabine, A. (1999) 'Prisons and resistance: agency, gender and power.' Paper presented at the British Criminology Conference, Liverpool, 13–16 July.

Bottoms, A.E. (1999) 'Interpersonal violence and social order in prisons', in M. Tonry and J. Petersilia (eds) *Prisons*. Chicago, IL: University of Chicago Press.

Bottoms, A., Hay, W. and Sparks, R. (1990) 'Situational and social approaches to the prevention of disorder in long-term prisons', *The Prison Journal*, 70: 83–95.

Bottoms, A.E and Light, R. (1987) *Problems of Long-term Imprisonment*. Aldershot: Gower.

Bourdieu, P. (1990) *The Logic of Practice*. Cambridge: Polity Press.

Bourne, I. and Oliver, B. (1998) *A Model for Counselling Survivors of Trauma*. Extract from a training manual for the RSA Diploma in Post-traumatic Stress Counselling, Richmond Fellowship, Bristol.

Boyle, J. (1977) *A Sense of Freedom*. London: Pan Books.

Boyle, J. (1984) *The Pain of Confinement*. London: Pan Books.

Brewer, J.D. and Magee, K. (1991) *Inside the RUC: Routine Policing in a Divided Society*. Oxford: Clarendon Press.

Brogden, M., Jefferson, T. and Walklate, S. (1988) *Introducing Policework*. London: Unwin Hyman.

Brookes, M. (1988) *Control and Restraint Techniques: A Study into its Effectiveness at HMP Gartree*. DPS report, series II, no. 156, January.

Brown, J.M. and Campbell, E.A. (1990) 'Sources of occupational stress in the police', *Work and Stress*, 4: 305–18.

Bryans, S. and Wilson, D. (1998) 'The prison governor: theory and practice', *Prison Service Journal*.

Bull, I. and Horncastle, P. (1986) *Police Recruit Training in Human Awareness: An Independent Evaluation*. London: Police Foundation.

Burke, M. (1993) *Coming Out of the Blue*. London: Cassell.

Cain, M. (1973) *Society and the Policeman's Role*. London: Routledge & Kegan Paul.

Canada (Sub committee on the Penitentiary System in Canada) (1977) *Report to Parliament*. Ottawa: Ministry of Supply and Services.

Carlen, P. (1983) *Women's Imprisonment: a study in Social Control*. London: Routledge and Kegan Paul.

Chan, J. (1996) 'Changing police culture', *British Journal of Criminology*, 36(1): 109–34.

Chatterton, M. (1979) 'The supervision of patrol work under the fixed points system', in S. Holdaway (ed.) *The British Police*. London: Edward Arnold.

Cheek, F.E. and Miller, M.D.S. (1983) 'The experience of stress for correction officers: a double-bind theory of correctional stress' *Journal of Criminal Justice*, 11: 105 20.

Chinoy, E. (1955) *Automobile Workers and the American Dream*. Garden City, NJ: Doubleday & Co.

Clarke, D. (1996) 'Therapeutic communities for drug misusers', *Prison Service Journal*, issue 111.

Clarke, J., Cochrane, A. and McLaughlin, E. (eds) (1994) *Managing Social Policy*. London: Sage.

Clemmer, D. (1940) *The Prison Community*. Boston, MA: Christopher Publishing Company.

Cohen, S. and Taylor, L. (1972) *Psychological Survival*. Harmondsworth: Penguin Books.

Colvin, E. (1977) 'The English prison officer: a sociological study.' Unpublished PhD thesis, University of Cambridge.

Connell, R.W. (1987) *Gender and Power*. Cambridge: Polity Press.

Cooke, D.J. (1991) 'Violence in prisons: the influence of regime factors', *The Howard Journal*, 30(2).

Cooper, C.L., Davidson, M.J. and Robinson, P. (1982) 'Stress in the police service', *Journal of Occupational Medicine*, 24: 30–6.

Cooper, R. and Law, J. (1995) 'Organization: distal and proximal views', *Research in the Sociology of Organizations*, 13: 237–74.

Coyle, A. (1989) 'Incidents in the Scottish prison service: history and response', *The Howard Journal*, 26(2).

Crawley, E.M. (2000a) 'Identities, expectations, conflicts: how prison officers see their work, themselves and each other.' Paper presented at the British Society of Criminology conference 2000, Leicester University, 5–7 July.

Crawley, E.M. (2000b) 'Reflections on the sex offender treatment programme', *Howard League Magazine*, February.

Crawley, E.M. (2002) 'Bringing it all back home? The impact of prison officers' work on their families', *Probation Journal*, 49(4).

Crawley, E.M (forthcoming) 'Emotion and performance: prison officers and the presentation of self in prisons', *Journal of Punishment and Society*.

Crawley, E.M. and Sparks, J.R. (2003) 'Surviving prison in later life.' Paper presented at the Punishment and Society Roundtable, 2003 American Society of Criminology conference, 18–22 November, Denver, CO.

Crouch, B.M. (1980) *The Keepers: Prison Guards and Contemporary Corrections*. Springfield, IL: Charles C. Thomas.

Crouch, B. and Marquart, J.W. (1980) 'On becoming a prison guard', in B. Crouch (ed.) *The Keepers: Prison Guards and Contemporary Corrections*. Springfield, IL: Charles C. Thomas.

Cupach, W.R. and Metts, S. (1994) *Facework*. London: Sage.

Czarniawska-Joerges, B. (1992) *Exploring Complex Organizations*. London: Sage.

Daniels, E. (1985) 'Nostalgia and hidden meaning', *American Imago*, 42(4): 371–82.

Davis, F. (1979) *Yearning for Yesterday: A Sociology of Nostalgia*. New York, NY: Free Press.

Deal, T.E. and Kennedy, A. (1982) *Corporate Cultures*. Reading, MA: Addison Wesley.

Denzin, N.K. (1970) *The Research Act*. Chicago, IL: Aldine.

Denzin, N.K. and Denzin, Y.S. (eds) (1994) *Handbook of Qualitative Research*. London: Sage.

Dilulio, J. (1987) *Governing Prisons*. New York, NY: Free Press.

Ditchfield, J. (1990) *Control in Prisons: A Review of the Literature. Home Office Research and Planning Unit Report*. London: HMSO.

Douglas, M. (1970) *Purity and Danger: An Analysis of Concepts of Pollution and Taboo*. Harmondsworth: Penguin Books.

Duffee, D. (1980a) *Correctional Management: Change and Control in Correctional Organizations*. Englewood Cliffs, NJ: Prentice Hall.

Duffee, D. (1980b) 'The correction officer subculture and organizational change', *Journal of Research in Crime and Delinquency*, 11: 155–72.

Dunbar, I. (1985) *A Sense of Direction*. London: HM Prison Service.

Eaton, M. (1986) *Justice for Women? Family, Court and Social Control*. Milton Keynes: Open University Press.

Ellison, J.W.G. (1997) 'Professionalism in the Royal Ulster Constabulary: an examination of the institutional discourse.' Unpublished PhD thesis, University of Ulster.

Enterkin, J. (1998) 'Prison service cross-posting policy and female prison officers', *Prison Service Journal*, issue 117.

Evans, R. (1990) 'Management models and performance monitoring in the prison service', *Prison Service Journal*, issue 78.

Fairweather, L. (1995) 'Does good design help those inside?', *Prison Service Journal*, issue 101.

Farmer, R. (1977) 'Cynicism: a factor in corrections work', *Journal of Criminal Justice*, 5: 237–46.

Farnworth, L. (1992) 'Women doing a man's job: female prison officers working in a male prison', *Australia and New Zealand Journal of Criminology*, 25.

Feeley, M.M. and Rubin, E.L. (1998) *Judicial Policy Making and the Modern State*. Cambridge: Cambridge University Press.

Fielding, N. (1994) 'Cop canteen culture', in T. Newburn and E.A. Stanko (eds) *Just Boys Doing Business?* London and New York: Routledge.

Fielding, N. (1995) *Community Policing*. Oxford: Clarendon Press.

Finch, J. (1983) *Married to the Job: Wives' Incorporation in Mens' Work*. London: Allen & Unwin.

Fineman, S. (1993) *Emotion in Organizations*. London: Sage.

Fineman, S. and Gabriel, Y. (1996) *Experiencing Organisations*. London: Sage.

Finkelstein, E. (1993) *Prison Culture: An Inside View*. Aldershot: Avebury.

Fisher, J. (1998) 'Staff management in the prison service: a cultural critique', *Prison Service Journal*, issue 86.

Fitzgerald, M. (1977) *Prisoners in Revolt*. Harmondsworth, Penguin Books.

Fitzgerald, M. and Sim, J. (1982) *British Prisons*. Oxford: Blackwell.

Fitzpatrick, J.S. (1980) 'Adapting to danger: a participant observation study of an underground mine', *Sociology of Work and Occupations*, 7(2): 131–58.

Flam, H. (1990) 'Emotional man', *International Sociology*, 5(10): 39–56.

Fleming, R. (1994) *Scotland Yard*. London: Signet.

Foucault, M. (1979) *Discipline and Punish*. London: Penguin Books.

Fox, S. (1990) 'The ethnography of humour and the problem of social reality', *Sociology*, 24(3): 431–46.

Gabriel, Y. (1993) 'Organizational nostalgia – reflections on the "Golden Age", in S. Fineman (ed.) *Emotion in Organizations*. London: Sage.

Gadamer, A.G. (1975) *Truth and Method*. London: Sheed.

Garfinkel, H. (1967) *Studies in Ethnomethodology*. Englewood Cliffs, NJ: Prentice-Hall.

Garland, D. (1985) *Punishment and Welfare*. Aldershot: Gower.

Garland, D. (1990) *Punishment and Modern Society*. Oxford: Oxford University Press.

Geertz, C. (1973) *The Interpretation of Cultures: Selected Essays*. New York, NY: Basic Books.

Gelsthorpe, L. and Morris, A. (1988) 'Feminism and criminology in Britain', in P. Rock (ed.) *A History of British Criminology*. Oxford: Oxford University Press.

Gennep, A. van (1960) *The Rites of Passage*. Chicago, IL: University of Chicago Press.

Gergen, K.J. (1999) *An Invitation to Social Construction*. London:Sage.

Gerth, H. and Mills, C. (1954) *Character and Social Structure: the psychology of social institutions*. London: Routledge and Kegan Paul.

Giacalone, R.A. and Rosenfeld, P.R. (1991) *Applied Impression Management*. Newbury Park, CA: Sage.

Giddens, A. (1984) *The Constitution of Society*. Cambridge: Cambridge University Press.

Glaser, B. and Strauss, A. (1967) *The Discovery of Grounded Theory*. Chicago, IL: Aldine.

Gluckman, M. (1963) 'Gossip and scandal', *Current Anthropology*, 4(3).

Goffman, E. (1959) *The Presentation of Self in Everyday Life*. New York, NY: Doubleday.

Goffman, E. (1961) *Encounters*. Indianapolis, IN: Bobbs-Merrill.

Goffman, E. (1963a) *Stigma*. Englewood Cliffs, NJ: Prentice Hall.

Goffman, E. (1963b) *Behaviour in Public Places*. New York, NY: Free Press.

Goffman, E. (1967) *Interaction Ritual: Essays on Face-to-face Behaviour*. New York, NY: Pantheon.

Goffman, E. (1968) *Asylums*. Harmondsworth: Penguin Books.

Goffman, E. (1971) *Relations in Public*. New York, NY: Basic Books.

Goldstein, J.H. and McGhee, P.E. (1972) *The Psychology of Humour: Theoretical Perspectives and Empirical Issues*. New York, NY and London: Academic Press.

Gordon, I.E. (1989) *Theories of Visual Perception*. Chichester: Wiley.

Graef, R. (1989) *Talking Blues*. London: Fontana.

Gunn, J., Robertson, G., Dell, S. and Way, C. (1978) *Psychiatric Aspects of Imprisonment*. London: Academic Press.

Haas, J. (1977) 'Learning real feelings: a study of high steel ironworkers' reactions to fear and danger', *Sociology of Work and Occupations*, 4: 147–70.

Habermas, J. (1984) *The Theory of Communicative Action. Vol. 1*. Cambridge: Polity Press.

Harding, M. (1997) *Private Prisons and Public Accountability*. Buckingham: Open University Press.

Hawkins, G. (1976) *Prison: Policy and Practice*. Chicago, IL: University of Chicago Press.

Hawkins, R. and Alpert, G.P. (1989) *American Prison Systems: Punishment and Justice*. Englewood Cliffs, NJ: Prentice Hall.

Hay, W. and Sparks, R. (1991) 'What is a prison officer?', *Prison Service Journal*, summer issue.

Hearn, J. (1993) 'Emotive subjects: organizational men, organizational masculinities and the (de)construction of "emotions"' in S. Fineman (ed.) *Emotion in Organizations*. London: Sage.

Heidensohn, F. (1985) *Women and Crime*. Basingstoke: Macmillan.

Heidensohn, F. (1992) *Women in Control? The Role of Women in Law Enforcement*. Oxford: Clarendon Press.

Henning, K. (1976) 'Management styles and organizational climate', in G. Killinger *et al.* (eds) *Issues in Corrections and Administrations*. St Paul, MN: West Publishing.

Herbert, T.T. (1981) *Dimensions of Organizational Behavior*. New York, NY: Macmillan.

Hewitt, J.P. and Stokes, R. (1975) 'Disclaimers', *American Sociological Review*, 40: 1–11.

HMCIP (1995) *Report on HM Young Offender and Remand Centre Lancaster Farms*. London: Home Office.

HMCIP (1996) *HM Young Offender Institution Portland: Report of an Unannounced Short Inspection by HM Chief Inspector of Prisons* 2–3 July. London: Home Office.

HMCIP (1997) *HM Prison Garth: Report of a Full Inspection 9–13 June*. London: Home Office.

HMCIP (1999) *Annual Report of HM Chief Inspector of Prisons for England and Wales*. London: Home Office.

Hochschild, A. (1983) *The Managed Heart*. Berkeley, CA: University of California Press.

Hochschild, A. (1998) 'The sociology of emotion as a way of seeing', in G. Bendelow and S.J. Williams (eds) *Emotions in Social Life*. London:

Routledge.

Hockey, J. (1986) *Squaddies*. Exeter: Exeter University Publications.

Holdaway, S. (1983) *Inside the British Police*. Oxford: Blackwell.

Holdaway, S. (1994) 'Academic whistleblowing on the beat: the policeman's lot', in G. Vinten (ed.) *Whistleblowing: Subversion or Corporate Citizenship?*. London: Paul Chapman Publishing.

Home Office (1984*)* *Managing the Long-term Prison System (The Report of the Control Review Committee)*. London: HMSO.

Home Office (1985) *Staff Attitudes in the Prison Service*. London: HMSO.

Home Office (1986) *HM Prison Service*. London: Home Office

Home Office (1989) *Special Security Units. Research Study 109*. London: HMSO.

Home Office (1994) *Report of the Enquiry into the Escape of Six Prisoners from the Special Security Unit at Whitemoor Prison, Cambridgeshire on Friday 9 September 1994 (The Woodcock Report)*. London: HMSO.

Home Office (1995) *Review of Prison Service Security in England and Wales and the escape from Parkhurst Prison on Tuesday 3 January (The Learmont Report)*. London: HMSO.

Home Office (1999) *HM Prison Wormwood Scrubs, Report of an Unannounced Inspection 8–12 March 1999*. London: HMSO.

Hopfl, H. and Linstead, S. (1993) 'Passion and performance: suffering and the carrying of organizational roles', in S. Fineman (ed.) *Emotion in Organizations*. London: Sage.

Howard League (2000) 'Institutional abuse', *The Howard League Magazine*, 18(1).

Hughes, E.C. (1958) *Men and their Work*. Glenco, IL: Free Press.

Hughes, E.C. (1971) 'Good people and dirty work', in *The Sociological Eye*. Chicago, IL: Aldine.

Hughes, J.A. (1976) *Sociological analysis: Methods of Discovery*. London: Nelson.

Ignatieff, M. (1978) *A Just Measure of Pain: The Penitentiary in the Industrial Revolution 1750–1850*. Harmondsworth: Penguin Books.

Irwin, J. (1980) *Prisons in Turmoil*. Boston, MA: Little, Brown.

Jacobs, J.B. (1978) 'What prison guards think: a profile of the Illinois force', *Crime and Delinquency*, 24.

Jacobs, J. (1983) *New Perspectives on Prisons and Imprisonment*. Ithaca, NY: Cornell University Press.

Jacobs, J.B. and Retsky, H.G. (1980) 'Prison guard', in B. Crouch (ed.) *The Keepers: Prison Guards and Contemporary Corrections*. Springfield, IL: Charles C. Thomas.

James, A.L., Bottomley, A.K, Leibling, A. and Clare, E. (1997) *Privatizing Prisons: Rhetoric and Reality*. London: Sage.

James, N. (1989) 'Emotional labour; skill and work in the social regulation of feelings', *Sociological Review*, 37(1): 15–42.

Jameson, N. and Allison, E. (1995) *Strangeways 1990: A Serious Disturbance*. London: Larkin Publications.

Janis, I.L. (1983) 'Groupthink', in H.H. Blumer *et al.* (eds) *Small Groups and Social*

Interaction. Vol. 2. Chichester: Wiley.

Janowitz, M. (1964) *Professional Soldier: A Social and Political Portrait.* New York, NY: Free Press.

Jefferson, T. (1998) 'Muscle, "hard men" and "Iron" Mike Tyson: reflections on desire, anxiety and the embodiment of masculinity', *Body and Society,* 4.

Johnson, J.C. (1990) *Selecting Ethnographic Informants.* London: Sage.

Johnson, R. (1988) *Hard Time: Understanding and Reforming the Prison.* New York, NY: Wadsworth.

Jones, C. (1993) 'Auditing criminal justice', *British Journal of Criminology,* 33(2).

Jones, M. (1956) 'The concept of a therapeutic community', *American Journal of Psychiatry,* 112: 647–50.

Jorgensen, D.L. (1989) *Participant Observation.* Newbury Park, CA: Sage.

Jurik, N.C. and Musheno, M.C. (1986) 'The internal crisis of corrections: professionalization and the work environment', *Justice Quarterly,* 3(4).

Kalinich and Pitcher (1984) *Surviving in Corrections.* Springfield, IL: Charles C. Thomas.

Kaplan, H.A. (1987) 'The psychopathology of nostalgia', *Psychoanalytic Review,* 74(4): 463–86.

Katz, D. and Kahn, R. (1966) *The Social Psychology of Organizations,* New York, NY: Wiley.

Kauffman, K. (1988) *Prison Officers and their World.* Cambridge, MA: Harvard University Press.

Kelman, H.C. (1973) 'Violence without moral restraint', *Journal of Social Issues,* 29: 29–61.

Kilmann, R., Saxton, M. and Serpa, R. (1985) *Gaining Control of the Corporate Culture.* San Francisco, CA: Jossy Bass.

King, R.D. and Elliot, K. (1977) *Albany: Birth of a Prison, End of an Era.* London: Routledge & Kegan Paul.

King, R.D. and Maguire, M. (1994) 'Contexts of imprisonment: an international perspective', *The British Journal of Criminology,* special issue, 'Prisons in context', 34.

King, R. and McDermott, K. (1990) 'My geranium is subversive: some notes on the management of trouble in prisons', *British Journal of Criminology,* 41(4): 445–71.

King, R. and McDermott, K. (1995) *The State of our Prisons.* Oxford: Oxford University Press.

King, R.D. and Morgan, R. (1980) *The Future of the Prison System.* Farnborough: Gower.

Kirmeyer, S. and Diamond, A. (1985) 'Coping by police officers: a study of role stress and Type A and Type B behaviour patterns', *Journal of Occupational Behaviour,* 6: 183–95.

Kleinman, S. and Copp, M.A. (1993) *Emotions and Fieldwork.* London: Sage.

Kluckholn, F. (1940) 'The participant observer technique in small communities', *American Journal of Sociology,* 46.

Kroes, W., Margolis, B. and Hurrel, J. (1974) 'Job stress in policemen', *Journal of Police Science and Administration*, 2: 145–85.

Kuper, A. (1983) *Anthropology and Anthropologists*. London: Routledge.

Lasch, C. (1980) *The Culture of Narcissism*. London: Abacus.

Law, J. (1994) *Organizing Modernity*. Oxford: Blackwell.

Law, J. and Cooper, R. (1995) 'Organization: distal and proximal views', *Research in the Sociology of Organizations*, 13: 237–74.

Law, J. and Lodge, P. (1984) *Science for Social Scientists*. London: Macmillan.

Lawler, J. (1994) *Behind the screens: nursing, somology, and the problem of the body*. Melbourne: Churchill Livingstone.

Layder, D. (1993) *New Strategies in Social Research*. Cambridge: Polity Press.

Lee, R. (1993) *Doing Research on Sensitive Topics*. London: Sage.

Lee, R. (1995) *Dangerous Fieldwork*. London: Sage.

Leech, M. (1995) *The Prisoners' Handbook*. Oxford: Oxford University Press.

Lella, J.W. and Pawluch, D. (1988) 'Medical students and the cadaver in social and cultural context', in M. Lock and D.R. Gordon (eds) *Biomedicine Examined*. Dordrecht: Kluwer Academic.

Lewis, D. (1997) *Hidden Agendas*. London: Hamish Hamilton.

Liebling, A. (1992) *Suicides in Prison*. London: Routledge.

Liebling, A. (1998) 'Managing to prevent prison suicide: are staff at risk too?', in J. Kamerman (ed.) *Negotiating Responsibility in the Criminal Justice System*. Carbondale, IL: Southern Illinois University Press.

Liebling, A. (1999) 'Prisoner suicide and prisoner coping', in M. Tonry and J. Petersilia (eds) *Prisons*. Chicago, IL: University of Chicago Press.

Liebling, A. and Krarup, H. (1993) *Suicide Attempts in Male Prisons*. London: Home Office.

Leibling, A., Muir, G., Rose, G. and Bottoms, A. (1997) *An Evaluation of Incentives and Earned Privileges: Final Report to the Home Office*. London: Home Office.

Liebling, A., Price, D. and Elliott, C. (1999) 'Appreciative inquiry and relationships in prison', *Punishment and Society*, 1.

Liebling, A. and Price, D. (2001) *The Prison officer*. Leyhill: HM Prison Service.

Livingstone, S. and Owen, T. (1995) *Prison Law*. Oxford: Clarendon Press.

Loader, I. (1996) *Youth, Policing and Democracy*. London: Macmillan.

Lombardo, L.X. (1981) *Guards Imprisoned: Correctional Officers at Work*. New York, NY: Elsevier.

Loo, R. (1986) 'Post-shooting stress amongst police officers', *Journal of Human Stress*, 12: 27–31.

Louis, M.R. (1980) 'Surprise and sense-making: what newcomers experience on entering unfamiliar organizational settings', *Administrative Science Quarterly*.

Lowenstein, L.F. (1999) 'Treating stress in the police force', *The Police Journal*, 72(1).

Lygo, R. (1991) *Management of the Prison Service*. London: HMSO.

Lyon, J. and Evershed, S. (1999) 'The impact on staff or working with difficult young prisoners', in *What Works with Young Prisoners? Report of a Conference organised by the Institute for the Study and Treatment of Delinquency (ISTD)*. London: ISTD.

Malinowski, B. (1922) *Argonauts of the Western Pacific*. London: Routledge.

Mangham, I.L. and Overington, M.A. (1987) *Organizations as Theatre*. Chichester: Wiley.

Manning, P.K. (1997) *Police Work: The Social Organization of Policing*. Prospect Heights, IL: Waveland Press.

Martin, C.A., McKean, H.E. and Veltkamp, L.J. (1986) 'Post-traumatic stress disorder in police and working with victims: a pilot study', *Journal of Police Science and Administration*, 14: 98–101.

Martin, J. and Powers, M. (1983) 'Truth or corporate propaganda? The value of a good war story', in L. Pondy *et al.* (eds) *Organizational Symbolism*. Greenwich, CT: JAI Press.

Martin, S. and Jurik, N. (1996) *Doing Justice, Doing Gender*. London: Sage.

Mathiesen, T. (1965) *The Defences of the Weak*. London: Tavistock.

Mawby, R.C. (2002) *Policing Images: Policing, Communication and Legitimacy*. Cullompton: Willan.

May, J. (1979) *Report of the Committee of Inquiry into the United Kingdom Prison Services* (Cmnd 7673). London: HMSO.

McCleery, R. (1960) 'Communication patterns as bases of systems of authority and power', in R. Cloward (ed.) *Theoretical Studies in the Social Organization of the Prison*. New York, NY: Social Science Research Council.

McDermott, K. and King, R. (1988) 'Mind games: where the action is in prisons', *British Journal of Criminology*, 28(3): 357–77.

McDonald, D.C. (1994) 'Public imprisonment by private means: the re-emergence of private prisons and jails in the United States, the United Kingdom and Australia', in R. King and M. Maguire (eds) *Prisons in Context*. Oxford: Clarendon Press.

McFarlane, A.C. (1988) 'The longitudinal course of post-traumatic morbidity: the range of outcomes and their predictors', *Journal of Nervous and Mental Disease*, 176(1): 30–9.

McLaughlin, E. and Muncie, J. (1994) 'Managing the criminal justice system', in J. Clarke *et al.* (eds) *Managing Social Policy*. London: Sage.

McLean, A. and Marshall, J. (1988) *Cultures at Work: How to Identify and Understand Them*. Luton: Local Government Training Board.

Mead, G.H. (1964) *Mind, Self and Society*. Chicago, IL: University of Chicago Press.

Meek, L. (1992) 'Organisational culture: origins and weaknesses', in G. Salaman (ed.) *Human Resource Strategies*. London: Sage.

Meerabeau, L. and Page, S. (1998) 'Getting the job done: emotion management and cardiopulmonary resuscitation in nursing', in G. Bendelow and S.J. Williams (eds) *Emotions in Social Life*. London: Routledge.

Menzies-Lythe, I. (1988) *Containing Anxiety in Institutions. Selected Essays*. London: Free Association Books.

Mercier, V. (1926) *The Irish Comic Tradition*. Oxford: Clarendon Press.

Merton, R. (1949) *Social Theory and Social Structure*. Glencoe, IL: Free Press.

Mitroff, I. and Kilmann, R. (1976) 'On organizational stories: an approach to the design and analysis of organizations through myths and stories', in R.

Kilmann *et al.* (eds) *The Management of Organizational Design.* New York, NY: Elsevier.

Morgan, D. (1988) *Focus Groups as Qualitative Research.* Newbury Park, CA: Sage.

Morgan, R. (1997) 'Imprisonment: Current concerns and A Brief History since 1945' in M. Maguire, R. Morgan, and R. Reiner (eds.) *The Oxford Handbook of Crimonology.* pp. 1137–94. Oxford: Clarendon Press.

Morris, A. (1987) *Women, Crime and Criminal Justice.* Oxford: Blackwell.

Morris, P. (1963) 'Staff problems in a maximum security prison', *Prison Service Journal,* issue 6.

Morris, T. and Morris, P. (1963) *Pentonville: A Sociological Study of an English Prison.* London: Routledge & Kegan Paul.

Mulcahy, A. (1995) '"Headhunter" or "Real Cop"? Identity in the world of internal affairs officers', *Journal of Contemporary Ethnography,* 24(1).

Murton, T. (1976) *The Dilemma of Prison Reform.* New York, NY: Holt, Rinehart & Winston.

NACRO (1995) *Criminal Justice Digest No. 86.* London: NACRO.

Narey, N. (1999) 'Taking the prison service into the 21st century' (extract from the Eve Saville Memorial Lecture), *Criminal Justice Matters,* 36: 29–30.

Neale, K. (1991) 'The European prison rules: contextual, philosophical and practical aspects', in J. Muncie and R. Sparks (eds) *Imprisonment: European Perspectives.* London: Sage.

Nichols, T. and Benyon, H. (1977) *Living with Capitalism.* London: Routledge & Kegan Paul.

Noon, M. and Blyton, P. (1997) *The Realities of Work.* Basingstoke: Macmillan Business.

Norman, C. (1986) 'Prison staff attitudes: a serious case of insecurity', *Prison Service Journal,* April issue.

Olesen, V. and Bone, D. (1998) 'Emotions in rationalizing organizations: conceptual notes from professional nursing in the USA', in G. Bendelow and S.J. Williams (eds) *Emotions in Social Life.* London: Routledge.

Paine, R. (1967) 'What is gossip about?', *Man,* 278–85.

Parisi, N. (ed.) (1982) *Coping with Imprisonment.* London: Sage.

Parkin, W. (1993) 'The public and the private: gender, sexuality and emotion', in S. Fineman (ed.) *Emotion in Organizations.* London: Sage.

Peters, T.J. (1978) 'Symbols, patterns and settings: an optimistic case for getting things done', *Organizational Dynamics,* 7: 3–23.

Peters, T.J. and Waterman, R.H. (1982) *In Search of Excellence.* New York, NY: Harper & Row.

Pierce, C.S. (1940) 'Logic as semiotic: the theory of signs', in J. Buchler (ed.) *The Philosophical Writings of Pierce.* New York, NY: Dover.

Pogrebin, M.R. and Poole, E.D. (1997) 'The sexualized work environment: a look at women jail officers', *American Jails,* July/August.

Pollitt, C. (1993) *Managerialism and the Public Services.* Oxford: Blackwell.

Poole, E.D. and Regoli, R.M. (1980) 'Work relations and cynicism among prison guards', *Criminal Justice and Behaviour*, 7(3).

Prescott, J. (1976) *Hull Prison Riot, August 31 to September 3, 1975: Submissions, Observations and Recommendations*. London: HMSO.

Price, D. and Liebling, A. (1998) 'Staff–prisoner relationships: a review of the literature'. Unpublished report submitted to the Prison Service.

Prison Officers Association (1991) *POA Submission: Stage 2 of the Woolf Inquiry*. Edmonton: POA.

Prison Officers Association (1994) *Criminal Justice and Public Order Act*. Edmonton: POA.

Prison Officers Association (1996) *Annual Report 1995*. Edmonton: POA.

Prison Reform Trust (1998) *Help the Aged. Prison Report 43*. London: Prison Reform Trust.

Prison Service (1996) *Weekly Bulletin*, 1(18).

Prison Service (1992) 'The way forward: caring for prisoners at risk of suicide and self-injury'. Information paper. London: Home Office.

Prison Service (1997) *Prison Service Review*, October. London: HMSO.

Prison Service (2000) *Restorative Justice, HMYOI Huntercombe*. Leaflet produced for HMYOI Huntercombe personnel.

Punch, M. (1985) *Conduct Unbecoming*. London: Tavistock.

Punch, M. (1986) *The Politics and Ethics of Fieldwork*. Beverly Hills, CA: Sage.

Punch, M. (1994) 'Politics and ethics in qualitative research', in K. Denzin and Y. Denzin (eds) *Handbook of Qualitative Research*. London: Sage.

Putnam, L. and Mumby, D. (1993) 'Organizations, emotions and the myth of reality', in S. Fineman (ed.) *Emotion in Organizations*. London: Sage.

Radcliffe-Brown, A.R. (1952) *Structure and Function in Primitive Society*. London.

Ramsbotham, GCB, CBE, Sir David (1999) 'Back to the future: the way for imprisonment'. A talk given to a North Eastern Prison After Care Society (NEPACS) meeting 22 June.

Raphael, B., Meldrum, L. and McFarlane, A.C. (1995) 'Does de-briefing after psychological trauma work?', *British Medical Journal*, 310: 1479–80.

Regoli, R., Poole, E. and Shrink, J. (1979) 'Occupational socialization and career development: a look at cynicism among correctional institution workers', *Human Organization*, 38: 183–6.

Reiner, R. (1978) *The Blue-coated Worker*. Cambridge: Cambridge University Press.

Reiner, R. (1985) *The Politics of the Police*. New York, NY: Harvester Wheatsheaf.

Reuss-Ianni, E. (1983) *The Two Cultures of Policing: Street Cops and Management Cops*. New York, NY: Transaction Books.

Rosaldo, R. (1993) *Culture and Truth*. London: Routledge.

Ross, P.D. and Jakubczyk, A. (1992) *One-Off (Felo de se)*. HM Prison Hull.

Rubenstein, J. (1973) *City Police*. New York, NY: Farrar, Strauss & Giroux.

Rutherford, A. (1993) *Criminal Justice and the Pursuit of Decency*. Oxford: Oxford University Press.

Ryder, R. (1994) 'Violence and the role of machismo', in E.A. Stanko (ed.) *Perspectives on Violence*. London: Quartet.

Sampson, A. (1994) *Acts of Abuse*. London: Routledge.

Schwartzman, H.B. (1993) *Ethnography in Organizations*. London: Sage.

Scottish Home and Health Department (1971) 'Report of the Departmental Working Party on the treatment of certain male long term prisoners and potentially violent prisoners.' Unpublished.

Scraton, P., Sim, J. and Skidmore, K. (1991) *Prisons Under Protest*. Buckinghamshire: Open University Press.

Seidler, V. (1992) 'Rejection, vulnerability, and friendship', in P. Nardi (ed.) *Men's Friendships*. Newbury Park, CA: Sage.

Serge, V. (1977) *Men in Prison*. London: Writers & Readers Publishing Co-operative.

Shearing, C.D. and Ericson, R.V. (1991) 'Culture as figurative action', *British Journal of Sociology*, 42(4): 481–506.

Sheath, M. (1990) 'Confrontative work with sex offenders: legitimised nonce-bashing?', *Probation Journal*, 37(4): 159–62.

Shover, N. (1979) *A Sociology of American Corrections*. Homewood, IL: Dorsey Press.

Sim, J. (1994) 'Tougher than the rest? Men in prison', in T. Newburn and E.A. Stanko (eds) *Just Boys Doing Business?*. London: Routledge.

Sims, D., Fineman, S. and Gabriel, Y. (1993) *Organizing and Organizations*. London: Sage.

Skolnick, J. (1975) *Justice without Trial*. New York, NY: Wiley.

Smircich, L. (1983) 'Concepts of culture and organizational analysis', *Administrative and Science Quarterly*, 28: 339–56.

Smith, K. (1989) *Inside Time*. London: Harrap.

Snyder, M. (1987) *Public Appearances, Private Realities*. New York, NY: Freeman.

Sohn, L. (1983) 'Nostalgia', *International Journal of Psychoanalysis*, 64: 203–11.

Sparks, J.R. (1993) 'Out of the digger: the Barlinnie Special Unit as prison and escape.' Paper presented at the British Criminology Conference, Cardiff University, July.

Sparks, J.R. (1996) '"Penal austerity": the doctrine of less eligibility reborn?', in R. Matthews and P. Francis (eds) *Prisons 2000: An International Perspective on the current State and Future of Imprisonment*. London: Macmillan Press.

Sparks, J.R. and Bottoms, A.E. (1995) 'Legitimacy and order in prisons', *British Journal of Sociology*, 46(1).

Sparks, J.R., Bottoms, A.E. and Hay, W. (1996) *Prisons and the Problem of Order*. Oxford: Clarendon Press.

Spradley, J. (1970) *You Owe Yourself a Drunk*. Boston, MA: Little.

Spradley, J. (1979) *The Ethnographic Interview*. New York, NY: Holt, Rinehart & Winston.

Spradley, J. (1980) *Participant Observation*. New York, NY: Holt, Rinehart & Winston.

Stanislavski, C. (1961) *Creating a Role*. New York, NY: Theatre Arts Books.

Steele, J. (1992) *The Bird that Never Flew*. Princeton, NJ: Princeton University Press.

Stewart, D. and Shamdasani, P. (1990) *Focus Groups: Theory and Practice*. Newbury Park, CA: Sage.

Stirling, J.W. (1974) 'The college level entry requirement: a real or imagined cure-all', *The Police Chief*, August.

Swanson, C.R. (1977) 'An uneasy look at college education and the police organization', *Journal of Criminal Justice*, 5: 311–20.

Sykes, G. (1958) *The Society of Captives*. Princeton, NJ: Princeton University Press.

Talarico, S.M. and Swanson, C.R. (1982) 'Police perceptions and job satisfaction', *Work and Occupations*, 9: 59–78.

Tehrani, N. (1999) 'Post trauma care.' Paper presented at the 'Work-related violence conference', Scarman Centre for the Study of Public Order, University of Leicester, 25 February.

Territo, L. and Vetter, H.J. (1981) *Stress and Police Personnel*. Boston, MA: Allyn & Bacon.

Thames Valley Police (1999) *A Balanced Approach: Restorative Conferencing* (training package).

Thomas, E. (1972) *The English Prison Officer since 1850*. London: Routledge & Kegan Paul.

Thomas, G. (2000) 'The availability of counselling for staff and inmates within the prison service in England and Wales.' Unpublished MA dissertation, Counselling Studies Department, Keele University.

Thomas, J.E. (1994) 'Woolf and prison staff: still looking for good gaolers', in E. Player and M. Jenkins (eds) *Prisons after Woolf*. London: Routledge.

Thompson, P. and McHugh, D. (1995) *Work Organizations: A Critical Introduction*. London: Macmillan.

Toch, H. (1977a) *Police, Prisons, and the Problem of Violence*. Washington, DC: Government Printing Office.

Toch, H. (1977b) *Living in Prison: The Ecology of Survival*. New York, NY: Free Press.

Toch, H. (1994) 'Prison violence in perspective', in E. Stanko (ed.) *Perspectives on Violence. Vol. 1. Howard League Handbooks*. London: Quartet.

Tracy, K. (1990) 'The many faces of facework', in H. Giles and W.P. Robinson (eds) *Handbook of Language and Social Psychology*. New York, NY: John Wiley.

Trauer, T. (1984) 'The current status of the therapeutic community', *British Journal of Medical Psychology*, 57: 71–9.

Tumim, S. (1994) *HM Prison, Leeds: Report by HM Chief Inspector of Prisons*. London: Home Office.

Turner, B. (1971) *Exploring the Industrial Subculture*. London: Macmillan.

Turner, B. (1990) *Organizational Symbolism*. Berlin: De Gruyter.

Turner, J.C. (1991) *Social Influence*. Milton Keynes: Open University Press.

Van Maanen, J. (1975) 'Police socialization', *Administrative Science Quarterly*, 32: 207–28.

Van Maanen, J. (1979) 'The self, the situation, and the rules of interpersonal relations', in W. Bennis *et al.* (eds) *Essays in Interpersonal Dynamics.* Holmewood, IL: Dorsey Press.

Van Maanen, J. (1988) *Tales of the Field.* Chicago, IL: University of Chicago Press.

Van Maanen, J. and Barley, S.R. (1984) 'Occupational communities: culture and control in organizations', *Research in Organizational Behaviour,* 6: 287–365.

Van Maanen, J. and Kunda, G. (1989) '"Real feelings": emotional expression and organizational culture', in L.L. Cummings and B.M. Staw (eds) *Research in Organizational Behaviour,* Greenwich, CT: JAI Press.

Waddington, P.A.J. (1999) 'Police (canteen) sub-culture: an appreciation', *British Journal of Criminology,* 39(2): 286–309.

Waite, I. (1994) 'Too little, too bad', *Probation Journal,* 41(2): 92–4.

Walker, C.R. and Guest, R.H. (1952) *The Man on the Assembly Line,* Cambridge, MA: Harvard University Press.

Walmsley, R. (1989) *Special Security Units. Home Office Research and Planning Unit Report 109.* London: HMSO.

Walmsley, R., Howard, L. and White, S. (1991) *The National Prison Survey. Home Office Research Study 128.* London: HMSO.

Waplington, D. (1996) 'Memories of Leicester Prison in the 70s', *Prison Service Journal,* issue 105.

Webb, B. and Webb, S. (1932) *Methods of Social Study.* London: Longman.

Webb, G.L. and Morris, D.G. (1980) *Prison Guards: The Culture and Perspectives of an Occupational Group.* Texas: Coker Books.

Websdale, N. and Johnson, B. (1997) 'The policing of domestic violence in rural and urban areas: the voices of battered women in Kentucky', *Policing and Society,* 6(4): 297–317.

Westley, W. (1953) 'Violence and the police', *American Journal of Sociology,* 59: 34–41.

White, M.E. (1974) 'Therapeutic communities', *Prison Service Journal,* issue 15.

Whyte, W.F. (1955) *Streetcorner Society.* Chicago, IL: University of Chicago Press.

Wilkins, A. and Martin, J. (1980) *Organizational Legends.* Working paper, Graduate School of Business, Stanford University.

Williams, A., Dobson, P. and Walters, M. (1993) *Changing Culture: New Organisational Approaches.* London: Institute of Personnel Management.

Willis, P. (1977) *Learning to Labour: How Working Class Kids get Working Class Jobs.* Farnborough: Gower.

Wintrob, R.M. (1969) 'An inward focus: a consideration of psychological stress in fieldwork', in F. Henry and S. Saberwal (eds) *Stress and Response in Fieldwork.* New York, NY: Holt, Rinehart & Winston.

Woolf, Lord Justice (1991) *Prison Disturbances 1991* (Cm 1456). London: HMSO.

Worrall, A. (1997) *Punishment in the Community.* London: Longman.

Wright, M. (1982) *Making Good: Prisons, Punishment and Beyond.* London: Burnett Books.

Young, M. (1991) *An Inside Job.* Oxford: Clarendon Press.

Zeeman, E.C., Hal, C.S., Harrison, P.J., Marriage, G.H. and Shapland, P.H. (1977) 'A model for prison disturbances', *British Journal of Criminology*, 17: 251–63.

Zijderveld, A.C. (1983) 'The sociology of humour and laughter', *Current Sociology*, 31(3).

Zimmer, L. (1986) *Women Guarding Men*. New York, NY: Elsevier.

Zimmer, L. (1987) 'How women reshape the prison guard role', *Gender and Society*, 1(4): 415–31.

Zurcher, L.A. (1983) *Social Roles: Conformity, Conflict and Creativity*. Beverly Hills, CA: Sage.

Index